PORTRAITS
OF AMERICAN
WOMEN

Volume I
From Settlement
to the Civil War

PORTRAITS OF AMERICAN WOMEN

Volume I
From Settlement to the Civil War

G. J. Barker-Benfield
State University of New York at Albany

Catherine Clinton
W. E. B. Du Bois Institute at Harvard University

St. Martin's Press
New York

Senior editor: Don Reisman
Production supervisor: Katherine Battiste
Text design: Nancy Sugihara
Cover design: Darby Downey

Library of Congress Catalog Card Number: 89-60952

For information, write:
St. Martin's Press, Inc.
175 Fifth Avenue
New York, NY 10010

ISBN: 0-312-02428-2

Acknowledgments

"Pocahontas" by Philip Young. Originally published as "The Mother of Us
    All: Pocahontas Reconsidered," *Kenyon Review,* Vol. 24, Summer,
    1962, rights owned by Young.
"Anne Hutchinson," by M. J. Lewis. This essay has been revised by the
    editors from a work in progress by M. J. Lewis.
"Phillis Wheatley" by Charles Scruggs. Parts of this essay were published
    previously in "Phillis Wheatley and the Poetical Legacy of Eighteenth-
    Century England," *Studies in Eighteenth-Century Culture,* Vol. 10.
    Courtesy of University of Wisconsin Press.
"Catharine Beecher" by Kathryn Kish Sklar. Previously published as "Catha-
    rine Beecher's *A Treatise on Domestic Economy:* A Document in Do-
    mestic Feminism," edited by Earl A. French and Diana Royce, *Portraits
    of a Nineteenth-Century Family* (Hartford, Conn.: Stowe-Day Founda-
    tion, 1976), Courtesy of Stowe-Day Foundation.
"Margaret Fuller" by Bell Gale Chevigny. Reprinted with permission of
    Charles Scribner's Sons, an imprint of Macmillan Publishing Company,
    from *American Writers,* Supplement II, edited by Leonard Unger and A.
    Walton Litz. Copyright © 1960, 1961, 1963, 1964, 1965, 1968, 1969,
    1970, 1971 by the University of Minnesota.

Acknowledgments and copyrights are continued at the back of the book on
    page 247, which constitutes an extension of the copyright page.

To all students in women's history,
past, present, and future.

Preface

The title of our book reveals much about our goals. The word *portrait* emphasizes the individuality of a particular woman and the historian's representation of her. By combining *American* and *women*, we include the general features of the cultural life that individuals shared with others who were American and who were women. Scholars always have to balance two dimensions of their subject: the distinctive and the common, the exceptional and the representative. So in each "portrait" the reader will find references to many other women as well as generalizations about the period in which they lived. Our text attempts to paint a picture of not only women's history in general, but the history of gender roles and relations in the United States, in the context of the broad scope of social history. Clearly, women's lives provide a vital perspective through which the great panorama of social change in the American past can be understood.

We have placed introductory essays before each grouping of portraits to provide connections between our subjects and their times. Insofar as it is possible to do so in so brief a space, these essays aim to locate the histories of women and men together by period and to provide a sense of their continuities through the whole gallery of the American past. We hope these introductory passages will make the major themes of American history and women's role in these significant transformations accessible to general readers. Until recently, the "womanless" American history was the norm. But in fact, without a history of women we neglect consideration of gender dynamics, sex roles, and family and sexual relations—the very fundamentals of human interaction.

We want to emphasize that the individuality of each portrait is a distinguishing feature of the book. We decided on this for two reasons. First, the portraits demonstrate the sheer quality and variety of women's experiences and contributions throughout American history. The ways in which individual women have been able to push beyond the ideological myths attempting to define them as the "second sex" provide absorbing material. Perhaps one of the most notable developments in the history of the American nation, one which can be detected in the following pages, has been the mass "awakening" of women.

Second, it could be said that our portraits are representative in that they represent for many women the possibilities of their historical circumstances. At the same time, we do not mean that these women "typify" female experience in the American past. A typical woman was more subordinated to productive and reproductive labors and was denied the possibilities of finding her own voice and of leaving us a record of it. It was only recently that, inspired by the changes of the 1960s, social historians developed ingenious ways of recovering the pasts of the uneducated, the poor, and the oppressed; we applaud these efforts, which enrich our historical horizons through their studies of women of color and others who left behind only the faintest traces of their lives.

There are many paths to the past, and we wish to provide you with some of the principles that shaped the composition of our gallery of portraits. First and foremost, we decided to include in our collection women who made significant contributions in the public realm. The second was the availability of accessible source material to allow us a viable portrait of each subject. In a few cases we could find neither suitable primary papers nor scholars involved in biographical research to undertake such a project. In some instances, we found a few previously published essays that suited our needs, and we adapted these to our text. But the majority of our portraits are commissioned pieces, written by scholars engaged in ongoing research on their subjects. Our selection process was also guided by our desire to maintain as diverse and balanced a group as possible to represent coverage within each chronological era. The portraits are fashioned to appeal to a wide range of readers, but all include sound scholarship and accessible prose and raise provocative issues to illuminate women's lives within a broad range of historical transformations.

Our second goal in thus presenting a series of individual histories is derived from our experience as scholars and teachers. Students of American history seem to find biographical approaches very appealing, and we obviously share that view. As exciting and revealing as other approaches to women's history have been over the last quarter century—and we have incorporated these findings where relevant—the lives of individuals continue to defy generalizations and to create compelling reading.

Our portraits are of women who realized their potential more than did the majority of their sisters, for a whole range of reasons, which we challenge you to consider. Between the introductory essays and the portraits, we would like our readers to ponder the question, What distinguished each individual woman portrayed from other women of her time and place? By making our intentions and assumptions about the book explicit, we encourage you to question our choices and think of alternatives. Most of all, we want *Portraits of American Women* to stimulate you to fresh ways of thinking about the history of women, of America, and of yourselves.

We would like to thank the following scholars for their anonymous but very welcome reviews of an early draft of our manuscript: Jo Ann Argersinger, University of Maryland, Baltimore County; Kathleen Berkeley, University of North Carolina, Wilmington; Victoria Brown, San Diego State University; Miriam Cohen, Vassar College; Janet L. Coryell, University of Dayton; Barbara Epstein, University of California, Santa Cruz; Barbara L. Green, Wright State University; Jaclyn Greenberg, University of California, Los Angeles; Susan M. Hartmann, Ohio State University; Ann J. Lane, Colgate University; Carol Lasser, Oberlin College; Joanne Meyerowitz, University of Cincinnati; Fred M. Rivers, Towson State University; Jean R. Soderlund, University of Maryland, Baltimore County; and Margaret B. Wilkerson, University of California, Berkeley. We would also like to thank all those at St. Martin's Press who helped to produce this book: Elise Bauman, Don Reisman, Abigail Scherer, Heidi Schmidt, Bob Sherman, Jean Smith, and Richard Steins.

All of our friends and colleagues give us indispensable support, but several gave generously of their time and skills in specific ways: Anne Braden, Ellen Fitzpatrick, Jacqueline Jones, Debbie Neuls, Tammy Rich, Angie Simeone, and Bennett Singer. We received invaluable institutional support from the Department of American Studies at Brandeis University, the W. E. B. Du Bois Institute at Harvard University, and the Department of History at the State University of New York at Albany.

We thank our families, Patricia West, Daniel Colbert, and Drew and Ned Colbert for their sacrifices and support.

Our part introductions are the distillation of courses we have taught for years, and the best aspects of them represent the fine work of historians whose gratifyingly large number make them impossible to specify here. But we can single out the fellow scholars whose work makes up this volume. They have given us much more than their chapters. Along with helping us to meet the inevitable challenges of the process, they strengthened old friendships, established new ones, and reaffirmed our faith in the great enterprise of writing women's history.

G. J. Barker-Benfield
Catherine Clinton

Contents

Preface *vii*

PART I
Colonial Beginnings *1*

Pocahontas (1596?–1617)   Philip Young 13

Anne Hutchinson (1591–1643)   M. J. Lewis 35

PART II
Many Revolutions *55*

Eliza Lucas Pinckney (1722–1793)   Constance B. Schulz 65

Nancy Ward (1738?–1822)   Theda Perdue 83

Phillis Wheatley (1753–1784)   Charles Scruggs 103

Mercy Otis Warren (1728–1814)   Marianne B. Geiger 121

PART III
The Flowering of Antebellum Culture *137*

*Maria Weston Chapman
   (1806–1885)*   Catherine Clinton 147

Catharine Beecher (1800–1878)   Kathryn Kish Sklar 169

Margaret Fuller (1810–1850)   Bell Gale Chevigny 189

PART IV
Divided Loyalties   209

Elizabeth Cady Stanton
   (1815–1902)   Bruce Miroff 221

Mary Todd Lincoln (1818–1882)   Jean Baker 241

Varina Howell Davis (1826–1906)   Joan Cashin 259

Charlotte Forten (1837–1914)   Brenda Stevenson 279

About the Authors 300

PORTRAITS
OF AMERICAN
WOMEN

Volume I
From Settlement
to the Civil War

PART I

Colonial Beginnings

Cultures from three continents came together in seventeenth-century North America; they were remarkably different from one another. Already present were dozens of nations of indigenous peoples, who possessed at least a thirty-thousand-year history on the continent. These peoples had created complex societies and political systems, between which there had been long traditions of international relations that included trade, diplomacy, and war. The people from across the Atlantic, seen by the native inhabitants as invaders, came from several European countries. They brought an increasing number of Africans to the land they saw as the "New World." The Africans, like the Indians and the Europeans, came from a wide range of nations, each with a long and complex history.

The different native inhabitants may be grouped together by their common languages. For example, along the Atlantic seaboard, the large number of diverse nations can be divided into four distinct language groups: the Muskogean, Algonkian, Iroquoian, and Siouan. All of their economies were based on a mix of farming and hunting. Within most nations women farmed while men hunted, traded, negotiated, and fought. Those nations in which farming predominated tended to be matrilineal, that is, children traced their lineage through their mothers. Nations in which hunting was the chief source of food tended to be patrilineal; lineage was traced through fathers. The religions of these people shared certain characteristics, among them the belief in spirits, a divine creator, the presence on earth of both the natural and supernatural, and the power of prayer and ritual.

In some matrilineal nations, women may have exercised significant political and social influence. However, it is important not to romanticize the "precontact" authority of Indian women. The political power of Iroquois women was real but indirect. Their greater autonomy within their economic domain may have been derived from their physical separation from their menfolk, who were frequently absent hunting. And if in some nations the women were beneficiaries of greater sexual freedom (notably, divorce was exceedingly simple), they were also subordinated and feared by men because of their reproductive capacities. Childbirth and menstruation were hedged around with powerful taboos; men used the term "woman" as an insult, and in some tribes mutilated women for sexual transgressions.

As ethnohistorians have shown us, the relationship between Europeans and Indians was a two-way street. Europeans introduced guns, alcohol and other kinds of trade goods into the Indian economy. The native peoples taught the Europeans how to understand the new environment, even while fighting them and resisting their encroachments.

By early in the seventeenth century, the English, the Dutch, the French, and the Swedes had all established permanent colonies on the North American mainland. All of these had been preceded by the Spaniards in "New Spain," who had fanned out from Central America and explored vast areas from Florida to California during the previous century. The Spanish conquistadors had taken over the indigenous empires of the Aztecs and the Incas, ransacking them for gold and capitalizing on forced native labor. As other European powers attempted to emulate these exploits, they were frequently in deadly competition with each other as well as with the indigenous nations. The English eventually triumphed over rival Europeans on North America's eastern seaboard. Their settlements grew within two chief regions, along the Chesapeake in the south and on Massachusetts Bay in the north.

The first English settlers on the Chesapeake, organized as the Virginia Company, were an uneasy assortment of male adventurers with fantasies of getting rich quick. After starvation, disease, and deadly warfare led to the near disintegration of the Jamestown, Virginia settlement they found they could flourish only by the exhausting manual labor of tobacco cultivation.

The six Algonkian groups inhabiting that part of the Chesapeake region were confederated under the leadership of Powhatan. Although characterized by raids and skirmishes, relations between the English and Powhatan Confederacy at first served the purposes of both groups. The English were enabled to survive largely because of the food they received from the native peoples in exchange for steel knives and guns, which were adapted by the Indians to their own cultural purposes, including use as weapons in disputes with their neighbors. Pacts of mutual interest between the English and the Powhatans were formalized by a treaty in 1614, of which the marriage between Powhatan's daughter Pocahontas and the English settler John Rolfe was a symbol.

The profitability of tobacco led more and more settlers to encroach onto Powhatan land. On Good Friday in 1622, Opechancough, Powhatan's successor attacked the English and killed about a quarter of the settlement's population. The rest escaped only because of forewarning by two Christianized Indians. With the help of reinforcements from England, the settlers eventually defeated Opechancough; however, the severity of this raid led the English king to take over the Virginia Company. The settlement became a royal colony, to be ruled directly by the king's representative, a development that demonstrates the crucial influence of native peoples' resistance on shaping European settlement as a whole.

Though Opechancough's attack killed 347 English, that figure was only a fraction of the staggering number of deaths incurred by the early settlers. Between 1607 and 1624, over 80 percent of the 8,500 whites who came to Virginia had died. Maintaining the population in the face of disease and a difficult climate meant that the Chesapeake colonies of Virginia and Maryland (chartered in 1632) required a continual flow of immigrants, the majority of whom were men.

The colony failed to "self-reproduce" until the turn of the century. English women had come to Virginia as early as 1608, although in much smaller numbers than men. Most women were indentured servants, but they were also intended as wives. The disproportionate number of men was seen as contributing to the colony's anarchic tendencies. In 1619 the colony's promoters dispatched the list of several boatloads of "maids" to Virginia. Their rationale was the one generally given for encouraging the shipment of women: "the plantation can never flourish till families be planted and the respect of wives and children fix the people on the soil." Women continued to come as indentured servants. They tended to be in their teens and early twenties, looking to get married after their term of servitude expired. Because of the greater proportion of men and the relative freedom from family control, former servants found it easier to get married than in England. They were also able to carve out a more prosperous life than they would have had in England: if women survived to marry and then to outlive their husbands, they would, as widows, gain greater independence than would be the case once the population of the colony began to stabilize demographically.

Regardless of these opportunities during the early years of settlement, women led a hardscrabble life. Many servants worked in
the tobacco fields when their masters found it necessary. They
encountered the hardship of seasoning (the physical and psychological adjustment to the climate) and diseases such as malaria,
and they faced higher rates of death in childbirth and infant mortality. Families were broken continually by early death. But
many women survived where the men of their families did not.
The premature death of a father and sons made patriarchal authority and lineage more difficult to enforce.

By 1700, the plantation patriarchy, or plantocracy, emerged out
of the terrible struggles of early settlement. This caste dominated
the social ideals and organization of society from courthouse to
household. By then, because it was clear they could depend upon
the forced agricultural labor of slaves imported from Africa, Chesapeake plantation owners identified themselves still more closely
with Old Testament patriarchs. Furthermore, the hierarchical restraints on women were reinforced by the region's interracial character. As white men attempted to preserve an unmixed white
lineage within their own class, they prohibited white women from
intercourse with black men. The sexual double standard allowed
male slave owners to increase their slave stock by their own intercourse with slave women, and furthermore, African-American
women had no legal recourse in cases of rape.

The circumstances of immigrants to Virginia and Maryland
differed significantly from those migrating to Massachusetts and
other northern colonies. The English women settling in New
England came as parts of whole families within communally
organized social experiments. They were inspired and led by two
kinds of Puritans. In England some Protestant reformers were
called Puritans because they believed that the English or "Anglican" Church, while separated from Rome since 1529, had not
been "purified" enough from its entanglement with what they
saw as worldly corruptions, and the presumption that the individual could buy or work his or her way into heaven. As dissenters,
they believed the power of salvation resided with God, not with
worldly institutions. Among themselves they differed over the
extent to which Puritans should work within the Anglican
Church or separate themselves from it. A small group of those
who believed they should separate entirely, the Separatists,

landed in 1620 at a place they called Plymouth. A much larger group of "non-separating" Congregationalists settled at Massachusetts Bay, beginning in 1628. These later immigrants dispersed very quickly, settling in townships in what would later become the colonies of Connecticut and New Hampshire and the state of Maine. All of the early settlements required exhausting work, but in the northern climate and with communal efforts, the physical strains were dramatically less than those faced by Chesapeake residents.

With a more balanced ratio of men and women, and possessing a more cohesive set of social values, the population and culture of New England reproduced itself virtually from the beginning. This meant a rapid duplication of the traditional gender hierarchy; indeed, with their strict interpretation of scripture, these Puritans attempted to establish a state on an even more patriarchal basis than the one that existed in England. The male heads of household believed that they directly embodied the authority of their Calvinist God. In 1630, a Massachusetts minister publicly praised his wife for her "incomparable meekness of spirit, toward myself, especially." The female members of a clergyman's family, above all, his wife, held exemplary positions in the community as his agents, and they were expected to instill virtue in their household servants and take notes during a husband's sermons. But they were also subordinate to men. They faced a rigid male hierarchy bent on implementing the will of a patriarchal "masculine" God.

Puritanism, therefore, had ambiguous meanings for women. That some were charged with taking notes on sermons indicated that women were literate and were assumed to be intelligent. Women could attain salvation, the most important value of the culture, just as men could. Nevertheless, they were excluded from the operations of the formal, hierarchical institutions of Puritan belief, which in effect defined the terms on which salvation could be reached. The ministry was entirely male. At the same time the ideal in Protestantism of a direct relation between the believer and God promised some self-expression for women which was unmediated by men. The Protestant emphasis on exposure to the word of God in the printed and vernacular Bible could lead to considerable literacy, one of the greatest resources for modern individualism. Two of the most famous women of

early Massachusetts history, Anne Hutchinson and Anne Bradstreet, owed their educations to the Protestant beliefs of their
fathers. Both fathers were wealthy enough to provide their daughters with access to libraries, all of which were private at the time.
But Hutchinson and Bradstreet's literacy led them in different
directions. On the one hand, Anne Hutchinson's story illustrates
the terrible obstacles that were faced even by a skilled theologian. On the other, the poet Anne Bradstreet was able to turn the
possibilities of Protestantism to her own advantage. Born in
1612, Bradstreet survived migration from England to Massachusetts, frequent illness, the birth of ten children, and the demands
of women's work in the new colony. While doing so she probed
Puritan ideology, just as Hutchinson had done. Bradstreet came
down on the side of gender orthodoxy, as her epitaph to her
mother illustrates: "A worthy Matron of unspotted life/A loving
Mother and obedient wife." Whereas the outspoken Anne Hutchinson was banished and killed, Anne Bradstreet became the greatest artist of seventeenth-century colonial America. Bradstreet's
verses show she was "a learned lady," a Renaissance humanist of
enormous philosophical sophistication.

Both of these women were exceptional because they were well-
known in their own age and were able to leave documentary
traces. Bradstreet was a member of the ruling elite and received
support from male kin. In England she had been educated in a
nobleman's household, where her father held the important office of steward. Spending her adult life in a small distant colony,
she was in a position to write "The Dialogue between Old England and New." Hutchinson and Bradstreet had found intellectual and moral inspiration in Protestantism, despite its domination by men. Protestantism would continue to provide women
such resources and may be seen as one root of nineteenth-
century feminism.

In 1681 the English king granted his friend, the Quaker William Penn, the huge territory that became known as Pennsylvania. The Quaker commitment to toleration, even of Indians, at
first made Pennsylvania a haven for many groups of European
dissenters, including Swiss Mennonites, French Huguenots, and
German Protestants. Philadelphia, along with New York (as
"New Amsterdam" had been renamed in 1664 when the English
conquered it from the Dutch), became the chief ports of entry for

the immigration which poured in during the next century. The New England colonies meanwhile remained far less receptive to non-English or non-Puritan immigrants. One of Anne Hutchinson's supporters, Mary Dyer, had been converted to Quakerism by George Fox, founder of the sect, during a sojourn to England in the 1650s. She returned to Boston to preach her faith but was hanged by the Puritans in 1660, twenty-two years after Anne Hutchinson met her fate.

Seventeenth-century America was a frontier of red, white, and black. Enslaved Africans were brought first to the Caribbean sugar colonies (far and away the most profitable part of the European New World empire through the eighteenth century) and then to the later-established mainland colonies. They mostly came from the agricultural and trading kingdoms between the Senegal and Niger rivers and the Gulf of Benin, and from the Kingdom of Angola. Various in economies and cultures, Africans' long, complex histories rivalled those of European nations. In certain respects their religions resembled the religions of indigenous peoples of America: Africans did not separate the sacred and secular as dramatically as did Protestants, and they invested natural phenomena with spiritual forces. Africans held that their dead ancestors entered a pantheon of gods existing under a supreme being; ancestors could mediate with gods on behalf of their earthly descendants, as could certain living priests.

African gender arrangements varied from nation to nation. In many regions of Africa from which slaves were bought or stolen, women tilled the soil and cultivated crops. (Rice cultivation, unknown in Europe, was probably introduced to the Carolinas by African technology.) Among the Ibo, the sexes worked together throughout the whole agricultural cycle, while among the Yoruba, the men did most of the agricultural labor and women helped only with harvest. In addition to farmwork, African women had the tasks of childcare, spinning, and weaving.

Though traumatized by enslavement and the horrors of the "middle passage" (the transatlantic crossing), the Africans, no less than the Europeans, brought cultural baggage with them to the New World. However, because they arrived in comparatively small numbers throughout the seventeenth century, were drawn from several regions and disparate language groups, and were scattered among aliens and exposed to the full force of European power, Africans had far less opportunity to recreate their Old World than did the English. Their age at their time of capture and the circumstances of their lives in slavery would dictate the terms on which they would attempt to rebuild their culture. By far the largest proportion of Africans was shipped into southern colonies for clearing the land and for harsh field labor. The greater demand for males led to an unbalanced sex ratio. Together with the damaging physical conditions under which Africans were forced to work, this severely reduced African-American prospects for a more stable family life, a condition which lasted until the eighteenth century.

Ætatis suæ 21. Aº. 1616.

Matoaks als Rebecka daughter to the mighty Prince
Powhatan Emperour of Attanoughkomouck als Virginia
converted and baptized in the Christian faith, and
Wife to the worⁿ Mʳ Tho: Rolff.

Pocahontas

(1596?–1617)

Philip Young

From the little verifiable evidence that exists, a remarkable legend about the life of Pocahontas has been passed down through the years. Disputes over her actual role in early America continue to the present day. We do know she was the daughter of a Virginia tidewater chieftain, Powhatan. But even her name creates controversy: although she is referred to as Pocahontas—which means "playful one"—her birth name might have been Matoaka.

At the heart of the legend is the story that she "saved" Captain John Smith from execution by her father's hand. She was held captive in Jamestown, and later converted to Christianity and was baptized Rebecca. In 1614 she married an English widower, John Rolfe; their marriage was meant to symbolize peace efforts between natives and European settlers. In 1616 Rolfe took his wife and their son Thomas to London on a diplomatic mission with the colonial governor, where Pocahontas was sought after in English society and presented at court. In March 1617 she died before she could return to her home and people.

. . . having feasted him after their best barbarous manner they could, a long consultation was held, but the conclusion was, two great stones were brought before *Powhatan:* then as many as could layd hands on him, dragged him to them, and thereon laid his head, and being ready with their clubs, to beate out his braines, *Pocahontas* the Kings dearest daughter, when no intreaty could prevail, got his head in her armes, and laid her owne upon his to save him from death: whereat the Emperour was contented he should live to make him hatchets, and her bells, beads, and copper. . . .

Of course it may never have happened at all and even if it did we think we may be a little tired of it. Yet three and a half centuries have elapsed, and this interminable sentence about an incident from the travels of Captain John Smith still lives. Americans, their literature swarming with its offspring, still without revulsion can summon up the old image: Smith pinned down by savages, his head on a rock, all those clubs about to smash it; and the lovely Indian princess, curiously moved out from the crowd and across all the allegiances of her family, home and land, her religion and her race, lowering her head to his. Why can this commonplace, even banal, picture absorb us yet?

Shopworn by sentimentality, Pocahontas endures and stands with the most appealing of our saints. She has passed subtly into our folklore, where she lives as a popular fable—a parable taught children who carry some vague memory of her through their lives. She is an American legend, a woman whose actual story has blended with imaginary elements in time become traditional. Finally, she is one of our few, true native myths, for with our poets she has successfully attained the status of goddess, has been beatified, made holy, and offered as a magical and moving explanation of our national origins. What has happened to her story, why did it happen—and in fact what really was her story? It may be that our very familiarity with Pocahontas has kept us from looking at her closely enough to see what is there.

I

Even in the sketchiest of outlines, the story from which all the folklore and legends take off is a good one. As every schoolchild knows, the English arrived in Jamestown in 1607. During December of that year, while exploring the Chickahominy River, Smith—who had worked his way up from prisoner to leader of the expedition—was captured by men of chief Powhatan, and two of his companions were killed. It was at this time that he reputedly was rescued from

15

death by the chief's favorite child, a young girl—no more than
twelve or thirteen—called Pocahontas. Then, after what struck him
as some very odd behavior on the part of the Indians, he was allowed
to return to Jamestown, a place where—the great majority of its
members dying within a year of their arrival—one of the most appalling casualty rates in history was being established. By placating
Indians and planting corn, and with the help again of Pocahontas,
who is said often to have brought supplies, and once to have come
through the forest on a dark night to warn of an attack by her father,
Smith is usually credited with having temporarily saved the colony.
He gave the credit to her, however, as having done most, "next under
God," to preserve the settlers.

The Captain returned to England in 1609, and in that year ships
under Sir Thomas Gates brought relief to a group of people so desperate that one man had eaten his wife. The *Sea Venture*, flagship of the
fleet, was wrecked in Bermuda, but its survivors somehow built a
new vessel, and with it made Jamestown. One of its passengers was
an Englishman named John Rolfe. Some time elapsed before he saw
Pocahontas, because for a while she had no connection with the
vicissitudes of the colonists. But in 1613, while visting the chief of
the Potomacs, she was tricked into captivity by an Indian bribed
with a copper kettle, and taken as security for English men and
equipment held by Powhatan. Now she met Rolfe, whose first wife
had died in Virginia, and soon they expressed a desire to marry.
Powhatan gave his approval but Rolfe had to get permission from his
own superiors, and wrote Sir Thomas Dale a passionate, tedious
letter protesting that he wished to marry Pocahontas despite, as he
put it, her "rude education, manners barbarous and cursed generation," for the good of the plantation, the honor of England, the glory
of God, and his own salvation—not "to gorge myself with inconti-
nency" but, according to God's wish, to convert the girl. Even Smith
had said that conversion was the first duty of the settlers; permission was granted. Dale gave the girl a good deal of religious instruction, christened her Rebecca—it was the first such conversion by the
colonists—and in April of 1614 she and Rolfe were married.

Rolfe, it is generally believed, was primarily responsible for the
production of the tobacco—detested by both King James and Smith—
which made the colony permanent, and in 1616 he and his wife and
their son Thomas were taken abroad by Dale to publicize the success
of Jamestown. Thus it was that Pocahontas, less than six weeks after
the death of William Shakespeare, arrived in England. In the party too
was an Indian named Tomocomo, whom a thoughtful Powhatan had
sent as a scout. He had a sheaf of sticks in which he was to place a
notch for each white person he encountered, and some equally trou-

blesome instruction to see this "God" about whom the English talked so much.

Pocahontas fared better, for a time. She was honored by the church and feted by the King and Queen, to whom Smith in glowing terms had commended her as his savior. James Stuart demanded to know if her commoner husband had not committed a treasonable act in marrying a princess. The Lady Rebecca became the toast of London, where alert pubs changed their names to "La Belle Sauvage." But not everything went well. She saw Smith again and was mysteriously displeased. Then while preparing for her return to Jamestown she was taken sick, very likely with smallpox, and died. She made a godly end, according to Smith, at the age of perhaps twenty-two, and was buried on the 21st of March, 1617, at Gravesend, on the banks of the Thames.

Her father survived her by only a year. Her husband returned to Virginia alone, married once again, and was killed four years later by Indians. Her son Thomas grew up in England, and then came back to this country to start the line of proud Virginians—of Jeffersons and Lees, of Randolphs, Marshalls, and an estimated two million other people—who to this day trace their ancestry back to the Indian girl. Smith transferred his affections to New England, which he named, but was never able to get the colonial job he wanted and died in bed in 1631. As for Pocahontas, the exact place of her burial is unknown, and the only tangible remains of her are a pair of earrings and a portrait, done in 1616, showing a dark and handsome if uncomfortable young lady, incongruously overdressed in English clothes.

There are other details of a more or less factual nature that have been added to this story by people who knew Pocahontas, or who wrote of her during her lifetime. Smith himself supplies some of them. It is he who describes that day in England when he somehow so upset her, and she "turned about, obscured her face," on seeing him—an event which, since Smith either could not explain it or did not wish to, has tantalized generations of romantics.

There is also the testimony of Samuel Purchas, who was present when Pocahontas was received by the Lord-Bishop of London with even more pomp than was accorded other great ladies of the time, and who records in *Hakluytus Posthumus* or *Purchas his Pilgrimes* (1625) the impressive dignity with which the young lady received her honors. And in his *True Discourse of the Present Estate of Virginia* (1615) Ralph Hamor put down the pious details of her conversion and marriage.

But not all these additions conform to the somewhat stuffy reputation that has been built for her. Smith, for instance, coldly comments that he might have married the girl himself—or "done what he listed" with her. He also supplies a colorful but usually neglected incident relating how she and "her women" came one day "naked out of the woods, onely covered behind and before with a few green leaves . . . singing and dauncing with most excellent ill varietie, oft falling into their infernall passions"; and also tells how, later, "all these Nymphes more tormented him than ever, with crowding, pressing and hanging about him, most tediously crying, Love you not me?"

In addition, William Strachey, in his *Historie of Travaile into Virginia Britannia*, written about 1615, supplies information which does not appear in Sunday School versions of the story. The first secretary of America's oldest colony and the friend of great poets, including Donne, Jonson, and probably Shakespeare, Strachey disturbs the tenderhearted by noting that Rolfe's future bride is already married, to a "private captaine, called Kocoum." Even worse is his description of Pocahontas in earlier days as a "well-featured but wanton yong girle" who used to come to the fort and "get the boyes forth with her into the markett place, and make them wheele, falling on their hands, turning their heels upwards, whome she would followe and wheele so herselfe, naked as she was, all the fort over."

These are all the important sources of the Pocahontas story. Strachey's intelligence was not published until some 234 years after he wrote. Smith's swashbuckling accounts of his own adventures were taken as gospel for even longer, though for quite a while the story of Pocahontas had very little circulation, and was seldom repeated outside a couple of books on Virginia. But when about the start of the nineteenth century Americans began to search intensely for their history the romance was resurrected, and Pocahontas began to loom large as the guardian angel of our oldest colony. Exaggerating even Smith's accounts of her, historians entered into a quaint struggle to outdo each other with praise, concentrating of course on the rescue story. Considering the flimsiness of the evidence, it is odd that for a long time no one seems to have entertained the slightest doubt of its authenticity. On all sides, instead, sprung up the most assiduous and vigilant defense of the lady. Here the case of the Honorable Waddy Thompson is instructive. Poor Thompson, who had been our minister to Mexico, published in 1846 his "Recollections" of that place, and in his desire to praise a girl named Marina, "the *chère amie* and interpreter of Cortez," he let slip a remark he must have regretted the rest of his days. He said that Pocahontas was "thrown into the shade" by her.

The response to these imprudent words was dreadful; an anonymous Kentuckian rushed into print a whole pamphlet Vindicating her Memory. He appealed to all Virginians, to all Americans, and finally "to the admirers of virtue, humanity, and nobleness of soul, wherever to be found," against this Erroneous Judgment. Pocahontas had every gift Marina possessed, and—no *chère amie*—she had also, he added, her "good name." Indeed, it is not possible to improve on her, and to demonstrate either this or his scholarship the gentleman from Kentucky appended long accounts of her from the work of twenty-six historians, including French, German, and Italian representatives. Her character is "not surpassed by any in the whole range of history" is one estimate.

The author of this pamphlet also spoke of "proof" that Pocahontas rescued Smith, which he called "one of the most incontestable facts in history": "The proof is, the account of it given by Captain Smith, a man incapable of falsehood or exaggeration . . . hundreds of eyewitnesses . . . and to this may be added tradition." Here the gentleman defends, somewhat ineptly, what no one is known to have attacked, despite the fact that there have always been excellent reasons for contesting the rescue. For one thing, the Captain had a real inclination toward this sort of tale. His *Generall Historie* of 1624, which tells the full story for the first time, reveals a peculiar talent for being "offered rescue and protection in my greatest dangers" by various "honorable and vertuous Ladies." Most striking of these is the Lady Tragabigzanda, who fell in love with him when he was in bondage, not this time to her father but to her husband, the powerful Bashaw Bogall of Constantinople. She delivered him from this slavery, and sent him to her brother, "till time made her Master of her selfe"—before which, however, Smith made a fantastic escape.

Then, much worse and apparent from the beginning, there is the well-known fact that Smith's *True Relation* of 1608, which tells of his capture by Powhatan, and speaks also of the chief's kindness and assurances of early release, contains no mention at all of any rescue. He had plenty of other opportunities to tell the story, too, but neither he nor anyone else who wrote on Jamestown is known to have referred to the event until 1622, when he remarked in his *New England Trials*, which includes his third version of his capture: "God made Pocahontas the King's daughter the means to deliver me." Then in 1624 when his *Generall Historie* was published he told the story as we know it, and also printed for the first time his letter of eight years before to Queen Anne.

The obvious inference here is that if the rescue was actually performed Smith would have said so in the first place or, if he had not, would have told the story to others who would have repeated it. His *Historie* is boastful; it is hard to know how much of it he may have made up or borrowed from other travelers of the period. And there was a historical precedent for the Pocahontas tale: the story of a soldier, Juan Ortiz, who was lost on an expedition to Florida in 1528 and was found there by De Soto about twelve years later. Ortiz said he had been captured by Indians, and saved at the last second from burning at the stake by the chief's daughter, who later came at night in peril of her life to warn him of her father's plot to kill him. This story had appeared in London, in an English translation by Richard Hakluyt, in 1609, the year of Smith's return to that city.

Despite all grounds for suspicion, however, Smith's tale went unchallenged for well over two centuries—until about 1860, that is, when two historians, Edward D. Neill (who became known as the scavenger of Virginia history) and Charles Deane, began to make what now seem the obvious objections. These men were quickly joined by others, and in order to publicize Deane's case there entered the cause no less an intellect than that of Henry Adams. Writing anonymously in the *North American Review* in 1867, Adams lowered his biggest guns and patiently blasted what he called "the most romantic episode" in our history into what must have seemed to him and his crushed readers total oblivion. Henry Cabot Lodge concurred that the rescue belongs to fiction. Many other great men expressed themselves on the question, and quickly it became the custom to speak of the Pocahontas "legend."

Other historians, however, rushed to the defense. Chief among these were John Fiske, the philosopher and historian, and William Wirt Henry. Fiske in 1879 flatly dismissed the dismissals, and went on to champion the story. Why is it not in the *True Relation* of 1608? Because the editor of that work had obeyed an injunction against printing anything that might discourage potential colonists, and in a preface had explained that Smith had written "somewhat more" than was being published. Certainly the Captain was not allowed simply to go free, after having killed two Indians. The rescue by Pocahontas was quite in accordance with Indian custom. Any member of a tribe had a right to claim a prisoner as son or lover—but how could Smith have known enough about this to invent the tale? That scene in which he describes the weird behavior of his captors following his rescue was clearly a ceremony of adoption into the tribe, the natural consequence of Pocahontas' act. Why didn't Smith tell the story to his compatriots? Because he feared that if they knew the favor of an Indian woman was possible they would desert.

And so the battle, which continues to the present day, was on. There is a rebuttal. Why for example censor from Smith's first book a charming rescue story (which might cause desertions) and include as the editor did an excessively discouraging description of one of Smith's companions, "John Robbinson slaine, with 20 or 30 arrowes" in him? There is no easy answer to that. But, after the short period of the story's disrepute (conveniently passed in time for the Jamestown Tercentenary of 1907), wide acceptance ruled again— especially with proudly celebrating Virginians, who appeared to have forgotten that by their rules the girl was colored. Credence in the story, however, is of course not limited to the South. Indeed by 1957, when the 350th anniversary of the founding was elaborately solemnized, most Americans, including a majority of the published authorities, seemed to subscribe to the tale as fact. For the celebrations Paul Green wrote a "Symphonic Outdoor Drama" called *The Founders*, in which the key events of the young lady's life took on the force of ritual observance in performances at Williamsburg. Since the evidence is not decisive, perhaps everybody has a right to believe as he wishes.

II

Exactly what happened would not seem to make any enormous difference anyway. What counts more is the truly extraordinary way in which the story—despite the profound awkwardness of a climax that comes in the very opening scene—pervades our culture. Pocahontas is represented in countless paintings and monuments; she gives her name to ships, motels, coal mines, towns, counties, and pseudonymous writers, to secret orders and business firms. There are histories of her and Smith by everyone from poet (John Gould Fletcher) to politician ("Alfalfa Bill" Murray, a descendant). But all other signs of her fade before the plays, poems, novels, and children's books which for the last 150 years have flooded our literature. Dramatizing the story from the alleged facts, and filling gaps or inadequacies with invented material usually presented as fact, there are so many different treatments, ranging from the serious to the absurd, that they begin to look numberless.

But they fall into patterns. The first person to make literary use of Pocahontas was no less a writer than the rare Ben Jonson, who included an obscure reference to her in his *Staple of News* of 1625. Then, much later, she was treated at length in a little novel called *The Female American* (1767). Here the story as we know it is, however, simply a rehearsal for far greater events, and the really memorable thing about the book is that its author was an English lady known as Unca Eliza Winkfield, who changed Pocahontas' name to Unca, and Smith's to Winkfield, and gave her a daughter called, once more, Unca.

The writer who really started things, by first romanticizing the story in a proper way, was still another Englishman—an adventuresome fellow named John Davis, a sailor who came to this country in

1798 and spent nearly five years traveling about on foot. Very young and romantic, hyperthyroid, chronically tumescent and rather charming, Davis wrote a book about his journey called *Travels of Four Years and a Half in the United States of America.* As a part of this work he "delivered to the world" the history of Pocahontas which, he announced, was reserved for his pen. Possessed of a lively and libidinous imagination, which he seemed unable to distinguish from his written sources, Davis tore into the story with hearty masculine appetite.

He begins with Smith in the hands of Powhatan, who keeps offering his prisoner a woman. The squaws fight fiercely for the honor, but to Pocahontas' "unspeakable joy" Smith is stern and turns them all down. After she has rescued him she comes to Jamestown, weeping "in all the tumultuous extasy of love." In order to cure her Smith slips off to England, instructing his compatriots to tell the girl he has died. She prostrates herself on his empty grave, beats her bosom, and utters piercing cries. One night while she is strewing flowers about his resting place she is come upon by Rolfe, secretly in love with her and of late much given to taking moonlight walks while composing love poems. ("Of these effusions I have three in my possession," says Davis, and he prints them.) Surprised by Rolfe's appearance, Pocahontas inadvertently falls in his arms, whereupon he seizes his opportunity and drinks from her lips "the poison of delight." A woman is "never more susceptible of a new passion than when agitated by the remains of a former one," is Davis' dark but profitable explanation, and thus it is that hours later, come dawn, Rolfe "still rioted in the draught of intoxication from her lips." Eventually they marry ("nor did satiety necessarily follow from fruition," the author adds anxiously). They go to England, and Pocahontas dies there.

Davis made it clear that he wrote as a historian: "I have adhered inviolably to facts; rejecting every circumstance that had not evidence to support it," he insisted, speaking of "recourse to records and original papers." The man was too modest, for of course these were, like Rolfe's poems, original enough but with him. And he should be given credit too for having seen the possibilities of uniting richly embroidered history with a mammary fixation (habitually the bosoms of his Indian women are either "throbbing" or "in convulsive throes"). That he did see the promise of this combination, and in advance of his time, is indicated by the fact that he himself soon wrote what he called a "historical novel" on "Pokahontas." The book is formally titled *First Settlers of Virginia* (1806), but it simply pads the previous account of the girl's adventures to novel length. Dropping Rolfe's claim to the poetry, Davis managed to add a couple of mildly pornographic native scenes, to use Smith's story of the enamored Indian girls ("Love you not me?") twice, and to present

Pocahontas as "unrobed" in her first scene with Rolfe. He also prefaced a second edition with a letter from Thomas Jefferson to the effect that the President of the United States "subscribed with pleasure" to this Indian Tale.

After Davis, the deluge. This began with a vast number of plays now mostly lost, but including four prominent and commercially successful ones which are preserved. To James Nelson Barker, ex-mayor of Philadelphia and future first controller of the Treasury in Van Buren's cabinet, goes a series of firsts: his *Indian Princess* of 1808 (although anticipated in 1784 by the little-known German *Pocahontas* of Johann Wilhelm Rose) was the first important Pocahontas play and the first to be produced of the Indian plays which soon threatened to take over our stage completely; it is generally cited also as the first American play to appear in London after opening in this country. Hugely popular, and rather deservedly so, Barker's success was followed by that of George Washington Parke Curtis, step-grandson of our first president, with his *Pocahontas* of 1830, and by Robert Dale Owen. The latter, son of the more famous Robert Owen, founder of the radical Owenite communities, and himself a very early advocate of birth control, the free discussion of sex, and the rights of women, made his Pocahontas (1837) an anachronistic feminist. His play, though over-long, is not incompetent and reads very well beside *The Forest Princess* (1844) of Charlotte Barnes Conner. Mrs. Conner, an actress, stuck close to the worst nineteenth-century concepts of theatre and produced a series of unlikely postures which are epitomized in her final scene, where a pious Rebecca dying in England, hand stretched heavenward, speaks her last iambics:

> I hear my father—Husband, fare thee well.
> We part—but we shall meet—above!

after which the hand drops with the curtain.

John Brougham's *Pocahontas* (1855) was honorably designed to stop this sort of thing, and his travesty did stop the production of "serious" Pocahontas plays for quite a time, greatly diminishing the popularity of the Indian drama to boot. But today his play is, to speak politely, "dated," for the humor depends mainly on puns ("What *iron* fortune *led* you to our shores?" "To now ill-use us would be base *illusion!*") (italics his), line after line for two long acts.

Brougham's burlesque was extremely well-received, however, and it performed a service for our drama that nothing has adequately performed for our poetry. Pocahontas poems, produced in the nineteenth century by the carload, are almost uniformly dull, tasteless, and interminable. The efforts of Lydia Huntly Sigourney and William Makepeace Thackeray stand out only a little from the average.

Most nineteenth-century Pocahontas poems seem to begin either with some silly sylvan scene or with "Descend O Muse, and this poor pen . . ." Smith always arrives as expected, but the Muse invariably has other things to do.

Equally forbidding are the Pocahontas poems written in the manner of Henry Wadsworth Longfellow. Longfellow neglected to produce any Pocahontas items himself, but there are a great many poems, and several plays in verse, which have sought to rectify his oversight. These pieces are all distinguished by lines of unrimed trochaic tetrameter ("By the shore of Gitche Gumee / By the shining Big-Sea-Water") which produce a stultifying effect the poets seem to equate with an Indian atmosphere; they suffer from what might properly be known as the Curse of Hiawatha. Of course Longfellow got his famous Hiawatha line from a German translation of a national epic of the Finns, but this is not known to have stopped anyone, and on they go:

> Then the maiden Pocahontas
> Rushes forward, none can stop her,
> Throws her arms about the captive,
> Cries,—"oh spare him! Spare the Paleface!"

What burlesque and abuse cannot destroy will just have to wear itself out. Although the machinery that mass-produces low-quality Pocahontas literature has long shown signs of collapse, the end is not yet. As recently as 1958 a Pocahontas novel by one Noel B. Gerson, with nothing to recommend it but the story, was smiled on by a very large book club. And so still they come with the story, juggling the climax or devising a new one, and trying to make up somehow for the fact that Smith never married the girl. Both problems can of course be solved at once by ending with the scene from Smith in which he and Pocahontas meet in London. Here Rebecca is overcome at the sight of her lost Captain and dies in his arms, usually of a broken heart; indeed it has become a convention to do it that way. But that has not helped, and it is the plays, particularly, which indicate that an industry really is exhausted. The best written and most interesting parts of their scripts are those that deal with such matters as the construction of campfires with electric fans, logs, and strips of red cloth.

One last sign of the popular Pocahontas drama's waning was the appearance (once Brougham was well-forgotten) of an Everything but the Kitchen Sink School. There exists, for instance, an operetta in which Smith has a "regulation negro" servant, comically named Mahogany, who plays a banjo. A better sample is the *Pocahontas* (1906) of Edwin O. Ropp. Mr. Ropp named three of his Indians Hiawatha, Minnehaha, and Geronimo; and there is a rough spot in the action when a man named simply Roger (Williams?), insisting on the freedom of religious thought, disappears for good in the Virginia forest. As for Pocahontas, she is taken through her marriage with Rolfe, to England and back again to Virginia, where she lives out her days in the wilderness with her husband, two children, and their Christian grandpapa, Powhatan, singing the praises of home sweet home, as the play ends with lines lifted from the poem of that name. Mr. Ropp dedicated his play, it should be recorded, to a Moral Purpose, to the Jamestown Exposition of 1907, and to Those Who Construct the Panama Canal. The world was ready for another burlesque when, in 1918, Philip Moeller published his *Beautiful Legend of the Amorous Indian*. In this play only one character, the senile mother of Powhatan, speaks Hiawathan, and there is a heart-warming moment in the dialogue when Powhatan's wife says of her aging mother-in-law: "When she talks in that old manner it nearly drives me crazy."

III

It is not hard to find reasons for the low quality of a large part of our Pocahontas literature: the writers had no talent, for instance. A less obvious difficulty has been that most of the poets and playwrights have prided themselves that their works were founded firmly on "historical sources." This impeded the imaginations of most of them, who tried to romanticize history instead of letting the facts act as a stimulus to fiction. As a result of sentimentality and inaccuracy, there is little or no historical value in their products. And because the works are based so solidly on "history," often footnoted, they seldom have any value as fiction, for invariably events are related not because they are dramatic but because they happened—which is aesthetically irrelevant. If the story is to satisfy a modern audience, it must be treated imaginatively.

Properly told it could be a truly epic story. This is indicated by the fact that elements in the relationships of the characters are so like those in other epics of other countries—the *Aeneid*, for instance. Aeneas, we recall, was an adventurer who also sought a westward land and finally anchored at the mouth of a river. The country there was ruled by a king, Latinus, who had a beautiful daughter, Lavinia. Latinus had dreamed that his daughter's husband would come from a foreign land, and that from this union would spring a race destined to rule the world, so he received Aeneas and feasted him. Later tradition goes on to record the marriage, the birth of a son, and the founding of the city in which Romulus and Remus were born. Other parallels—with the stories of Odysseus and Nausicaa, and of Jason and Medea—likewise suggest the epic possibilities of the American tale.

To be sure, a few writers, usually in a far more modest fashion, have tried to make something of Pocahontas. Fewer still have succeeded, but even some of the failures are interesting. Working from the probability that a letter by Strachey, who was on the wrecked *Sea Venture* with Rolfe, provided Shakespeare with material for *The Tempest*, John Esten Cooke wrote a polite novel called *My Lady Pocahontas* (1885) in which he made Shakespeare dependent on the lady and Smith for his characters Miranda and Ferdinand. At the climax, Pocahontas recognizes herself on the stage of the Globe.

Much of this invention has been blithely repeated as history, but such an attempt at legend fails anyway for being too literary. Other attempts have failed for not being literary enough. Mary Virginia Wall in 1908 wrote a book on Pocahontas as *The Daughter of Virginia Dare*—the child, that is, of this first native-born "American," who mysteriously disappeared, and Powhatan. Thus it is the spirit of Virginia Dare which accounts for the Indian girl's compassion. Now this could be a fruitful merger, uniting two of our best stories and giving Americans a kind of spiritual genealogy. The fact that to have been Pocahontas' mother Virginia would have had to bear a child at eight does not really matter much. But such scenes as the one in which the daughter comes to her end matter a good deal. On her deathbed, a place that has proved scarcely less fatal for authors than for their heroine, Pocahontas stoutly carols "Hark the Herald Angel Sings" (the Amen "begun on earth and ending in heaven"), and what started with some small promise has backed all the way out of it.

Another, but much better, novel which tries to do something with the story is the *Pocahontas* (1933) of David Garnett. This is a good historical novel with a thesis. In scenes of hideous but authentic brutality, Garnett shows the Indian women torturing their naked prisoners to death in orgies of obscene cruelty. These lead directly to orgies of sexual passion which act as a purge. To this sequence he contrasts the cruelty of the whites, which they sanction with self-righteousness and piety and follow with guilt. Garnett's book is a romantic and primitivistic performance after the manner of D. H. Lawrence which uses Pocahontas, more tender than her compatriots, as a vehicle for a lesson on the superiority of uncivilized peoples. Doctrinaire, and intellectually a little sentimental, this is still probably the best Pocahontas novel.[1]

Equally good, or maybe better, are two twentieth-century plays, Margaret Ullman's *Pocahontas* (1912) and Virgil Geddes' *Pocahontas and the Elders* (1933). More interesting than the plays themselves, however, are prefatory remarks their authors made about their material. In an introductory quotation Miss Ullman speaks of her heroine as a "Sweet-smelling sacrifice to the good of Western Planting." Geddes writes that his play is a "folkpiece" and his characters "part of the soul's inheritance." Both writers, in other words, were pointing to some pregnant quality of the story which goes beyond its facts. This was a direction which an informal group of modern poets was taking too. The result was the elevation of Pocahontas to myth.

It is Vachel Lindsay who was primarily responsible for this development. In his "Cool Tombs" Carl Sandburg had asked a question:

> Pocahontas' body, lovely as a poplar, sweet
> as a red haw in November or a pawpaw in May—
> did she wonder? does she remember—in the
> dust—in the cool tombs?

About 1918 Lindsay quoted this passage, answered yes, she remembers, and went on to explain in a poem which transforms the savior of Jamestown into a symbol of the American spirit. He supplies a magical genealogy whereby the girl becomes, as in his title, "Our Mother Pocahontas." Powhatan is the son of lightning and an oak; his daughter is the lover and bride of the forest. Thus

> John Rolfe is not our ancestor.
> We rise from out the soul of her
> Held in native wonderland,
> While the sun's rays kissed her hand,
> In the springtime,
> In Virginia,
> Our mother, Pocahontas.

Though she died in England, Lindsay acknowledges, she returned to Virginia and walked the continent, "Waking, / Thrilling, / The midnight land," and blending with it. We in turn are born not of Europe but of her, like a crop, and we are sustained by our inheritance.

One statement does not make a myth, but this concept was passed to other poets, notably to Hart Crane. First, though, came William Carlos Williams. A part of his prose study of the national past, called *In the American Grain* (1925), was devoted to an excoriation of the Puritans, after the fashion of the '20s, and to praise for the sensual joy of the Indians, who are again taken over as an element of our spiritual ancestry. Williams gave only brief notice to Pocahontas, but he quoted Strachey's description of a naked, wheeling Indian girl.

These are the materials from which Crane, in *The Bridge* (1930),

raised Pocahontas to full mythic stature. In some notes he made for
the poem, Crane saw her as "the natural body of American fertility,"
the land that lay before Columbus "like a woman, ripe, waiting to be
taken." He followed his notes, and the part of his long poem called
"Powhatan's Daughter" develops them. Starting with the quotation
from Strachey (which he took from a *transition* review of Williams
by Kay Boyle) the poet in a waking dream at the harbor dawn finds
someone with him ("Your cool arms murmurously about me lay . . .
a forest shudders in your hair!"). She disappears, then, from his
semiconsciousness to reappear later as the American continent,
most familiar to hoboes who "know a body under the wide rain," as
the poet himself is familiar with trains that "Wail into distances I
knew were hers." The land blooms with her, she becomes a bride
(but "virgin to the last of men"), passes herself then to a pioneer
mother, a living symbol of the fertility of the land, and makes her
last appearance as the earth again—"our native clay . . . red, eternal
flesh of Pocahontas. . . ."

Like these four poets, Archibald MacLeish in his *Frescoes for Mr.
Rockefeller's City* (1933) was discovering his own land and his faith
in its future. Dedicating his book to Sandburg, and deriving a symbol from Crane, MacLeish describes a "Landscape as a Nude"—the
American continent as a beautiful naked Indian girl, inviting lov-
ers. With this repetition the concept has taken hold. Thus we have
a sort of American Ceres, or Demeter, or Gaea, developed from
Pocahontas—a fertility-goddess, the mother of us all. We, by our
descent from her, become a new race, innocent of both European
and all human origins—a race from the earth, as in ancient my-
thologies of other lands, but an earth that is made of her. We take
on a brave, free, mythical past as our alternative to the more pro-
saic, sordid explanation of history. And the thing is alive, as an
image of the beautiful Indian girl is set in perpetual motion, and
comes cartwheeling through our veins and down our generations.

IV

For all our concern with Pocahontas, one of the most interesting
facts about her seems to have escaped everyone: the story John
Smith told, which we have embraced so long, is one of the oldest
stories known to man—not just roughly speaking, as in the Odysseus and Aeneas myths, but precisely in all essential parts. The tale
of an adventurer, that is, who becomes the captive of the king of
another country and another faith, and is rescued by his beautiful
daughter, a princess who then gives up her land and her religion for
his, is a story known to the popular literatures of many peoples for

many centuries. The theme was so common in the Middle Ages that medieval scholars have a name for it: "The Enamoured Moslem Princess." This figure is a woman who characteristically offers herself to a captive Christian knight, the prisoner of her father, rescues him, is converted to Christianity, and goes to his native land—these events usually being followed by combat between his compatriots and hers.[2] . . . Latin anecdotes from the *Gesta Romanorum*, which contains the germs of plots used by Chaucer and Shakespeare, were widely read in translation in late sixteenth-century England (hence Smith may have known them). Tale V, called "Of Fidelity," is about a youth wasting away as a prisoner of pirates. Their chief has a lovely and virtuous daughter who frees the young man and, being promised marriage, goes to his country. The origins of this version may be in Seneca the Elder, who at the beginning of the Christian era formulated precisely the same situation in his *Controversia* as an imaginary legal case for debate. It is possible that he in turn got the story from the Greek Sophists, who had a lively interest in literature and disputation. . . . It has always been an uncomfortable fact of the Pocahontas story, and an apparently formidable obstacle to its survival, that after appearing to offer herself to Smith the heroine never married the hero. It is a startling fact, and bewildering, that this curiosity has been an element of the story from the beginning. . . . [I]t is extremely curious that there appear to be no accounts in which we are told specifically that what we might expect invariably to happen actually happens.[3]

The presence of a disturbing element in a popular story is hard to explain. The notion that melodies unheard are sweetest and cannot fade, that the lover who has not his bliss then can love forever and she be fair does not seem to account for this peculiarity; it was never that way at all. Yet there must be something obscurely "right" about an apparently unsatisfactory ending, or over the many centuries we should have succeeded in changing it. And the durable popularity of the story also urges the presence of some appeal that is not on the surface, some force that has given an advantage in the struggle for survival which we should make out if we can. The notion that the story is symbolic of something is not new. The monks who used it for religious instruction hundreds of years ago sensed this and had their own reading: the young man, they said, represents the human race. Led irresistably by the force of original sin into the prison of the devil, he is redeemed by Christ, in the form of the girl. But this interpretation incongruously makes Jesus the daughter of Satan, and seems also a little arbitrary. It is too utilitarian—but in that it offers one clue to the story's longevity.

Nothing survives indefinitely without filling some function, and the usefulness of this story is clear: the tale approves and propagates the beliefs of anyone who cares to tell it. An informal survey of the children's sections of two small Midwestern libraries disclosed twenty-six different books on Pocahontas—and no wonder. Quite apart from the opportunity she presents to give children some notion of self-sacrifice, she is, in addition to all her other appeals, perfectly ideal propaganda for both church and state. The story has long been, among other things, a tale of religious conversion, and in its American form is so eloquent a tribute to accepted institutions that there is no need to deflate its power by so much as even mentioning the obvious lesson it teaches. Of course the thing is a little chauvinistic. It is always either indifferent to the attitudes of the betrayed or unconscious of them. Indeed it is a tribute to the high regard we have for ourselves that Pocahontas has never once been cast as a villainess, for she would make an excellent one. From the point of view of her own people her crimes—repeated acts of treason, and cultural and religious apostasy—were serious. But one does not resent a betrayal to his own side, and we can always bear reassurance: love exists, love matters, and we are very eligible, Pocahontas tells us.

The story will work for any culture, informing us, whoever we are, that we are chosen, or preferred. Our own ways, race, religion must be better—so much better that even an Indian (Magian, Moor, Turk), albeit an unusually fine one (witness her recognition of our superiority), perceived our rectitude. But it nicely eases the guilt we have felt, since the start of its popularity, over the way we had already begun, by 1608, to treat the Indians. Pocahontas is a female Quanto, a "good" Indian, and by taking her to our national bosom we experience a partial absolution. In the lowering of her head we feel a benediction. We are so wonderful she loved us anyway.

And yet the story has an appeal which easily transcends such crude and frequently imperialistic functions—especially in the rescue scene, which implies all the new allegiances that follow from it. There is a picture there, at least in the American rendering, which has compelled us for so long that it must certainly contain meanings that go beyond the illustrations of it in the children's books. It is characteristic of all hallowed images that they cannot adequately be put into words, and no single rendering would articulate all that might be stated anyway. But these are feeble excuses for total silence, and it does not take any great sensitivity to perceive that Pocahontas' gesture—accomplished not by any subterfuge, but by the frank placing of her own body between Smith's and death—is fairly ringing with overtones. This is because we see her act as a rite, a ceremonial sign which bestows life. A surface part of that symbolism has always been clear. The Indians understood it as we do, and immediately Smith was alive and free. But what we have not been conscious of, though the modern poets sensed something like it, is that her candor was that of a bride. That is one thing, buried beneath awareness, that has dimly stirred us. Unable to put it into words, we have let the girl keep her secret, but the ritual that we feel in her action is itself an unorthodox and dramatic ceremony of marriage, and we are touched. We see Pocahontas at the moment of womanhood, coming voluntarily from the assembly to the altar, where she pledges the sacrifice of her own integrity for the giving of life. This is an offering up of innocence to experience, a thing that is always—in our recognition of its necessity—oddly moving. It is an act which bespeaks total renunciation, the giving up of home, land, faith, self, and perhaps even life, that life may go on.

Perhaps this helps to explain why it is that what, in its flattery of him, is at first glance so much a man's story should also be greatly promoted by women. Apparently it is a very pleasant vicarious experience for us all. Yet in the depths of our response to the heart of the story, the rescue, there is something more profoundly wishful than a simple identification with persons in a touching adventure. All myths have an element of wish somewhere in them. But there is something about this one that is also wistful, as though it expressed a wish that did not really expect to be gratified. It is as though something in us says "if only it were true. . . ."

We surely ought to know what it is we wish for. In our fondness for Pocahontas can we make out a longing that is buried somewhere below even the affection we bear for our fair selves and white causes? This yearning might be for another kind of love entirely, a love that has forever been hidden under the differences that set countries, creeds, and colors against each other. From the freedom and noble impracticality of childhood, we as a people have taken this Indian girl to heart. Could we be hinting at a wish for a love that would really cross the barriers of race? When the beautiful brown head comes down, does a whole nation dream this dream?

But it is still only a dream. And that fact helps to explain why it is that from the very beginning the story has had what looks like the wrong ending, why the wedding of the protagonists remains a symbol that was never realized. To be sure the girl eventually married, and the groom was usually the hero's compatriot, but by then the event has lost its joy and its force—seems a substitute for the real thing, and not at all satisfactory. But the story might have died centuries before us, and we would have made much less of Pocahontas, if the substitution were not in some way fit and right. We sense that the adventure has to end the way it does partly because we know the difference between what we dream and what we get. We are not particularly happy with the denouement, but we feel its correctness, and with it we acknowledge that this is all just make-believe.

To understand the rest of our dim and reluctant perception of the propriety of the story's outcome, Americans must see the Indian girl in one last way: as progenitress of all the "Dark Ladies" of our culture—all the erotic and joyous temptresses, the sensual, brunette heroines, whom our civilization (particularly our literature: Hawthorne, Cooper, Melville, and many others) has summoned up only to repress. John Smith is the first man on this continent known to have made this rejection; his refusal to embrace "the wild spirit" embodied in the girl was epic, and a precedent for centuries of denial. Prototypes too, and just as important, were the arrogantly hypocritical Rolfe and the rest of the colonists, who baptized, christened, commercialized, and ruined the young lady. With censorship and piety as tools, American writers—a few poets, far too late, aside—completed the job, until Pocahontas was domesticated for the whole of our society, where from the very start any healthy, dark happiness in the flesh is supposed to be hidden, or disapproved. Pocahontas is the archetypal sacrifice to respectability in America—a victim of what has been from the beginning our overwhelming anxiety to housebreak all things in nature, until wilderness and wildness be reduced to a few state parks and a few wild oats. Our affection for Pocahontas is the sign of our temptation, and our feeling that her misfortunes in love have a final, awkward fitness comes from our knowing that all that madness is not for us.

Notes

[1] It is not nearly so good as John Barth's *The Sot-Weed Factor* (1960), but this unprecedented novel is only incidentally about Pocahontas. Included in it, however, are John Smith's *Secret Historie,* parallel—but far superior—to John Davis' discovery of John Rolfe's poems, and the *Privie Journall* of a rival character. In the course of these extended tours-de-force a tribal custom is revealed that requires a prospective suitor to take the maidenhead of his bride before marrying her. In the case of Pocahontas no man has been successful in fracturing this membrane (indeed "most had done them selves hurt withal, in there efforts"). But with the aid of a fantastically invigorating vegetable device Smith publicly accomplishes the feat. In its review of the book, entitled "Novelist Libels Pocahontas Story," the *Richmond News-Leader* demanded to know if, in view of the respectability of the lady's descendants, all this was not "actionable."

[2] See, for instance, F. M. Warren, "The Enamoured Moslem Princess in Orderic Vital and the French Epic," *PMLA*, XXIX (1914), 341–58. It is a mistake, however, to speak of this theme as if it were wholly a matter of the distant past. For instance, the Enamoured Moslem Princess figures prominently in the Fourth Canto (1821) of Byron's *Don Juan.* Here she is Haidée, whose mother was a Moor; her father is Lambro, a pirate leader who holds the Christian Juan captive. The chieftain is about to kill his prisoner "When Haidée threw herself her body before; /... 'On me,' she cried, 'let death descend. . . .' " Juan is saved, but is taken off, and Haidée withers away and dies.

[3] The widely known and excellent ballad called "Young Beichan" seems an exception, but only because a new element, the motif of promised marriage, has been grafted on. Beichan is London-born, and longs strange lands for to see, but is taken by a savage Moor whose daughter, Susan Pye, steals her father's keys and releases him from a prison, after which he goes back to England, having promised to marry the girl in seven years. Later she abandons her country for England, is converted to Christianity, and gets a new name. She arrives in England to discover that Young Beichan has just married. But the ceremony is not yet consummated ("of her body I am free") and Susie Pye, now Lady Jane, is able to marry him after all. F. J. Child prints fourteen versions of this ballad in his *English and Scottish Popular Ballads,* while mentioning many related items in Norse, Spanish, Italian, and German. In its various forms it may have been affected by a fairly well-known legend on more or less the same theme, originating in the thirteenth century and concerning Gilbert Beket, father of St. Thomas à Becket. This also has the happy ending.

Anne Hutchinson
(1591–1643)

M. J. Lewis

Born Anne Marbury in 1591, in Alford, England, Anne Hutchinson was educated at home, where she had the benefit of her clergyman father's library. At twenty-one she married William Hutchinson, a successful Alford merchant. They had fifteen children together. In 1634, the Hutchinsons emigrated with a group of fellow Puritans, following their minister, Rev. John Cotton, to Massachusetts Bay Colony in New England. In the aftermath of a fierce political and religious struggle that erupted soon after they arrived, Anne Hutchinson was accused of supporting a church opposed by John Winthrop, the first governor of the colony. In three trials, one by the Bay's General Court and two by the Boston Church. Hutchinson was excommunicated from the church and banished from the colony. The charges against her are virtually all that are known of her life. The falsified official trial records in Winthrop's political pamphlets, published after her death, contribute to a myth surrounding Hutchinson that prevails today. The following essay focuses on the theological and political issues at stake in Hutchinson's public ordeal.

*This essay has been revised by the editors from a work in progress by M. J. Lewis.

Early in this century one of America's very few statues of a woman was erected in Boston on the State House grounds. It was a memorial to Anne Hutchinson, one of the settlers in the first great English migration to this continent in the 1630s and the first woman to be martyred for her beliefs. The statue's design and its reception, however, are as charged with ambiguity as the historical record of her life. Nearly three hundred and fifty years after her death, she remains a shadowy legend. The plaque at the base of the large bronze memorial recognizes her as a "courageous exponent of religious toleration," but the statue itself conveys a very different message. The figure is passively pious: her throat bared submissively, her eyes weakly appealing to heaven.

Moreover, the memorial was grudgingly received. The federated Women's Clubs of Massachusetts presented the statue to the Commonwealth in 1920, just two months before the Nineteenth Amendment granted women suffrage. The legislature, however, did not formally accept it for three years and has never, apparently, officially dedicated it. Reluctance to do so centered on Anne Hutchinson's reputation. In 1922 a reporter asked a legislator to explain the hesitation to accept the gift. His reply, that the statue represented her "as an idealist while many think she was aggressive," mirrors attitudes about her as strong today as they were in the twenties. The biographical dictionary *Notable American Women* portrays her as "impulsive . . . confused . . . anarchistically subjective; [she] broods morbidly . . . [is] menopausal . . . no champion of religious freedom . . . irrational," yet "a remarkably intelligent and courageous woman."[1]

This reputation and these contradictory attitudes derive entirely from documents fabricated in the seventeenth century by her opponents. Although these documents are obvious political propaganda, they have since been accepted by historians as factual and read literally. Even today, Hutchinson is celebrated as a midwife and an Antinomian* when she was neither.[2] Every effort was made to create a fiction, an official story. John Winthrop, who led one of the two groups in the conflict associated with her and was judge and prosecutor in her civil trials, is responsible for the condition of the records we have. He wrote most of the story, destroyed contrary evidence, and saw to it that most public records were altered or rewritten to be consistent with his version of the events; for example, the General Court records for the three-year period at the height of the conflict are not original, having been mysteriously recopied; the entire Boston Church record was recopied and the entries for eighteen months were removed.

*Antinomian: one who believes that faith alone, not adherence to biblical law, is necessary for salvation.

Winthrop directed the Massachusetts Bay Company's 1630 expedition to New England. Apart from two brief periods, he was governor of the colony until his death in 1649. His writings, in particular the journal he intended to transform into a history of the new country, are the primary sources for subsequent study of the conflict as well as for the first twenty years of New England history.[3] So skillfully does he write and so objective and judicious does he seem, that countless scholars have since accepted his work at face value. In fact, no modern historian has suspected the extent of his efforts to conceal his regime's illegal acts. Yet in spite of his efforts, the conflict was so profound, affected so many people, and had such momentous consequences, that it could not be completely hidden. Enough documents survived to prove beyond reasonable doubt that Winthrop's account was fraudulent. He fabricated a myth to serve his own political ends.

By comparing these documents with Winthrop's writings, we can for the first time begin to distinguish fact from fiction, a believable woman from a caricature. The woman Anne Hutchinson had dignity, self-command, and unusual intellectual and moral courage. She was thoughtful and articulate, and enjoyed the devotion of her husband and family and the respect of her peers. Winthrop casts her in the role of woman as adversary. She is Eve, a seductress luring man into disobedience to his God; the "Whore of Babylon," a metaphor for a harlot church competing with the state for political supremacy. From this role come the derogatory epithets and insinuations— "Mistress Anne," "Jezebel," "prophetess" witch, midwife, woman preacher—characterizing her in the historical legend.

We know relatively little about the woman. Nothing she wrote, no pictorial likeness, little neutral contemporaneous writing about her have been found. Of her life before she emigrated to New England, we know that she was the daughter of Bridget Dryden and Francis Marbury, a silenced Church of England minister, who was tried, imprisoned twice and silenced by church courts for his attacks on incompetent clergy. She was born in Alford, Lincolnshire, and baptized July 20, 1591. When she was fourteen, she moved with her family to London. On August 9, 1612, at twenty-one, she married William Hutchinson, an affluent merchant and native of Alford. They returned to Alford, where they lived for the next twenty years. During this time she bore fourteen children, only two of whom died in childhood—a survival rate that testifies to her great vigor and remarkably competent childrearing. In 1634, when she was forty-three, the family joined a large contingent of emigrants from Lincolnshire to New England. We know little of the first two years of her life in Boston, except that she bore a fifteenth child, baptized in Boston Church in 1636.[4]

The Lincolnshire settlers were followers of the dissident minister John Cotton, who had accepted the pulpit of Boston Church the year before. Rich merchants and minor gentry, their number and quality made them prominent in Bay society. Most joined Boston Church, among them Anne and William Hutchinson. The men assumed leading positions in state and church; William became a Boston town commissioner, inferior court judge, deputy to the Bay's chief governing body, and was ordained a deacon in Boston Church.

The heart of the conflict that eventually drove most of the Lincolnshire settlers into exile seems to have been control of the pulpit. From its beginning, the Bay Company exercised authority over the church: hired ministers, paid passage for them and their families to New England and guaranteed return, provided housing and handsome stipends, determined the number of churches, and limited the franchise to church members. These and other practices transformed a private company into an independent and illegal state government, with the church as a subordinate arm.

John Winthrop later claimed that John Cotton's first sermon in Boston argued against a state-salaried ministry and for the congregation's obligation to pay its own minister. Implicit in Cotton's argument was the power to elect the minister, or lay control of the pulpit—a power exercised in England by hiring lecturers, ministers who preached, but did not dispense the sacraments. Cotton submitted to state support, but the debate over congregational control continued in private meetings. Many, if not most, of those in the influx of new settlers were part of groups led by ministers expecting to form their own congregations. Fearing loss of its authority over the pulpit, Winthrop's government denied these groups permission to congregate separately. Rather than join the established churches, many of them met privately. When increasing numbers chose such meetings, which were, in effect, competing churches, they became a threat to political stability. The meetings deprived the legal churches of members and implicitly repudiated their state-salaried ministers. More importantly, they were powerful vehicles for dissent and resistance to state control. Thus they had to be suppressed. (Roger Williams, for example, was forced into exile for holding such meetings.)

After offering some resistance, many groups gave up and moved out of the Bay jurisdiction. But one minister and his followers, part of the group from Lincolnshire, challenged state control of the pulpit when they were denied the right to form a church. The minister, John Wheelwright, who was Anne Hutchinson's brother-in-law, had arrived in June 1636 with his family, including William Hutchinson's mother. According to John Winthrop's deeply-biased account, a dispute with Wheelwright and his allies began in late October 1636, when most of Boston Church tried to hire him as a lecturer. When their efforts were thwarted by John Winthrop, the group proposed a church at Mount Wollaston, nine miles away, where many of them had large farms. By this time, the group enjoyed considerable power. Among its leaders was Henry Vane, a brilliant young nobleman who came to New England in the fall of 1635 representing enormously wealthy and powerful English investors and political interests. Within months of his arrival, Vane attracted so wide a following that in May 1636 he was elected governor, forcing Winthrop to serve as deputy-governor under a man half his age who had far greater political and economic resources.

Perhaps their strength led Wheelwright's supporters to underestimate the resistance to the proposed church, which was led by the formidable John Winthrop. In the succeeding months, painful strife erupted among the members of Boston Church and bitter controversy among the Bay clergy.[5] To intimidate Wheelwright and his supporters, Winthrop brought charges of sedition against Wheelwright for a sermon he preached by invitation in Boston Church. Unable to control a court over which Vane presided, Winthrop could not silence Wheelwright, who had begun to preach at Mount Wollaston and in Boston, presumably at the Hutchinson farm at the Mount and house in Boston. Faced with such defiance, Winthrop called for a church synod to condemn the doctrines supporting what had become by this time a profound dispute over church-state relations and in May seized the government from Vane by coup d'état. After engaging in written dispute with Winthrop concerning the respective jurisdictions of church and state,[6] Vane returned to England in August, shortly before the September church synod condemned doctrines supporting the dissenters' position. Within two months after the synod, Winthrop had broken the dissident party. When a duly-elected General Court, the colony's governing body, met in October and refused for the fourth time to punish Wheelwright, Winthrop dissolved it and called for a new—and illegal—election. With nearly two-thirds of its members replaced with Winthrop allies, the new Court was considerably more tractable. It dismissed members of the Court who belonged to the dissenting group and disfranchised and banished its leaders, including Wheelwright. Then, after months of fierce quarreling in which Anne Hutchinson played no public part, the Court called her to appear to answer charges of being in alliance with the condemned party and maintaining a meeting in her house.

These charges argue that her Boston house was a center for the dissenters and a pulpit for Wheelwright. Her house was also the scene of women's meetings. Well before she arrived, women had begun the practice of gathering to discuss scripture during the public lecture or week-day sermon they were not permitted to attend. Although she later testified that she did not at first approve of such meetings, she had bowed to public pressure—accusations of pride— and begun to attend. She had, apparently, soon acquired a reputation for learning, for skill in scriptural exegesis. Such meetings were, of course, opportunities to proselytize. By now a strong leader among her sex, she was a threat to containing dissent. To weaken her influence and deprive the group of its meeting place, Winthrop summoned her before the Court. When he asked her to denounce the condemned leaders and agree to hold no more meetings, he must have expected her to submit quietly, to discontinue conduct "not fitting for your sex," as he put it. (Later in her trial he admitted that he "had not meant to deal with those of your sex.") But he underestimated her intellect and her powers of resistance. What seems to have begun as a mopping up of holdouts ended with Winthrop being forced to display the lengths he was willing to go to keep himself in power.

Although Winthrop managed to control the public record of the proceedings against the dissidents, a few documents survived. Among them is a transcript of Anne Hutchinson's civil trial. The text is long, thirty-six printed pages, and appears authentic.[7] Winthrop's opening charge, carefully planned to be extremely threatening, accused her of four grave crimes: sedition, blasphemy, heresy, contempt of court. He then asked her the question he had asked the leaders previously condemned, "whether you do not justify Mr. Wheelwright's sermon and the petition."[8] Unless she denounced the sermon (Wheelwright's doctrines)—and repudiated a petition to the Court protesting his punishment, compiled by her allies—she would receive heavy punishment.

Ignoring the question, she asked to be accused: "I am called here to answer before you but I hear no things laid to my charge." Her reply was dazzling; it proved that she was well-aware that the Court had no case against her, that she was prepared to challenge it to make a case it could prove or to prosecute her illegally. As she had not signed the petition, she could not be convicted on the same evidence as those who had. Furthermore, the Court had passed no order prohibiting private meetings. Forced to be specific, Winthrop countered that she had broken a law by "harboring" the petitioners. Her reply, "that's matter of conscience, Sir," proves that she was also prepared to defend her behavior and the beliefs informing it as matters of conscience. She was making a distinction between secular and sacred authority, defending an independent spiritual order.

Denying any distinction, Winthrop flatly asserted the Court's right to compel her conscience, "Your conscience you must keep or it must be kept for you."

Knowing that English law permitted peaceful petitions, she asked what law the petitioners had broken. Winthrop, extending the fifth commandment to honor parents to rulers of the state, replied: "The law of God and of the state," which requires you to "honour thy father and thy mother." Her answer, "Ay Sir in the Lord," accepted the Court's authority but added the condition that a Christian was bound in duty to obey only just laws.[9] This exchange, perhaps more than any other in what proved to be a long trial, goes to the heart of the matter. For Winthrop, state and church were inextricably fused; for the dissenters, they were separate realms. The political implications of the dispute, the proper relation between state and church, were and are profound. Having suffered under an oppressive church in England, Winthrop was determined to maintain state dominance in the new commonwealth.

Well instructed in the law and in biblical texts, Anne Hutchinson defeated every attempt to convict her. During two days of intense debate, six ministers witnessed against her. In her defense, three witnesses, one of whom was John Cotton, refuted their testimony, arguing that they had distorted her words, added things she did not say, and omitted crucial qualifications. In spite of these witnesses and her claim of a right to speak "what in my conscience I know to be truth," Winthrop relentlessly pursued a conviction. When his intent was clear, she submitted to the Court's authority but quoted a scriptural warning that their acts of persecution would bring a curse upon them and their posterity. When she further claimed that she would be delivered from this adversity, Winthrop seized the opportunity to ensnare her. Twisting her words to pretend that she was speaking prophecy, he asked: "Daniel was delivered by miracle do you think to be deliver'd so too?" Recognizing Winthrop's theological trap—Puritans denied miraculous intervention; God did not act through miracles, only through a predestined providential plan—she answered: "I do here speak it before the court. I look that the Lord should deliver me by his providence."[10] Unable to break her repeated insistence that she meant providential delivery—an appeal members of the Court frequently made—or to enlist Cotton's help to condemn her, Winthrop simply ignored her witnesses' testimonies and pretended that she had claimed a miraculous delivery. Announcing that she must be cut off, he stampeded the Court, declaring her the "ground of all these tumults and troubles."

Cotton recognized the great threat to her these new charges of blasphemy implied and tried to restrain him. Winthrop ignored his efforts. William Coddington, a member of the Court, a lawyer, and now leader of what had become a true political opposition party, also intervened in the face of this added danger. Coddington called attention to the many irregularities in the proceedings—no clear witnesses, her judges were her accusers, she had broken no law of God or man—and appealed to Winthrop: "I beseech you do not speak so to force things along." Winthrop was as undeterred by these pleas—from a man who had long been a personal friend, had been part of the original venture of settling New England, enjoyed nearly as much power and prestige as he, and with whom he was united in a church covenant of brotherhood—as he had been by Cotton's. Denouncing her as "unfit for our society," Winthrop ruled "that she shall be banished out of our liberties and imprisoned till she be sent away." After he imposed these extreme punishments, Anne Hutchinson defended her innocence and called attention to the Court's illegal proceedings by asking: "I desire to know wherefore I am banished?" Winthrop's blatantly arbitrary reply was, "Say no more, the court knows wherefore and is satisfied."

So unexpected and powerful had been her defense, so harsh her punishment that Winthrop feared retaliation—or pretended to. He ordered sympathizers to denounce the leaders or have their guns confiscated, imprisoned Anne Hutchinson in the neighboring town of Roxbury where his support was strong, and had the state's munitions moved from Boston to Roxbury. We have no evidence of anything but peaceful compliance. Yet called to account by Boston Church for the trial and these acts, Winthrop defended them as necessary for the preservation of the country.

In a final attempt to heal a breach that had torn Boston apart or anticipating Winthrop's next move, the leaders of the group petitioned Winthrop in January 1638. Although he promised no further punishment and virtually begged them to capitulate, he demanded surrender. In what appears to be the ultimate step to break their strength, he enlisted the help of ministers hostile to Cotton to force Boston Church to condemn Anne Hutchinson and through her the competing beliefs. After months of inquisition, the ministers contrived enough evidence of alleged heresy to pressure the Church into a public trial. Her allies, her husband among them, admitted defeat. Choosing to leave rather than resist further, they secured permission (careful as they had always been to respect the law) to depart the colony. In early March, as soon as the winter's unusually heavy snow permitted travel, they left Boston to seek a place to form a new settlement. Taking advantage of their absence to insure the unanimity necessary to condemn her, Boston Church peremptorily brought her to trial in mid-March.

Again, fortunately, a record of what became two church trials was preserved. Its text was written and edited by two ministers active in the prosecution, and "proved by four witnesses," none of whom was named.[11] By this time she was showing the debilitating effects of the civil trial, of four months' incarceration, of being without her husband and allies and knowing that their absence made excommunication likely, and of serious illness. A neoplastic growth, with symptoms indistinguishable from those of pregnancy, brought her near death soon after her exile.[12] At the opening of the first trial, the presiding elder apologized for her appearing late and explained that he was "to acquaint all this congregation, that whereas our Sister Hutchinson was not here at the beginning of this exercise, it was not out of any contempt or neglect to the ordinance, but because she hath been long [under] durance. She is so weak that she conceives herself not fit nor able to have been here so long together."[13]

Conducted and recorded in the same manner as the civil trial, the church proceedings were made up of elaborate and unsupported charges, increasingly antagonistic questioning, a shift from particular accusation to inference in the face of her refutation and strong denial, and the use of verbal tricks to justify imposing the heaviest penalties. After many hours of inquisition, she was condemned to be admonished, the church's most serious discipline short of excommunication. Her words interrupting the admonition show her to be greatly weakened but impressively self-possessed: "I desire to speak one word before you proceed: I would forbear but by reason of my weakness. I fear I shall not remember it when you have done."

During the week intervening before her second church trial, her situation was much as it had been at her civil trial: a choice between submission or heavy punishment, renunciation of her beliefs or excommunication. She brought to the second trial a written answer to specific charges of heresy. In the statement paraphrased by Cotton— apparently to make it audible to spectators—she made no mention of doctrinal error, but humbly expressed sorrow for offenses stemming from pride. She heartily regretted her behavior, but not, it must be assumed, her belief. Unappeased, aggravated, her clerical opponents denounced her submission and demanded further satisfaction. But in spite of repeated provocation and distortion of her words and meaning, they were unable to elicit evidence of heresy. By the end of a day of bitter theological dispute, the effects of their harassing and her weakened condition were apparent; she was visibly confused. At a crucial moment when she was being provoked to confess to lying, her son-in-law pleaded: "things is with her in distraction, and she cannot recollect her thoughts."[14] Physically but not spiritually broken, she refused to confess to a lie she had not told. She remained to the end, during harsh excommunication, self-controlled and dignified—at least no evidence of any other kind of behavior was recorded by her opponents.

After her banishment, Anne Hutchinson joined her husband, who, with the large number who chose exile, purchased from the Indians an unpatented tract on the Narragansett Bay, in a region that became Rhode Island, and settled in two towns. Unfortunately, the site they chose had long been coveted by Winthrop for its great intrinsic value and its strategic importance as a base of operations for exterminating intractable Indians and controlling sea trade. With its rich land, temperate weather, access to trade routes linking the Connecticut Valley, the Hudson and Delaware Valleys, Virginia, the Atlantic seaboard, and the West Indies, Narragansett Bay was considered a much more desirable place than Boston.[15]

From the time Winthrop learned of the acquisition, he began to undermine the exiles' efforts to establish a colony. Knowing the land was unpatented, he justified Bay moves to annex the region by denying the legitimacy of rights based on purchase from the Indians only. When the colony sought to protect itself by securing a patent from England, he tried to assume jurisdiction by sending, in the guise of "a brotherly mission of inquiry" from Boston Church, an armed expedition led by three military officers to "require some satisfactory answer about such things as we hear be offensive amongst them."[16] Frightened by the expedition and the assertion of jurisdiction implied in the mission's demand, the settlers established a government similar to that in the Bay. Soon thereafter, when Anne Hutchinson's young son Francis wrote Boston Church asking to be dismissed to join his own church, Boston Church refused, replying that it would dismiss only to a church it accredited; that is, one that became part of the established Bay church. Unable to accept this answer, Francis Hutchinson and his brother-in-law William Collins, a young minister ordained by the English Church, neither of whom had been involved in the earlier part of the conflict, went to Boston to question the refusal. The young men barely escaped with their lives: they were arrested without charge, fined outrageously, imprisoned for months, released under penalty of death if they returned to the Bay.

In an act that had much to do with Anne Hutchinson's ultimate fate, the same Court that dealt so threateningly with the young men admonished the leaders of groups in the Bay who had begun to plan a colony on Long Island under Dutch jurisdiction "not to go to the Dutch because of scandal and offense."[17] At this time New England was extremely vulnerable, its very existence threatened. Affluent, stable settlers were essential to attract and keep investment capital. The Bay's harsh practices deterred immigration from England and provoked large numbers of its own inhabitants to leave. In part because of the exodus, Lord Say, New England's richest English investor, had just written Winthrop that he was shifting his millions from investment in New England to the West Indies—an act that must have had much to do with Winthrop's vindictiveness toward those who left.

Anne Hutchinson and her family were so intimidated by the young men's experience and by the Bay's inexorable moves to annex the Narragansett region, that they and many of its other inhabitants sought the civil and religious freedoms offered by the Dutch. But a third exile did not spare them further hostility.[18] Strong circumstantial evidence suggests that their settlement near New Amsterdam was too opportune a target to miss: Anne Hutchinson and her associates could not be brought back into the fold; their wealth, stability, and reputation strengthened the Dutch and would attract followers; a violent death at the hands of "savages" would be a powerful deterrent to others and would promote the ruin of the Dutch plantation. Depicted as divine justice by the pulpit and in letters to England, such a death could help repair the Bay's reputation among English supporters and investors.

The massacre took place sometime in the early fall of 1643.[19] When news of it reached Samuel Gorton, Anne Hutchinson's Narragansett neighbor and friend, he wrote in outrage to Winthrop that her blood was "so savagely and causelessly spilt." Implying Bay complicity in the murders, his letter continued: "we have heard them [the dissenting exiles] affirm that she would never heave up a hand, no nor move a tongue against any that persecuted or troubled them, but only endeavor to save themselves by flight, not perceiving the nature and end of persecution. . . ."[20]

One contemporary description of the massacre survives in a propaganda tract published in England a decade later by Edward Johnson, a Bay military leader. Johnson's work was intended to counter criticism of New England's "too strict government." Writing his defense in the form of annals, Johnson linked divine retribution with her behavior by including her death in his 1638 description of the conflict. This tactic permitted him to obscure the years between the two events and impede recovery of the truth. (If such was his intent, he was successful; modern scholars still limit the conflict to less than two years.) "The grand Mistress of them all," he wrote, who ordinarily prated every Sabbath day, . . . withdrew her self, her husband, and her family also, to a more remote place; . . . The Indians in those parts forewarned them of making their abode there; yet this could be no warning to them, but still they continued, being amongst a multitude of Indians, boasted they were become all one Indian: and indeed, this woman, who had the chief rule of all the roost, being very bold in her strange revelations and misapplications, tells them, though all nations and people were cut off round about them, yet should not they; till on a day certain Indians coming to her house, discoursing with them, they wished to tie up her dogs, for they much bit[.] [T]he man, not mistrusting the Indians' guile, did so; the which no sooner done, but they cruelly murthered her, taking one of their daughters away with them, and another of them seeking to escape is caught, as she was getting over a hedge, and they drew her back again by the hair of the head to the stump of a tree, and there cut off her head with a hatchet; the other that dwelt by them betook them to boat, and fled, to tell the sad news.[21]

The impression Johnson created and the details he chose are consistent with the most probable facts and inconsistent with the claim that Anne Hutchinson and her family were the victims of a random Indian raid.

A likely reconstruction is that Johnson was a participant, for his narrative is filled with revealing details. The Bay government, not the Indians, warned against going to the Dutch. Raiding Indians do not walk up to "discourse" with their victims, nor do victims mindlessly tie their guard dogs. The settlers must have had good reason for trust; either they knew the Indians or the English who must have been with them. How else could Johnson know such particulars as a woman's trying to escape over a hedge being pulled back by her hair to a stump and decapitated with a hatchet. If no English were with the Indians, Johnson's story had to come from "the other" who "took them to boat" to tell the "sad news." But Winthrop claimed in his *Journal* that none survived, that sixteen were killed, including two men in a boat who came to help. John Underhill, who had been a member of the dissenting party in Boston and had a settlement nearby, wrote that only nine, all in the families of Hutchinson and Collins, were massacred. The child taken hostage, Anne Hutchinson's eight-year-old daughter, cannot have been the source because she had forgotten how to speak English when she was returned years later. (Winthrop neglected to mention in his *Journal* account that his October 1643 Court recorded but did not act on a request by Bay relatives and friends of the murdered families, to ransom the child— a request that strongly suggests Winthrop knew which Indians had her.) The inconsistency between Johnson and Winthrop leads us to suspect an attempt to bury the details in obscurity and conceal Johnson's presence.[22]

The present historical record reveals only these facts about the life of Anne Hutchinson. The fiction accepted as fact was created by John Winthrop and his London agents to exonerate his government in the face of heavy condemnation of its practices by investors and allies in England. Winthrop's version was first published anonymously, presumably without his awareness or consent, in a political pamphlet in mid-January 1644, seven years after the trials, at the height of what has been called a "wild and confused period, the very maelstrom of the revolution," the English Civil War. A large embassy sent to promote New England interests arrived in London shortly thereafter to discover the pamphlet and recognize from what immediately became a pamphlet war over its subject the damage it had done. By early February another edition, incorporating the first and prefaced with a long, virulent attack on Anne Hutchinson was rushed into print. Purely an instrument of propaganda, the second work has been accepted by modern scholars as a factual account of the conflict.[23]

But it was written to hide the truth and to defend the New England church and its government's oppression of dissent. Winthrop had to posit a powerful adversary, one for whom no sympathy was possible. Thus he created a demonic Anne Hutchinson, a divine John Winthrop. His narrative portrayed her as the cause of the entire conflict. Describing her behavior and treatment, his language became heavily charged and metaphoric: "All these (except Mr. Wheelwright) were but young branches, sprung out of an old root, the Court had now to do with the head of all this faction . . . a woman who had been the breeder and nourisher of all these distempers, one Mistress Hutchinson. She was "a woman of a haughty and fierce carriage, of a nimble wit and active spirit, and a very voluble tongue, more bold than a man, though in understanding and judgment, inferior to many women."[24] Among the qualities with which he endows her, "voluble tongue" deserves comment. The organ most feared and resented in a woman was her tongue; use of the tongue, the conduit of salvation, was a prerogative exclusive to the male ministry. Women were not permitted to even speak in the church, much less preach. That she did not have a "voluble tongue" Winthrop himself offered the strongest proof. In the record he cautioned the court: "It is well discerned to the court that Mrs. Hutchinson can tell when to speak and when to hold her tongue. Upon the answering of a question which we desire her to tell her thoughts of she desires to be pardoned." Nothing in the trial record resembles the impatient, fierce, boasting spirit who cannot "endure a stop in her way" he depicted in the pamphlet.[25]

Winthrop further claimed that she brought her heretical opinions from England and infected others in the infant church. To explain why such a woman was accepted by the Bay church, he wrote: "This woman had learned her skill in England, and had discovered some of her opinions in the ship, as she came over, which had caused some jealousy of her, which gave occasion of some delay of her admission, when she first desired fellowship with the Church of Boston, but she cunningly dissembled and colored her opinions, as she soon got over that block, and was admitted into the Church, then she began to go to work, and being a woman very helpful in the times of childbirth, and other occasions of bodily infirmities, and well furnished with means for those purposes, she easily insinuated herself into the affections of many."[26] Associating Anne Hutchinson with childbirth has led to the false assumption that she was a midwife. As midwives were a favorite target of witch hunters, Winthrop meant to tar her with the brush of witchcraft.

Winthrop further tampered with the trial record to distort her behavior and the court's acts. He twisted the civility, respect, and careful deference she showed the court into insolence and defiance by removing the Sir with which she prefaced most of her replies to his questions and by adding arrogant claims to her testimony. He changed a single, private meeting into multiple public meetings. He struck out her emphatic denial that she had taught men and put in a claim that she had asserted the right to teach men and had taught them publicly.[27] Of far greater importance in the light of her punishment, however, were Winthrop's pretenses that she presumed to be beyond the law and to have prophetic or miraculous powers. The first pretense, to be exempt from the law, was a way to associate her with the Antinomians, a sect much feared in 1644 by orthodox English clergy. She recognized in the court transcript the court's authority over her body, but not over her soul, her conscience. Winthrop has her deny the court's authority over her body. Although she repeatedly denied miraculous intervention, Winthrop not only removed her denials but contrived elaborate evidence that she claimed prophetic powers and spoke prophecy, permitting him to justify her severe punishment.[28] Winthrop even admitted that the court had insufficient proof to proceed against her, then tried to prove that she was self-condemned, that she had fully and freely convicted herself of everything suspected of her. Thus, he concluded with feigned regret, the Court had no choice but to find her guilty and sentence her accordingly.[29]

As a further pretense to authenticity, Winthrop wrote a summary description of her church trial. Needless to say, it bears no relation to her actual behavior and treatment.[30] In it he doubles her alleged heretical opinions, literally creating new offenses. He makes her behave repulsively, hypocritically, rashly, proudly, and obstinately. Winthrop also had to counter criticisms that she was put "to durance," illegally coerced, or treated harshly. Well-trained in the law, he wrote that she "pretended bodily infirmity" but had "only a favourable confinement, so as all of her family and divers others, resorted to her at their pleasure."

By the time the pamphlet was published, Anne Hutchinson and her immediate family were dead. She had no opportunity to defend herself. Winthrop had access to the press, controlled public records, and wrote the first history of New England. His authority has remained unchallenged for over three centuries. Yet his version of the conflict is that of the prosecution only. Having heard no defense, how can we judge? History never stops questioning its own assumptions, its own perspectives. We need to analyze the documents with appropriate rigor, separate fact from fiction, truth from myth. Change one assumption, and another world appears. If, for example, we see the missing dates in the Boston Church Records as an eighteen-month gap rather than a closed record, we ask who made it and why. A long overdue fair hearing would make the words at the base of her memorial, "courageous exponent of civil liberty," intelligible for the first time.

Notes

[1] Emery Battis wrote the entry; his *Saints and Sectaries* (Chapel Hill: University of North Carolina Press, 1962) has been the definitive text on the so-called Antinomian controversy for nearly thirty years.

[2] See G. J. Barker-Benfield, "Anne Hutchinson and the Puritan Attitude toward Women," *Feminist Studies* I, no. 2 (Fall, 1972) and Lyle Koehler, "The Case of the American Jezebels," *William and Mary Quarterly*, 3rd ser. 31 (1974).

[3] James Kendall Hosmer, ed., *Winthrop's Journal: "History of New England, 1630–1649,"* 2 vols. (New York, 1908).

[4] John Denison Champlin, "Hutchinson Ancestry and Descendants of William and Anne Hutchinson," *New York Geneological and Biographical Record*, v. 45 (1914), pp. 164–169.

[5] Scholars have confined their analyses of the conflict to the theological or doctrinal dispute, not recognizing that doctrinal quarrels stemmed from the

political implications of the state-established congregational polity; that is, the seemingly endless quibbling can be reduced to qualifications for church membership and for the ministry. Winthrop and his clerical allies tried to save their concept of church-state relations by making a distinction between discipline—organization, rules, admission practices—and doctrine-theological premises. But doctrine informs discipline; they are inseparable—as the clergy found when it presumed to confirm or deny church membership tied to political franchise rather than spiritual condition.

[6]To oversimplify a very complex issue, Vane's group maintained on the basis of Christ's imperative to render unto Caesar the things that are Caesar's and unto Christ the things that are Christ's that church and state were separate realms.

[7]"The Examination of Mrs. Anne Hutchinson at the Court at Newtown," in David Hall, *The Antinomian Controversy, 1636–1638: A Documentary History* (Middletown, CT: Wesleyan University Press, 1968). Hall reprinted the three documents—a pamphlet and two trial records—in the first selection of primary documents, Charles Francis Adams' *Antinomianism in the Colony of Massachusetts Bay, 1636–1638* (Boston: Publications of the Prince Society, 1894)—and added nine: two letters, five treatises and draft notes of a sixth, and Wheelwright's sermon. Breaks in continuity and defaced lines suggest corruption, but much discreditable detail is left intact.

[8]Hall, p. 312.

[9]Hall, pp. 312, 313.

[10]Hall, p. 338.

[11]Hall reprints the trial report from an eighteenth-century copy of the original that has disappeared. The punctuation "is so erratic as to make the manuscript almost unintelligible" (350).

[12]William Hutchinson wrote John Cotton of her grave illness. Hearing of it, John Winthrop wrote her physician, John Clarke, demanding a full description. Clarke's reply, part of which Winthrop paraphrased in his *Journal*, describes what was probably an hydatidi-form mole. A standard modern medical text calls the condition a "pathological pregnancy," a neoplastic lesion, usually spontaneously aborted by the third month, rarely beyond the sixth. In early stages it is indistinguishable from a normal pregnancy, except that hyperemesis, "morning sickness," is more frequent and apt to be more severe and protracted. The outstanding symptom is uterine bleeding (Nicholson J. Eastman, *Williams Obstetrics* [New York, 1982], pp. 528–532). Clarke wrote that he despaired of her life. Winthrop widely publicized in New and Old England what he called Anne Hutchinson's "monstrous birth."

[13]Hall, p. 351.

[14]Hall, pp. 372, 386.

[15]Cotton Mather called Rhode Island the paradise of New England, "the best garden of all the colonies." *Magnalia Christi Americana*, Hartford, 1853, p. 521.

[16]Richard D. Pierce, ed., *Records of the First Church in Boston 1630–1868,* Colonial Society of Massachusetts, *Publications,* vol. 39. (Boston, 1961), p. 27.

[17]Nathaniel B. Shurtleff, ed., *Records of the Governor and Company of the Massachusetts Bay in New England,* 5 vols. in 6 (Boston, 1853; reprint, New York: AMS Press, 1968), vol. I, p. 337.

[18]Forming a confederation with Connecticut, Plymouth, and New Haven, New England tried to contain the expansion of competing colonies, the Dutch in particular, and punish any who resisted. Winthrop refused to accept the Narragansett government into the confederation. He also used Indian agents to keep those driven from the Bay under close surveillance.

[19]Winthrop wrote of the murders in a letter dated October 10. His *Journal* account of the deaths is a brief, vague undated entry ostensibly made in July. He includes the telling detail that the same Indians went from Anne Hutchinson's settlement to attack Lady Deborah Moody's but found it too strongly defended with palisades and armed men. Lady Moody, Henry Vane's cousin, had found the Salem Church intolerable and had left the Bay to found a colony on Long Island.

[20]Samuel Gorton, *Simplicities Defence against Seven-Headed Policy* (London, 1646), p. 36. Even as he wrote, Gorton was defending his own settlement against annexation. Within days, it was under attack by a Bay military expedition that burned the houses, force-marched the men in shackles to Boston, and appropriated their livestock as booty. Winthrop greeted them with praise and drinks on the house. After keeping Gorton in chains and at hard labor until spring, Winthrop tried unsuccessfully to secure the death penalty on charges very similar to those brought against Anne Hutchinson.

[21]J. Franklin Jameson, ed., *Johnson's Wonder-Working Providence* (New York: Scribner's, 1910), p. 138.

[22]His intended Puritan English audience was particularly sensitive to this issue. Prosecutions and executions of witches in English history were concentrated in the second half of the sixteenth century and the first half of the seventeenth. Winthrop's 1644 smear of Anne Hutchinson coincided precisely with the activities of the most successful witch-hunter in English history, Matthew Hopkins. (For Hopkins, see Keith Thomas, *Religion and the Decline of Magic* (New York: Scribner's, 1971), p. 454.

[23]*A Short Story of the Rise, reign, and ruine of Antinomians, Familists, & Libertines. . . .* Page numbers refer to Hall, pp. 199–310. Spelling is modernized.

[24]Hall, p. 262.

[25]Hall, p. 275.

[26]Hall, p. 265.

[27]Hall, pp. 267, 314.

[28]Hall, pp. 338, 273.

[29]Hall, p. 265.

[30]This portrayal, indeed the entire pamphlet, should not be read as an attack on the person Anne Hutchinson. It was written to serve quite other political purposes. Winthrop used her figure to represent a recalcitrant church, one which resisted subordination to its divinely-appointed "godly" rulers, the magistrates.

PART II

Many Revolutions

B y 1720 the majority of the white population—north and south—had been born in the New World. Population growth was phenomenal throughout the eighteenth century, and competition for land continued to govern the history of European relations with the Indian nations. Decimated by European disease, then by genocidal practices, American Indians saw themselves forced off their ancient lands by European settlers who were relentlessly moving westward. In response, Indian nations formed more permanent confederacies, using all the arts of war and diplomacy to maintain their cultures.

The Cherokee, the largest Indian nation bordering the English, Spanish and French colonies in the South, had used their pivotal geographic position and large number to maintain their autonomy in the seventeenth and eighteenth centuries. They allied themselves with the English Carolinians, although they played off each European group, one against the other. However, after they joined the English for an expedition against the Spanish fort of St. Augustine in 1740–41, the Cherokees were decimated by smallpox. International warfare eventually took its toll as well, as the English proved that they could also play the game of "divide and conquer," by setting one Indian nation against another.

The eagerness of the Indians for European goods ultimately transformed their societies. The fur trade fundamentally altered Indians' relationships with the resources of their environment; some scholars believed this led indigenous peoples to destroy their own ecosystems. Men were drawn away from villages to hunt for prolonged periods of time, and the preparation of furs and skins for market were added to women's agricultural labor. Men's roles in hunting, trading, and diplomacy were aggrandized and the economic basis for women's matrilineal power was diminished. All of this may be interpreted as a form of successful resistance to European encroachment, because it strengthened Indians' economic and military power and their ability to deploy it. But the ability of Indian nations to play one imperial power against another was removed once the English pushed the French out of North America in 1763.

Increasingly, there was a general tendency among Indian nations to develop gender arrangements more like those of the Europeans with whom they intermarried as well as traded. While

Nancy Ward's life perhaps illustrates the resistance of native cultures to such a trend, it was one many American Indian women had to follow. Thomas Jefferson's presidential words in 1802 to Handsome Lake, a Seneca leader, symbolized the official expectations of the white man. "Go on, then, brother, in the great reformation you have undertaken. Persuade our red men to be sober and to cultivate their lands; and their women to spin and weave for their families." This was a message reinforced by missionaries, and Handsome Lake did in fact restructure Seneca life along more patriarchal lines.

By the early eighteenth century, the social order in both the northern and southern colonies had become more uniform in its patriarchal laws and customs. The pressure that the increasing population had on land increased paternal power as the resources that men controlled grew scarcer. Agricultural produce and land speculation were factors in a system of international trade and finance. Colonial economies required men to engage themselves in the market and the law. However, farm women were more isolated from travel and markets than their menfolk. While they seem largely to have accepted their subordination to "the small circle of domestic concerns," women frequently complained about tedium and drudgery. Moreover, a significant number were not so entirely immersed in household production from dawn to dusk as previously thought. The fact that many households did not have the equipment to manufacture clothing, candles, cheese, and butter—even as the production of such items was increasing—suggests that trade networks had come into existence among women.

The advantages of prosperity to women were most evident in colonial cities such as Boston, New York, Philadelphia, Baltimore, and Charleston. The number and misery of poor women in cities was striking, and class divisions were generally sharpened over the course of the century; however, women congregated in cities in part in hopes of the job opportunities (for example, as nurses and seamstresses) not available in the countryside. Other women in towns ran shops and inns, conducting businesses during men's temporary and long-term absences and often inheriting an enterprise to run as their own upon the male owner's death. The law tried to keep women off the charity rolls by according them "feme sole" status as traders—expanding their legal independence if they were adult and unmarried or widowed. Women used such concessions for their own advantage. Some became accomplished in matters of commerce, including Elizabeth Murray, a Scots immigrant. She became a successful merchant, making a fortune in retailing, real estate, and international trade. She profited from the mistakes of her first marriage by using prenuptial agreements to carve out a measure of economic autonomy in her two subsequent marriages. In her own words, she learned to cherish "a spirit of independence."

To be able to acquire education and broaden their interests, women need to be elevated above subsistence. Hence the most literate women throughout much of the eighteenth century came from the upper crust. Large aristocratic plantations emerged in the South after the early years. Plantation mistresses could escape much of the drudgery associated with running a large household by assigning that work to female slaves. Such relief allowed some women to diversify their talents, as exemplified by Eliza Lucas Pinckney. In addition to acquiring the upper-class accomplishments of decorative needlework, music, and French, Pinckney was versed in contemporary philosophy. She taught herself what she called "the rudiments of the law," before engaging in agricultural experiments. Still, with the ownership of slaves came responsibility for their supervision. A plantation mistress usually had far less time for leisure and intellectual interests than the privileged women in the burgeoning cities. There, a pool of female domestic labor provided wealthier women a significantly greater degree of freedom from domestic work. This was especially the case for younger, unmarried women. Some girls attended "dame schools," where an unmarried or widowed woman taught reading and writing. Later in the century, cities saw the growth of small private schools, many run by women trying to escape economic destitution. Such enterprises taught music, dancing, painting, and needlework, as well as academic subjects—accomplishments which enhanced a young woman's attractiveness on the marriage market for which she was destined.

So it is not surprising that we find most evidence of intellectual life among upper-class, urban women in the eighteenth century, especially women in the households of well-educated men. Ben Franklin's famous "Junto" club and his subscription library in Philadelphia are emblems of a growing appetite for education among men, but his daughter, Sarah Franklin Bache, also insisted on an education. In similar fashion, Jane Colden, educated and encouraged by her father, Dr. Cadwallader Colden, became a first-rate botanist—although she may well have given up her vocation when she married in 1759.

Advice books addressed to eighteenth-century female readers aimed to educate them primarily to serve men. Nonetheless, the published debates in England over the purposes of women's education, a daughter's choice in selecting a husband, and female subordination in marriage were echoed transatlantically. One of the most popular vehicles for the dissemination of these issues was the novel. The eighteenth century saw the rise of the first popular, middle-class literate culture among women, expressed in the writing and reading of novels. Their subjects were, above all, those human relationships which were necessarily of the most importance to women.

Many novels were "sentimental," celebrating the qualities of intuitive and instantaneous sympathy between like-minded people with the same "tastefulness" in aesthetic values. Sentimentalism identified human feeling with natural phenomena and celebrated compassion for the poor and exploited. Novelists believed that women could convert men from a hard, immoral approach to life and one contemptuous of women, to a softer, more selfless and Christian view, more respectful of women and more focused on the private delights of family life. The material context of these fictional themes was the changing domestic reality of home. For many it became more comfortable and entertaining over the century. It was the site for the gradual accumulation of domestic items. Chinaware that was easier to wash, manufactured knives and forks, and imported cloth signified a softening of manners and some easing of domestic labor. Among other domestic pleasures was the novel itself.

The popularization of the sentimental novel coincided with a growing religious fervor during the middle decades of the eighteenth century. During the 1730s, Jonathan Edwards, the first preacher identified with what became called the "Great Awakening," convinced thousands of inhabitants in the Connecticut Valley that they were in dire need of spiritual rebirth. In 1740 and 1741, he gathered flocks across New England, paving the way for crusades by fellow evangelicals George Whitefield, Gilbert Tennant, and Samuel Davies, among others, in the middle-Atlantic and southern colonies. Evangelism emphasized the power and value of instantaneous sympathy. It extolled expressive emotionalism—above all, of tears. Colonial congregations had become predominantly female in composition from the turn of the previous century. In the eighteenth-century's own view, religion was being "feminized." Now, in camp meetings, converts of both sexes gave free range to emotional outbursts; they fell down and wept before a God who was represented as a correspondingly more emotional and eventually more sympathetic figure. In this context, several female religious leaders emerged, including Sarah Hagger Osborn of Rhode Island, who made her home a center of religious revivalism in the 1760s.

Newly evangelized males, many from lower-class backgrounds, were (along with women and slaves) up against a formal patriarchy in established state churches. In Virginia, for example Baptists and Methodists challenged the traditional hierarchy of head and heart, of rote liturgy, of expensive church architecture, of a vestimentary code whereby rich clothing signified rank, and, indeed, whole layers of deference. Everywhere in the colonies, fervent converts split churches into opponents and supporters of the Awakening, "Old Light" and "New Light." Their challenges helped lay the groundwork for the American Revolution (1776–1783).

Literacy and religious evangelicalism encouraged individual self-assertion. From mid-century on some young people were more assertive in the private sphere, choosing their spouses for themselves and even restricting or planning pregnancies. Such relative freedoms were intensified by the experience of the American Revolution, the rhetoric for which sometimes drew upon the imagery of conflict between parents and children. The colonists depicted themselves as grown-up offspring, while the English government was portrayed as a decrepit and corrupt old parent. A number of women also extended the political notion of "tyranny" to the relationship of husbands to wives, most famously in the case of Abigail Adams telling her husband, "Remember, all men would be Tyrants if they could," as she implored him to "remember the ladies" during the making of the Constitution.

The Revolution was begun by a kind of economic warfare: the colonists' boycotts of British consumer goods, notably of tea and cloth, required women's cooperation. The majority of women were "patriotic," and enlisted in the rebel cause. Many organized themselves as "Daughters of Liberty," but some women sided with the "Loyalists" or "Tories," as they were derided by the revolutionaries. While men were off fighting, women ran farms, plantations, and businesses, gaining knowledge and self-confidence. As a consequence of such experience and because of the heightened interest in "liberty," the debate over women's education was decisively renewed in the 1780s and '90s. These decades also witnessed considerable debate over the future of American slavery.

The massive importation of Africans as slaves began late in the seventeenth century. This dramatic rise in the number of slaves in the colonies had several long-term consequences. It led to the codification into law of repressive practices which branded black people permanently with slavery. Slave status was automatically inherited by offspring through their mothers, thereby facilitating the economic and sexual purposes of white owners (children of white masters and female slaves were themselves slaves). African-Americans were forced to experience the terrible ambiguity of bearing and rearing children whom slave masters saw as livestock. A second distinctive feature of the lives of African-American women was being forced to labor in the fields along with men, when white women were by and large drawn away from such work. Women slaves worked both in commercialized agricultural gang labor and in households as skilled and drudge labor. Menial household work was the purpose for which Phillis Wheatley was bought.

Despite these circumstances, African-American family life was very significantly stabilized. This was partly one effect of the increased importation of Africans that resulted in a more balanced sex ratio by the 1740s. African-Americans established themselves with family characteristics and customs distinct from those of whites (for example, slaves observed a taboo against marriage between cousins). Even though family members were constantly subject to sexual exploitation and sale, the family was one important base for the creation and transmission of an African-American culture. The second base was religion. The Great Awakening converted slaves to evangelical Protestantism by the thousands. But the enslaved population, conscious of its origins in Africa and wishing to resist slavery, adapted European-American Protestantism and the King James version of the English Bible to its own needs. For example, because the story symbolized their own condition and hopes, African-Americans celebrated the survival, flight and triumph of the Israelites who had been enslaved by Egyptians. African influences permeated the Christian ceremonies of slaves. African-Americans celebrated their religious faith with their own familiar rituals and musical celebrations, in short their own religious culture.

Thus, the social history of African-Americans in the eighteenth century prepared them to meet the decisive changes through which slavery would pass in consequence of the Revolution. The disruptions of the war resulted in a numerically significant free black population in the cities, the staging ground for black abolitionism. Secondly, the Revolution and its rhetoric about freedom and independence added fuel to the religious impulses of a dawning anti-slavery movement. One by one, northern states ended slavery after the Revolution. However, several factors contributed to a counter-trend. The Revolution effectively removed all British roadblocks to restrict colonial expansion. This, along with the invention of the cotton gin in 1793 encouraged the spreading of slave culture into the fertile new lands. Slavery was therefore still more securely entrenched in the South, although cotton production for domestic manufacture and, above all, for exports, was vital to the growth of the nation's economy as a whole. While the Constitution of 1789 compromised U.S. sectional differences over slavery—writing slavery permanently into the new national laws but providing for the abolition of the slave trade in 1808—the stage was set for a potentially explosive division. Nonetheless, the outcome of the Revolution for whites was the achievement of a national identity. It also supplied a rhetorical legacy of revolution on which all Americans eventually could draw. From now on, women claimed a share in the nation's republicanism.

Eliza Lucas Pinckney

(1722–1793)

Constance B. Schulz

Born in the West Indies in 1722 and educated in England, Eliza Lucas was a privileged child of an upper-class planter who moved his family to Wappoo plantation in South Carolina when Eliza was fifteen. When her father was called back to Antigua in 1739, he left Eliza in charge of his three plantations. The young woman proved a talented manager, and successfully introduced the cultivation of indigo (a dye for textiles), a crop she imported from the West Indies in 1740. This agricultural breakthrough was a boon to the young colony, and became the source of fortune for many South Carolinian planters. In 1744 she married widower Charles Pinckney, a wealthy planter, and settled into the traditional role held by many wealthy southern women: plantation mistress and mother.

In 1753 Charles Pinckney's political career transplanted the family to England, where Eliza reestablished her childhood friendships and allegiances, but in 1758 business interests forced the Pinckneys to return to Carolina. The couple left their two sons in English schools and sailed home with their daughter. Within six weeks of their arrival home, Charles Pinckney died, and Eliza Lucas Pinckney was once again left to manage a large plantation on her own.

With the outbreak of the revolutionary war, Pinckney devoted herself to furthering the careers of her two sons, who had returned from England to participate in the colonial rebellion. In doing so, Pinckney rejected her former allegiances to an England she was fond of, and went so far as to lend a large sum of money to the new state of South Carolina in 1779. At war's end, her son Thomas served as governor of South Carolina, and her eldest son Charles Cotesworth became a delegate to the Constitutional Convention. At her death in 1793, George Washington

65

requested to serve as one of her pallbearers, in tribute to her devotion to the revolutionary cause.

Some say that the South Carolina low country is at its most beautiful in the fall. The great watery meadows of sea grass wave in the constant sea breezes behind the sheltering barriers of the outer islands, their tall seeded fronds bending with the tides. Thickets of live oak trees heavy with acorns dress in drifting curtains of Spanish moss, "where a variety of Airry Chorristers pour forth their melody." The newly fallen fresh-scented needles of the longleaf pine carpet the woods of the higher lands, while the great cedar groves reflect what Eliza Lucas Pinckney once called "an Autumnal gloom and solemnity."[1]

Approaching this bountiful land from the water, one can still see today much of what first greeted fifteen-year-old Eliza Lucas in the fall of 1738. Born in the West Indies in 1722, sent by her father to school in England, Eliza had traveled with her parents and younger sister Polly from their home in Antigua to take up residence on inherited Carolina lands that George Lucas hoped would be more healthful for his invalid wife. Eliza's grandfather, John Lucas, owned three properties in Carolina: a plantation of 1,500 acres on the Combahee River, another of 2,950 acres on the Waccamaw, and a third of 600 acres on a bluff overlooking Wappoo Creek, where it flowed into the Stono River not far from the canal constructed to connect the Stono to the Ashley River. This last plantation was the Lucas family's destination.

One can picture the excitement of an observant young woman who loved trees and gardens and the outdoor world around her as the West Indian ship skirted the sandy barriers of Folly, Morris, and James Islands south of the Cooper River, sailing majestically past the southern tip of Sullivan's Island (where slave ships were required to land their cargo for a ten-day period of quarantine lest they bring dreaded diseases like smallpox and malaria into port) and into sight of the bustling harbor city of Charles Town (renamed Charleston after the Revolution), secure on its peninsula between the Ashley and Cooper Rivers. By 1739, eight wharves, or "bridges," jutted into the Cooper, each having on its wooden deck warehouses, shops, and equipment for loading, unloading, and provisioning the numerous vessels docked at its sides. A 1739 painting by Bishop Roberts shows us a handsome urban waterfront, the foreground crowded with vessels of every size and shape: ships, schooners, brigantines, sloops in full sail, with canoes and plantation flats clustered around them.

Although we can see today the sights Eliza Lucas saw—the bustling waterfront of Charles Town, the quiet beauty of the salt marshes, the elegant homes along the city waterfront, and the comfortable plantation houses up the tidal rivers—we have no pictorial image of Eliza herself. That is odd, for by the mid-eighteenth century, Charles Town was becoming a center for the arts and boasted the works of resident and itinerant portrait artists. There are two handsome portraits of her husband, innumerable likenesses of her sons, a miniature of her daughter, and views of her imposing Charles Town home both in a waterfront prospect painted by Thomas Leitch in 1774 and in an 1861 photograph. Hampton plantation house, the home of her daughter Harriott Horry, where Eliza Lucas Pinckney lived after the American Revolution, still stands near Santee. Visitors there might imagine Eliza in 1791 with her daughter and granddaughters welcoming to breakfast George Washington, looking much like he does in the Gilbert Stuart painting, but we no more know what Eliza looked like in her graceful old age than how she appeared in girlhood. "No likeness of Mrs. Pinckney is ever known to have been taken," reported her great-granddaughter and earliest biographer.[2]

To create a portrait of this important woman of the colonial south, then, we must describe the world she lived in, the things she did, and the words she wrote, rather than her appearance at any given point in her life. And perhaps that is fitting, for hers was a life of action rather than of appearance, of the business of plantation agriculture and parental concerns rather than of fashion (although as a girl she gratefully accepted from her father "a piece of rich Yellow Lutstring consisting of 19 yards for my self," and as a young wife she knew enough about luxury apparel to send to London for weaving into damask the silk spun from the production of her own plantation, and to fashion from it three elegant dresses that demonstrated the possibilities of silk manufacture in Carolina).

Charles Town had in 1738 embarked on a remarkable period of growth that would span Eliza Lucas's entire lifetime. The capital of the English colony of South Carolina, it was also the most important English port on the Atlantic Coast south of Philadelphia. Founded in 1670, and moved to its more defensible present-day location in 1680, the city had grown from a struggling village in 1685 to a prosperous town of 6,800 in 1742, fourth largest in all the English mainland colonies. More than half of its inhabitants were black slaves; as early as 1708 blacks had equaled and begun to outnumber whites in the colony as a whole. The slave population had grown with the prosperity derived from the colony's rice cultivation. First introduced late in the seventeenth century, by 1730, rice replaced the earlier trade in deerskins from the Indian tribes of the interior as South Carolina's principal trade commodity. In 1750, the greatest concentration of slaves was in the low-lying coastal areas where rice cultivation based on a system of swamps and diked tidal creeks flourished.

Charles Town's crucial location at the center of an inland water system that stretched from the Cape Fear River in North Carolina to the St. John's River in Florida also made it a center for international commerce. Rice, and later indigo and cotton, fitted in particularly well with the English mercantile system, for all were commodities that England needed, but could not produce. Thus their cultivation and exportation were encouraged by favorable trade legislation, and even by the granting of bounties.

The wealth derived from staple crops and trade, and the commercial ties with England and the Continent, made "Charleston in the Age of the Pinckneys"[3] a remarkably cosmopolitan city. Freedom of religion, despite the firm establishment of the Church of England, attracted Methodists, Huguenots, Baptists, Presbyterians, Jews, Catholics, and Quakers; the presence of Germans, French, Scots-Irish, Dutch, and the majority population of African slaves gave a remarkable diversity to the city. Charles Town merchants intermarried with low-country planters, who maintained elegant homes in town to which they could retreat during the hot summers when "country fevers" (malaria and smallpox) plagued low-country plantations. During the "season," Charles Town offered its residents the best of society: music, theater, balls, a weekly newspaper, and (after 1748) a library society. Most of these amenities were in place, ready to welcome the Lucas family upon their arrival. As the eldest daughter of a wealthy planter family, Eliza Lucas was welcomed on visits to Charles Town where she danced at balls, flirted with naval officers, and attended elegant private dinners, feasting on "oyster soop," turtle, venison, boiled rice, and "dutch blumange" (recipes for all of which she later included in her own cookbook). "Charles Town, the principal one in this province, is a polite, agreeable place," she wrote to Mrs. Boddicutt, the woman with whom she had lived while a student in England.

> The people live very Gentile and very much in the English taste. . . . There is two worthy Ladies in Charles Town, Mrs. Pinckney and Mrs. Cleland, who are partial enough to me to be always pleased to have me with them, and insist upon my making their houses my home when in town and press me to relax a little much oftener than 'tis in my honor to accept of their obliging intreaties. But I some times am with one or the other for 3 weeks or a month at a time, and then enjoy all the pleasures Charles Town affords."[4]

Not all of what Charles Town offered was pleasant, of course, and just as Eliza and her family arrived in Carolina the city was plunged into a series of natural and human disasters. The Yamasee War in 1715 and its aftermath had virtually ended the early threat of Indian unrest to the city (though not to the frontier regions of the colony), but fears of slave revolt replaced those of Creek and Cherokee attack. No comment by Eliza survives on the Stono Rebellion in 1739, although it began less than five miles from her Wappoo plantation. On September 9, about twenty slaves broke into a store near the old Stono Bridge, killing two whites, and, under the leadership of a slave named Jemmy armed themselves. As they marched toward Savannah, their number grew to nearly eighty, many of them recently arrived Angolans. Overtaken by militia, the slaves resisted; by the end of the encounter twenty whites and forty blacks had lost their lives. In response, the Commons House of Assembly enacted a harsh Slave Code in 1740 that included heavy import duties levied on slaves brought from abroad, a financial burden which Eliza did write to her father about in the fall of 1741.

Slave rebellions were not the only source of fear and death in the city. A smallpox epidemic in Charles Town in 1738, and a yellow fever epidemic in 1739 decimated the population. No exact figures are given for the yellow fever attack; but by September 1738 the smallpox had infected 1,675 residents, of whom 295 died. Since 1720, the discovery of "variolation," or inoculation with live vaccine, had lessened the impact of smallpox on those who were willingly exposed to the virus while healthy and strong enough to survive a mild case of the disease and gain immunity. Charles Town became the first city in which this preventative measure was tried on a large scale; 437 citizens were inoculated, of whom only 16 died. Eliza Lucas had "taken the smallpox" while a student in England, and later used her own country house as a temporary hospital for the inoculation of her grandchildren and friends.

Scarcely had Charles Town recovered from the yellow fever attack, so severe that Governor Bull sent the Assembly home rather than risk their lives, when a great fire fanned by winds burned for six hours through the wooden buildings of the heart of the commercial district in November 1740, destroying more than 300 structures. Eliza recorded no comment on this disaster, even though her new friend Charles Pinckney, whose wife had so openly welcomed Eliza to their Charles Town home, lost considerable sums of money from it as one of the founders (with his brother William) of the "Friendly Society of Mutual Insuring of Houses against Fires."

The young woman who came to Wappoo in the fall of 1738 seems to have had both a traditional and an unusual education for a young

Englishwoman. Her lively letters show wit and style; she paid pretty compliments to friends of both sexes, quoted readily from scripture, wrote of playing the flute and taking harpsichord lessons with "Mr. Pachelbel,"[5] and of practicing French and needlework—all accomplishments expected of a young Englishwoman of wealth. But when the outbreak of the War of Jenkins Ear between England and Spain in the fall of 1739 recalled her father to Antigua to fulfill his duties as a lieutenant colonel in the British army and later as royal councilor and lieutenant governor of the colony, he had enough confidence in her practical skills to entrust the care of his estates to Eliza rather than to an outside agent or his ailing wife. "I have the business of 3 plantations to transact, which requires more business and fatigue of other sorts than you can imagine," wrote Eliza on May 2, 1740, to her "good friend Mrs. Boddicott."[6] To her father she wrote knowledgeably of local political and military news, reported complicated transactions of money and goods, and discussed the efficient use of the family's eighty-six Carolina slaves (whom she referred to as "servants").

In her stewardship of her father's property, young Eliza Lucas took on the roles of both plantation master and plantation mistress. In addition to managing the business of the plantation, she was busy concocting medicines for servants and friends, overseeing the activities of house servants, practicing her music, visiting neighboring women, and doing needlework projects—even though she admitted that "my father has an aversion to my employing my time in that poreing work."[7] One of her self-appointed duties was that of school-teacher to her younger sister Polly, insisting that she should not be sent away to school: "I will undertake to teach her French," she assured her father.[8] But Eliza did more. Despite the 1740 Slave Code prohibition against teaching slaves to read, Eliza included two black girls in her schoolroom; she wrote to her young friend Mary Bartlett, the visiting English niece of Mrs. Pinckney, "if I have my papas's approbation (my Mamas I have got) I intend [them] for school mistres's for the rest of the Negroe children."[9] It is instructive, both in the energy that it reveals, and in the mixture of plantation and household tasks it catalogs, to read the remainder of her lighthearted account to Mary Bartlett of her weekly activities:

> In general then I rise at five o'Clock in the morning, read till Seven, then take a walk in the garden or field, see that the Servants are at their respective business, then to breakfast. The first hour after breakfast is spent at my musick, the next is constantly employed in recolecting something I have learned least for want of practise it should be quite lost, such as French and short hand. After that I devote the rest of the time till I dress for dinner [dinner was served in

mid-afternoon] to our little Polly and two black girls who I teach to read. . . . [T]he first hour after dinner as the first after breakfast is at musick, the rest of the afternoon in Needle work till candle light, and from that time to bed time read or write. . . . I have particular matters for particular days, which is an interruption to mine. Mondays my musick Master is here. Tuesdays my friend Mrs. Chardon (about 3 miles distant) and I are constantly engaged to each other, she at our house one Tuesday—I at hers the next and this is one of the happiest days I spend at Wappoe. Thursday the whole day except what the necessary affairs of the family take up, is spent in writing, either on the business of the plantations, or letters to my friends. Every other Fryday, if no company, we go vizeting so that I go abroad once a week and no oftener. . . . O! I had like to forgot the last thing I have done a great while. I have planted a large figg orchard with design to dry and export them. I have reckoned my expence and the prophets [profits] to arise from these figgs, but was I to tell you how great an Estate I am to make this way, and how 'tis to be laid out you would think me far gone in romance.[10]

The "figg" experiment was no whim, for the Lucas estates and slaves were heavily mortgaged, and Eliza was determined to discover a profitable crop to increase their income. With her father's blessing and seed shipments, and under the tutelage of male neighbors and friends, including Charles Pinckney, she had tried a number of alternatives before the planting recounted in this spring 1742 letter to Bartlett. The first summer after her father's departure, she wrote to describe "the pains I had taken to bring the Indigo, Ginger, Cotton and Lucerne and Casadall[11] to perfection, and had greater hopes from the Indigo (if I could have the seed earlier next year from the West India's) than any of the rest of the things I had tryd."[12] Thus began the experiment that brought her lasting fame—the introduction of successful cultivation of South Carolina's second highly profitable staple crop, *Indigofera*, much prized as a source of the deep blue dye that was an important element in the rapidly expanding European and English textile industry.

Eliza Lucas was by no means the first to grow indigo in the English colonies. Indigo cultivation had been tried by the English in Virginia in the early seventeenth century, and further attempts at cultivating it were carried on in the first years of the Carolina settlement. A perennial native variety, *Indigofera caroliniana* grew wild in the province, but the manufacture of the prized dye either from the indigenous plant or from two imported strains that had to be planted each year from seed, "Guatamala" or "Bahama" (*I. suffruticosa*) and "French" or "Hispaniola" (*I. tinctoria*) eluded Americans until the mid-eighteenth century. It was a combination of her own persistence and luck of ideal timing that helped Eliza Lucas succeed in this enterprise where others had failed. The outbreak of the war with Spain created serious difficulties for planters shipping the bulky rice crop that was Carolina's principal export. A number of European ports were cut off to them altogether, and insurance costs for shipping elsewhere sharply reduced profits. Moreover, the war cut England's textile industry off from its usual supply of French West Indian indigo. Indigo proved to be a natural complement to rice: like rice, it was highly labor-intensive in its cultivation and harvest, but required that labor in the summer growing months, when rice needed less attention, thus promising efficient use of the plantation's slave labor force. Although indigo fared best in the rich loamy soils farther inland, where it was later extensively cultivated at the end of the eighteenth century, indigo was first grown at the coast on the high ground between the flooded rice fields.

The imported West Indian seeds Eliza received from her father grew reasonably well, although she wrote to him of her 1740 crop in June 1741 that "the frost took it before it [the seed] was dry." The difficulty with indigo was in the tedious manufacturing of small cubes of blue dye from the plant. Nothing in the plant itself is actually blue, although the leaves have a bluish tinge. The dye was produced by harvesting leaves and stems before the stem became woody, then immediately steeping them in water to ferment during the hot summer months. Next, at just the right moment, the foul-smelling fermented brew was drained into a second vat, where it was beaten with paddles to assist in the oxidation process that transformed the yellow liquid into the blue sediment. Lime was added at this stage to expedite oxidation. The dyemaker's skill determined when the beating should cease, allowing the dye particles to settle to the bottom of the vat while slaves drained off the excess liquid into a third vat. The sediment left in the second vat was shoveled into sacks and allowed to drip until nearly dry, then spread out to dry more completely until it could be cut into small cubes, which were packed into barrels for shipment. The sheds sheltering the three vats and pumps necessary for draining the liquid were built right in the indigo fields. Although West Indian planters could make up to eight cuttings, in South Carolina, the plants were cut twice (in a mild year, three times) before the plants were allowed to go to seed. Productivity in South Carolina varied with plant species and soil condition (indigo rapidly exhausted the soil in which it grew). An acre of the crop produced an average of thirty-five to forty pounds of commercial indigo; its cultivation and manufacture required the labor of one slave for every two to four acres planted.

Mastering this complicated procedure was the task that Eliza Lucas set herself, with the help and advice of her French Huguenot neighbor, Andrew Deveaux. Her father sent an experienced dye-maker, Nicholas Cromwell, to her in 1741, but she shortly afterward dismissed him on the discovery that he deliberately "threw in so large a quantity of Lime water as to spoil the color" to prevent Carolina indigo manufacture from succeeding and competing with that of his native Montserrat. Nicholas's brother Patrick proved a more loyal expert, and the Wappoo plantation produced "17 pounds of very good Indigo" in 1744, in addition to producing sufficient seed to distribute to her neighbors—a move that proved foresighted as well as generous, for within a year the French had forbidden the exportation of seed.[13] After five years of experimentation, the Lucas investment in indigo realized a return of £225 on dye sent to the London market in 1745 (although by then the plantation had passed out of the Lucas family control). Once the plant was domesticated in South Carolina, indigo cultivation spread rapidly: the colony exported 138,300 pounds of dye in 1747. A bounty of a shilling per pound of indigo voted by the English Parliament in 1748 (reduced to four pence in 1770) encouraged production even further, until South Carolina exports peaked at over one million pounds in 1775. Great fortunes were made in Carolina from indigo, particularly in the Winyah Bay area of Georgetown.

Although she must have rejoiced in the success of her efforts, by the time indigo was well established at Wappoo and the rest of the Carolina coast, Eliza's attentions and energies had shifted to quite a different role. Even before her 1744 crop had been harvested, on May 27, 1744, she married Charles Pinckney, Esq., a recent widower, former speaker of the Commons House of Assembly, member of the governor's Royal Council, extensive landholder—and at forty-four, nearly twice her age. His first wife, also named Elizabeth, was the kindly Mrs. Pinckney who had befriended Eliza on her arrival in Charles Town. She had borne no children, and perhaps regarded the engaging young Eliza almost as a daughter. For six years, the friendship between Eliza Lucas and Charles Pinckney had grown and deepened. In her father's absence, Charles Pinckney advised her on matters of business and law. She wrote to him in great amusement of her adventure in drawing up a will for a poor neighbor. He had loaned her books—Virgil, Plutarch, Malebranche—and taught her shorthand. Her letters to him, and messages to him in the letters she wrote to his wife's niece, suggest that he teased her for the seriousness he himself encouraged in her, and shared with her private jokes. The Pinckneys took Eliza with them when they traveled, and visited her at Wappoo.

Perhaps her father foresaw even in the first days of the Pinckneys' interest in her some danger for his daughter, for in the first letter she received from him after his 1739 departure for Antigua he apparently probed delicately whether she cherished some secret inclination, warned her against "an indiscreet passion for any one"—and offered her the choice of two gentlemen as potential husbands. Her response, carefully couched in the most obedient daughterly terms, had affectionately but firmly rejected both suitors:

> [A]s I know tis my happiness you consult [I] must beg the favour of you to pay my thanks to the old Gentleman for his Generosity and favourable sentiments of me and let him know my thoughts on the affair in such civil terms as you know much better than any I can dictate; and beg leave to say to you that the riches of Peru and Chili if he had them put together could not purchase a sufficient Esteem for him to make him my husband.

For the rest, she assured him:

> I hope heaven will always direct me that I may never disappoint you; and what indeed could induce me to make a secret of my Inclination to my best friend, as I am well aware you would not disapprove it to make me a Sacrifice to Wealth, and I am as certain I would indulge no passion that had not your approbation.

Whether in the spring of 1740 she had already an "Inclination" toward Charles Pinckney is impossible to say.[14]

When Elizabeth Pinckney died in January 1744 after a prolonged illness, the easy camaraderie so evident in the earlier correspondence between Charles Pinckney and Eliza Lucas had hastened to something more by the threat of her immediate removal to Antigua; financial difficulties and a lull in the hostilities led George Lucas to send for his family. The Pinckney "Family Legend" reports that the first Mrs. Pinckney had been "so averse to her [Eliza's] return to Antigua, that she had more than once declared that rather than have her lost to Carolina, she would herself 'be willing to step down and let her take her place.' "[15] Charles Pinckney also had strong affection for Eliza. Her mother and sister delayed their departure, first for George Lucas's permission for the marriage, and then for the wedding. Eliza's dowry was to have been the Wappoo plantation, and the first indigo crop a gift to the groom. Instead, the plantation was claimed by George Lucas's creditors. Ironically, Charles Pinckney distributed the indigo seed to neighbors, publicized widely the news of its successful cultivation, and pressed for the adoption of bounties both in the South Carolina Commons House of Assembly and in London.

The marriage was a happy one, and Eliza Lucas Pinckney threw herself with all her energies into her new life. She had often been a guest at the Pinckney country home, Belmont, on the Cooper River on the Charles Town neck. On her husband's plantation she continued her agricultural experimentation, growing flax and hemp and reviving earlier Carolina attempts at silk cultivation, while he was kept busy in Charles Town supervising the building of a handsome brick townhouse on East Bay Street, overlooking the harbor just up from Market Street. It was there, on February 14, 1746 (February 25, 1746 by today's calendar) that Eliza gave birth to their first son, Charles Cotesworth Pinckney. Motherhood delighted her: "I can discover all his Papa's virtues already dawning in him," she wrote to her friend Mary Bartlett when Charles Cotesworth was still only three months old; to Mary Bartlett's mother (the first Elizabeth Pinckney's sister) she wrote at the same time requesting her "to buy him the new toy . . . to teach him according to Mr. Lock's method (w[hi]ch I have carefully studied) to play himself into learning. Mr. Pinckney himself has been contriving a sett of toys to teach him his letters by the time he can speak, you perceive we begin by times for he is not yet four months old." The plan must have worked, for the proud mother later reported to her sister Polly, then in school in England, that twenty-two-month old Charles Cotesworth "can tell all his letters in any book without hesitation."[16]

The period of Eliza's second pregnancy was not so happy; her father had been taken prisoner by the French while en route to England, and died in captivity in January 1747. Charles Pinckney attempted to keep this news from her, for she loved her father dearly, and had often written of her agitation and concern for him during his military campaigns. Her discovery of the hidden letter so shocked her that she went into premature labor, and the infant, baptized George Lucas in honor of his grandfather, died on June 24, five days after his birth. Within a few months Eliza was pregnant again, and gave birth to a daughter, Harriott, on August 7, 1748. The young family was completed with the birth of Thomas on October 23, 1750. Eliza Lucas Pinckney's childbearing ended abruptly at the age of 28. Remarkably in an age of high infant and child mortality, all three of these children survived to adulthood, and outlived their mother.

Eliza now turned all the energy and dedication that had previously been directed into her plantation and gardening to her children. She did not nurse them as infants; we know this because in a visit with the English royal family several years later, the Princess Augusta asked Mrs. Pinckney directly if she had suckled her children, and Eliza responded "I had attempted it but my constitution would not bear it."[17] Their education, both temporal and spiritual, became one of her chief concerns. In an undated series of resolutions found in the family papers, the young mother resolved:

> to be a good Mother to my children, to pray for them, to set them good examples, to give them good advice, to be careful both of their souls and bodys, to watch over their tender minds, to carefully root out the first appearing and budings of vice, and to instill piety, Virtue and true religion into them; to spair no paines or trouble to do them good; to correct their Errors whatever uneasiness it may give myself; and never omit to encourage every Virtue I may see dawning in them.[18]

The happiness of these years must have been somewhat marred by concerns over Charles Pinckney's political fortunes. Joy at his appointment as chief justice for the colony in 1752 ended abruptly with the news that the king had disallowed the appointment in order to create a "place" for an English officeseeker. Charles accepted instead a position as "special" agent for South Carolina to the merchants in London, and in the spring of 1753 the entire family sailed for England. Eliza was pleased to return to the land where she had both fond memories of her girlhood and many friends. After hiring a house in Richmond (where Eliza supervised the inoculation of her children against smallpox) and traveling outside of London, the Pinckneys finally purchased a house near Ripley, in Surrey, enrolled the boys in school, and prepared to remain residents of England until their children's education was completed.

This plan came to an abrupt end on July 12, 1758. In the spring of that year, Charles Pinckney decided to return to Charles Town to look after his plantation and business interests. Leaving the boys at school, Eliza and Harriott returned with him on what was to have been only a brief visit. But weakened by a long voyage, unused after five years in England to the heat of the Carolina climate, Charles was infected with malaria, and within six weeks was dead. Eliza was almost inconsolable at his loss; too distraught to return to her own home in Charles Town for months, she filled her days and her letterbook writing long letters to their acquaintances in England and Antigua of her loss: "The greatest of human Evils has befallen me," she wrote again and again to friends, "My dear, dear Mr. Pinckney is no more! In him I have lost one of the best and worthiest of men, the tenderest and most affectionate of all husbands, and best of Fathers to my children. . . . I was for more than 14 years the happiest of mortals."[19]

Most difficult for her was breaking such overwhelming news to her young sons in England:

We have, my dear children, mett with the greatest of human Evils, but we must drink of the cup it has pleased God to Give us, a bitter Cup indeed! but aloted us by Infinite Wisdom, and let us ever remember, terrible and grievous as the stroke is, we have still reason to thank the hand from whence it comes for all his mercys to him, through life and through death, and to us for having given us this inestimable blessing, for having spared him so long to us, for all the Graces and Virtues he endowed him with, for the goodness of his understanding, and the soundness of his judgments.[20]

With her letter, she sent a barrel of rice, with instructions to the headmaster of their school about how to prepare it to their liking. Charles Cotesworth was then twelve, Thomas only eight. Although she missed them, she wished them to continue the education their father had planned for them. She would not see Charles Cotesworth again until May 1769, or Thomas until September 1771. She carried out her earlier resolves to them through a series of letters exhorting them to cultivate industry, piety, good manners, and above all—to write to her at every opportunity.

At the age of thirty-six, Eliza Lucas Pinckney, now a widow, returned to many of the same responsibilities of running a plantation and household that she had shouldered as a young woman. Named by her husband as executor in his will (to be assisted by a competent overseer), she returned to Belmont nearly a year after his death to discover that the estates had suffered greatly from neglect. She observed, "It has gone back to woods again."[21] The plantation needed to be returned to sound management, first to support the expenses of her boys in school, and then to be passed on to them as an inheritance. Once again, her letterbook is full of references to bills of exchange, of crops gathered, of purchases requested. But there is a profound difference from the letters of her youth: the personal letters are of affectionate instructions to her sons, or sent in thanks to those who befriended them in England, not to her beloved Mr. Pinckney; the letters of business are to Mr. Morley, her man of business, not to an indulgent father. As she returned to her tasks, she wrote to Morley:

I find it requires great care, attention and activity to attend properly to a Carolina Estate, tho' but a moderate one, to do ones duty and make it turn to account, that I find I have as much business as I can go through of one sort or another. Perhaps 'tis better for me, and I believe it is. Had there not been a necessity for it, I might have sunk to the grave by this time in that Lethargy of stupidity which had seized me. . . . A variety of imployment gives my thoughts a relief from melloncholy subjects, tho' 'tis but a temporary one, and gives me air and exercise, which I believe I should not have had resolution enough to take if I had not been roused to it by motives of duty and parental affection."[22]

The creativity and inventiveness of her earlier agricultural experiments were not repeated, though her love for her gardening continued. A long illness in 1760–61 sapped her energy. Although we do not know the name of the gentleman, she apparently received an offer of marriage, which she immediately rejected, "as entering into a second marriage never once entered my head"—although gossip about it reached her friends in England. For the next thirty years she remained faithful to the memory of her "dear, dear Mr. Pinckney."[23]

Her life might thus have passed uneventfully to its end in enjoyment of her children and grandchildren. Her daughter Harriott, who learned the skills of plantation management by observing and perhaps by assisting her mother, made an excellent marriage in 1768 to Daniel Horry, a widower with two children. She was then nineteen; a year later Eliza celebrated the birth of her first grandson, whose infant ways delighted her nearly as much as had those of her own first son. Charles Cotesworth Pinckney had by then returned to Carolina a mature and grave young man, trained in the law, ready to take the responsible role in the province urged upon him in his father's will; within months he had been elected to the Assembly, and in 1773 married Sarah Middleton, the daughter of planter and royal councilor Henry Middleton. Thomas too returned to Carolina: briefly in the fall of 1771, and permanently in 1774 after having been admitted to the bar in London. Eliza's pride in her children and their accomplishments seemed assured.

But public events now enlisted Eliza for yet another role. If she considered herself "on the whole a very loyal subject," with her "share of joy in ye agreable account of my Sovereign and his Consort,"[24] her sons had grown to adulthood in England loyal to their native America. The Stamp Act aroused in them such patriotic feelings that Charles Cotesworth Pinckney was painted in 1765 by the artist Zoffany proclaiming against the act, and Thomas Pinckney in his enthusiasm became known to his friends as "The Little Rebel."[25] Within a few years of their return to Charles Town, both young men were heavily involved in the revolutionary movement, receiving captain's commissions in the First Regiment of South Carolina troops. For Eliza the rush of events must have been disheartening; her childhood and many of her friends had been English, and some of the happy years of her marriage had been spent with the very English ruling class her sons and neighbors were now denouncing. But the loyalties of her sons became hers, and Eliza Lucas Pinckney earned through their military and political efforts and honors yet another honor of her own: "mother of patriots."

The revolutionary war years were not easy for South Carolina. By 1779, the British offensive campaign had shifted to the South. Responding to desperate appeals by the Assembly for funds to prepare the province's defenses, Eliza loaned £ 4,000 currency to the State of South Carolina at 10 percent interest in September 1779. In May 1780, Sir Henry Clinton's forces defeated General Benjamin Lincoln and captured Charles Town for the British. Charles Cotesworth Pinckney was captured in the fall of Charles Town; Thomas Pinckney escaped to rejoin Betsey Motte, whom he had married on July 22, 1779, but in August he too was captured, with his leg shattered by a bullet in the battle at Camden, South Carolina. The British confiscated the Pinckney properties in September 1780. To her English friend Mrs. Revance, Eliza wrote of her losses: "I have been rob[b]ed and deserted by my Slaves; my property pulled to pieces, burnt and destroyed; my money of no value, my Children sick and prisoners. . . . Such is the deplorable state of our Country from two armies being in it for nearly two years."[26]

Nor did the end of the war end Eliza's losses. Charles Cotesworth's wife Sarah died of tuberculosis in the spring of 1784, and within a short time, Harriott's husband Daniel Horry was dead of a "bilious fever." Charles Cotesworth brought his three young daughters to Harriott's Hampton plantation, which now became Eliza's permanent home. Like her mother, Harriott proved adept at running a plantation and directing the education of the assembled children.

In the early days of the new republic, Eliza's sons continued to distinguish themselves. Charles Cotesworth remarried, and shortly after, left for Philadelphia as a delegate to the Constitutional Convention of 1787; Thomas was elected governor of South Carolina in the same year, and presided over the state during the ratification debates. When newly elected President George Washington toured South Carolina in 1791 as part of his efforts to unite the country, he honored the two brothers by breakfasting at Hampton plantation with their mother and sister. The ladies greeted him "arrayed in sashes and bandeaux painted with the general's portrait and mottoes of welcome." He admired Harriott's rice fields, and knowing of Eliza's earlier agricultural contributions, spoke favorably of the indigo fields he had visited. Eliza's life had indeed come full circle.

Not long after, Eliza developed breast cancer. Told of Eliza's condition, Thomas, on a diplomatic mission in London, sent leeches home to be used as a cure, and in April 1793 Charles Cotesworth persuaded her to go to Philadelphia for additional treatment by Dr. William Shippen, a pioneer in the study of anatomy and midwifery, and James Tate. These doctors could do little for her, although while Eliza was there, Martha Washington and the wives of the cabinet officers honored her with visits. At her death, on May 26, George Washington at his own request served as one of her pallbearers. She was buried in Philadelphia's St. Peter's churchyard, far from her beloved Carolina.

Eliza Lucas Pinckney is not an unsung heroine; she has been honored by her country in many of its histories, beginning with David Ramsay's *History of South Carolina from Its First Settlement in 1670 to the Year 1808* (Charleston, 1809). Her contributions as described in these histories sometimes seem to suggest a paradox: Was she the independent young lady who ran a plantation by herself at the age of eighteen and singlehandedly introduced the crop that insured Carolina's wealth? Or was she the archetype of the faithful "republican mother," who sacrificed herself in raising two sons to become such splendid patriots? She is remarkable precisely because she did not herself see any contradiction in those two roles. Her own belief that it was natural and right for a southern woman to be prepared to run all aspects of a plantation can be seen in her willingness to give her daughter much the same training and opportunity that she herself had, and to the same good effect. Perhaps she was fortunate: the men who were closest to her respected her abilities, and encouraged her to use them. Her father provided her with a good education, and then trusted her with the management of his considerable properties. Her husband encouraged her serious reading, and paid her the ultimate compliment of leaving his estates in her competent care. Her sons brought their wives and children to her home when they themselves could not protect them. Eliza Lucas Pinckney was not an early feminist; she was not in open rebellion against the lot of women of her day. But she was a woman who took the considerable advantages with which she was gifted, and used her intelligence, her interest in the world around her, and her sense of duty to herself, her family, and her community to make important contributions, the benefits of which survive two centuries after her death.

Notes

[1]Elise Pinckney, *The Letterbook of Eliza Lucas Pinckney, 1739–1762* (Chapel Hill: University of North Carolina Press, 1972), pp. 61, 36.

[2]Harriet Horry Ravenel, *Eliza Pinckney* (Spartanburg, SC: The Reprint Company, 1967; reprint of Scribner's 1896 edition), p. 199.

[3]See *Charleston in the Age of the Pinckneys*, an excellent book by George C. Rogers, Jr., describing the evolution of Charleston from 1730 to 1830 (Columbia: University of South Carolina Press, 1969).

[4]Pinckney, *Letterbook*, pp. 7–8.

[5]This son of the composer Augustus Pachelbel served as organist in St. Philip's Church, and became one of the great early musicians of Charles Town; ibid., p. 25.

[6]Ibid., pp. 6–7.

[7]Ibid., p. 35.

[8]March 1740, ibid., p. 5.

[9]Ibid., p. 34.

[10]April 1742, ibid., pp. 34–35.

[11]Probably *cassava*, a root product that was a staple food of the tropics.

[12]July 1740, ibid., p. 8.

[13]Ravenel, *Eliza Pinckney*, pp. 104–05.

[14]Pinckney, *Letterbook*, p. 6.

[15]Ravenel, *Eliza Pinckney*, p. 68.

[16]Ibid., pp. 109–114.

[17]The conversation continued on the differences between "putting children" out to nurse in England, and the Carolina practice of using "Nurses in our houses." "Princess Augusta was surprized at the suckling blacks; the Princess stroakd Harriott's cheek, said it made no alteration in the complexion." Ravenel, pp. 151–152.

[18]Ibid., p. 117.

[19]To Mrs. Pocklington, 1759, Pinckney, *Letterbook*, p. 114.

[20]Ibid., pp. 94–95.

[21]Ravenel, *Eliza Pinckney*, p. 189.

[22]March 14th, 1760, Pinckney, *Letterbook*, p. 144.

[23]Ibid., p. 176.

[24]Ravenel, *Eliza Pinckney*, p. 217.

[25]Ibid., p. 247.

[26]Pinckney, *Letterbook*, p. xxiii.

Nancy Ward

(1738?–1822)

Theda Perdue

Although little is known of Nancy Ward's life in general and especially her early years, we suspect that she was born in a Cherokee settlement along the Little Tennessee River near Monroe County, Tennessee. She was the daughter of a Cherokee mother of the Wolf clan and a Delaware father. After her traditional Cherokee upbringing, Nanye'hi (her Cherokee name) married a Cherokee named Kingfisher, with whom she bore two children, Fivekiller and Catherine. Taking her husband's place after he fell in battle against the Creeks, the young Cherokee woman earned the title and privileges of "War Woman." She later married Bryant Ward, a white trader, took the name of Nancy Ward, and gave birth to a daughter, Elizabeth. Her husband eventually returned to South Carolina. She is reputed to have saved a white settlement in 1776 by warning of an impending Cherokee attack. She also used her prerogative as War Woman to save a white woman from being burned at the stake. Ward went on to assume many leadership roles, addressing treaty conferences between the United States and the Cherokee nation in 1781 and in 1785 and advising Cherokee leaders during negotiations in 1817. Political and economic changes in the Cherokee nation diminished the role of War Woman, but Nancy Ward adapted with the changes. She died an innkeeper in 1822 on the Ocoee River in a part of the Cherokee nation that today is eastern Tennessee.

In 1785, representatives of the Cherokee Indians met United States commissioners at Hopewell, South Carolina, to negotiate a peace treaty and land cession. Among the speakers at the conference was Nancy Ward, the War Woman of Chota, who addressed the assembly:

> . . . I look on you and the red people as my children. Your having determined on peace is most pleasing to me, for I have seen much trouble during the late war. I am old [about 47], but I hope yet to bear children, who will grow up and people our nation, as we are now to be under the protection of Congress and shall have no more disturbance. The talk I have given is from the young warriors I have raised in my town, as well as myself. They rejoice that we have peace, and we hope the chain of friendship will never more be broken.[1]

By addressing the treaty conference, Nancy Ward violated the Anglo-American convention that barred women from speaking publicly on political matters. As a Cherokee, however, her action embodied another tradition, one in which women enjoyed political status, acknowledged economic power, and a high degree of personal autonomy.

So alien was this tradition to Anglo-Americans, on whose written accounts we must rely for most information about preliterate native peoples, that few references to the political rights and roles of native American women exist in the traditional historical record. One reason for the paucity of information is that most Anglo-Americans who had contact with native peoples and left records were men. Because native men and women led very separate lives, these observers saw little of how Cherokee women lived, and what role they played in Cherokee society. These observers would have been excluded from women's councils, rituals, and ceremonies, as well as more mundane activities. Furthermore, Anglo-Americans had little interest in native women, except occasionally to buy corn from them or to take them as wives. The observers' ethnocentrism, the inability to interpret events from any perspective other than one's own culture, also poses problems for researchers using Anglo-American sources about native women. For example, many observers commented that Indian men were lazy and that women were virtual slaves who performed all the manual labor.[2] Europeans arrived at this conclusion because native women farmed while men hunted and fished, activities the Europeans considered to be sport instead of important contributions to subsistence. Yet we do have a few references, particularly to Nancy Ward, and through them, we can infer not only how Cherokee women lived in the late eighteenth and early nineteenth centuries but also how many of them obtained the privileges and extraordinary status of "War Women."

The Cherokees were a powerful people who lived in the southern Appalachians. Linguistically, they were related to the Iroquoian peoples of the north, but culturally, the Cherokees were part of the southeastern cultural complex. They shared many practices and beliefs with the Creeks, Choctaws, and Chickasaws; in particular, their economy was based on agriculture, a condition that was reflected in their ceremonial life. The Cherokees first came into contact with Europeans in the late seventeenth century. For much of the eighteenth century the Cherokees had access to the British along the Atlantic seaboard, the French in Canada and Louisiana, and the Spanish in Florida. Throughout this period they retained a degree of independence from any one group of Europeans, although their sentiments early in the century generally rested with the British. The eighteenth century was a period of recurring wars with European powers and with other native peoples. Cherokee warriors often participated in European military expeditions, and their chiefs traveled to colonial capitals and across the Atlantic on diplomatic missions. In the Seven Years' (French and Indian) War, most Cherokees supported the French—whose colonists were more interested in furs than land. The American Revolution found the Cherokee Nation divided, although the majority of Cherokees, motivated by the king's proclamation limiting expansion of colonial settlement, sympathized with the British.

Shifting diplomatic alliances were not the only changes the Cherokees experienced. By the early eighteenth century European traders had established trading posts among them. In response to the European demand for deerskins and their own desire for European goods, hunting came to dominate Cherokee economy. Warfare with European and native enemies disrupted village and family life, while defeat in the Seven Years' War and the American Revolution led to land cessions. Disease and famine took a heavy toll, calling into question the efficacy of certain religious rituals designed to ward off such hardships. By the time the Cherokees met with the representatives of the United States at Hopewell, their culture had begun a major transformation, best characterized as an attempt to preserve what they deemed truly valuable in their own way of life while adopting aspects of colonial culture in order to survive in the changing environment.

Nancy Ward's life spans these cultural changes. She was born about 1738 in Chota, the preeminent town of the Overhill Cherokees who lived in what is today eastern Tennessee.[3] It is thought that her Cherokee name was Nanye'hi, and that she was a member of the Wolf clan and a niece of Attakullakulla, or "The Little Carpenter." The Cherokees had no ruling clan, but many prominent eighteenth-century leaders came from the Wolf clan. One of the most distinguished was Attakullakulla, who visited England with a group of Cherokee chiefs in 1730 and returned to become a leading spokesperson for peace and friendship with Anglo-Americans. Atta-kullakulla was the brother of Nanye'hi's mother; in the Cherokees' matrilineal kinship system, this meant that he was the primary male figure in Nanye'hi's life.[4] According to the principle of ma-trilineal descent, a children's only kin were those on their mother's side—their mother's mother, sisters, other children (even those by different fathers), sisters' children, and brothers. Attakullakulla, as Nanye'hi's maternal uncle, assumed the role that Europeans as-cribed to fathers.

In the early 1750s Nanye'hi married Kingfisher, a member of the Deer clan. The Wolf and Deer clans were two of seven clans to which Cherokees belonged. Members of a clan believed that they shared a common ancestor, even if they did not know precisely who the ancestor was or how they were related. Clans were essential to Cherokee life because one's clan offered protection. The Cherokees had no formal laws or courts: any wrongdoing was punished by the victim's clan. For example, in the case of murder, the clan of the slain Cherokee would kill the murderer or one of the murderer's relatives. Within this system of justice, a person without a clan was often a target of violence because there would be no threat of retribu-tion to act as a deterrent.

In the eighteenth century, Cherokee towns reached from upcoun-try South Carolina into the mountain valleys of western North Caro-lina, eastern Tennessee, and northern Georgia. Most towns had households of each of the seven clans. Because of kinship customs, a Cherokee could expect a warm welcome in any household of his or her clan even if he or she had never met these people before. Because all members of a given clan were blood relatives, marriages were always between members of different clans. Cherokees usually mar-ried outside their father's clan. They considered a marriage to a member of the grandfather's clan to be the most desirable arrange-ment. Within these rules, Cherokees married whomever they chose; no one dictated spouses. Marriage did not alter clan affiliation; thus, Nanye'hi remained a Wolf and Kingfisher remained a Deer. Their two children, Fivekiller and Catherine belonged, because of the ma-trilineal system, to the Wolf clan.

Kingfisher and the children probably lived in Nanye'hi's household because the Cherokees were matrilocal as well as matrilineal. That is, a man lived with his wife and children in a house which belonged to her, or perhaps more accurately, to her family. Unmarried men lived with their mothers or their sisters, but they usually slept in the communal council house because they really had no house of their own. As the principal farmers, women also "owned" storage buildings, fields, crops, and agricultural produce—corn, beans, squash, sunflowers, and pumpkins. While the Cherokees technically held land in common and anyone could use unoccupied land, improved fields belonged to specific matrilineal households. In one sense then, Cherokees vested title to improved land in women.[5] Farming was essential to the Cherokees' way of life, and they highly regarded the economic role of women, which they commemorated in their most important religious festival, the Green Corn Ceremony. The central events of the Green Corn Ceremony were the rekindling of the sacred fire by the medicine man and the presentation of the new corn crop by the women.[6]

In 1755 Nanye'hi joined her husband on a military expedition against the Creeks, the Cherokees' ancient enemies to the south. Women sometimes accompanied war parties to draw water, gather firewood, and cook. In the Cherokees' rather rigid division of labor by gender, these activities were distinctly female. For a man to do them, particularly a warrior, jeopardized his manhood. That Nanye'hi went on an expedition at an early age may indicate a high status for her family or her husband, and it certainly suggests that she was regarded as knowledgeable of restrictions and scrupulous in observing them. For example, relations between men and women were strictly dictated. Men on the warpath, for example, did not engage in sexual intercourse because semen, coming from inside the body, possessed spiritual power. Other taboos prevented menstruating women from accompanying warriors; in fact, they sequestered themselves in special huts in the village during their menses. Even contact with meat from which blood had been spilled was considered potentially dangerous to a military expedition. Therefore, warriors (and, interestingly, menstruating women) ate only a little corn and never meat.[7] War parties that failed to follow these rules courted disaster.

At Taliwa in north Georgia, the Cherokees engaged the Creeks. As Nanye'hi lay behind a log, a Creek bullet found its mark, and Kingfisher dropped dead beside her. She seized his gun and took his place in the fray until the Creeks were driven off. By doing so, she became part of a tradition of women warriors among the Cherokees. Usually these women, like Nanye'hi, became warriors by circumstance, but according to John Howard Payne, who collected information about Cherokee customs in the 1830s, "women have in certain cases dressed in men's clothes and went [sic] to battle." In the American Revolution, one of the casualities of the Cherokee defeat by General Griffith Rutherford at Waya Gap in North Carolina was a woman "painted and stripped like a warrior and armed with bows and arrows." In the early nineteenth century, the Moravian missionary John Gambold had an opportunity to converse with one of these women warriors whose age he estimated to be 100: "The aged woman, named Chicouhla, claimed that she had gone to war against hostile Indians and suffered several severe wounds." The Cherokee Joseph Vann's wives verified this and said that she was "very highly respected and loved by browns and whites alike." One of anthropologist James Mooney's informants in the 1880s had known an old woman whose Cherokee name meant "Sharp Warrior." The Wahnenauhi manuscript that Mooney obtained from a Cherokee medicine man contained another account of a Cherokee woman who rallied the warriors when her husband died defending their village against enemy attack. This woman, Cuhtahlutah (Gatun'lati or "Wild Hemp"), saw her husband fall, grabbed his tomahawk, shouted "Kill! Kill!" and led the Cherokees to victory.[8]

Women who distinguished themselves in battle, like Nanye'hi, went on to occupy an exalted place in Cherokee political and ceremonial life. The eighteenth-century naturalist William Bartram translated the Cherokee title, which is no longer certain, as "War Woman," and he noted that a stream in north Georgia bore the name War Woman's Creek. A trader told him that the name of the stream came "from a decisive battle which the Cherokees had gained over their enemies on the banks of this creek, through the battle and strategem of an Indian woman who was present. She was afterwards raised to the dignity and honor of a Queen or Chief of the nation, as a reward for her superior virtues and abilities, and presided in the State during her life."[9] Anglo-Americans also translated the title as "Beloved Woman" and used the two interchangeably. Cherokees may, however, have reserved the term meaning "Beloved Woman" for postmenopausal women who had acquired unusual spiritual power by surviving both menstruation and warfare.

The Cherokees probably honored women who excelled in battle because these women challenged the usual categorization of the sexes. As we have seen, the Cherokee culture assigned specific roles to each sex. Neither sex was considered superior and neither set of roles was more important than the other. Both were essential to the Cherokee way of life, to their social well-being, and to cosmic order. For there to be harmony in the world, however, each sex had to fulfill its own role. Women were not supposed to engage directly in warfare; only men who had carefully prepared themselves for war through fasting and purification could expect to meet with success. How then could the Cherokees explain a woman who behaved like a man without bringing disaster, a woman who killed enemy warriors and led Cherokee men to victory? Such a woman was obviously an anomaly, and like certain other anomalies, had exceptional power.[10] She was no longer merely a woman nor, however, was she a warrior. She was a "War Woman," and the Cherokees permitted her to manifest her apparent spiritual power in a number of temporal ways.

Only War Women could perform martial dances along with the men. Mooney heard about a woman who had killed her husband's slayer in battle during the American Revolution: "For this deed she was treated with so much consideration that she was permitted to join the warriors in the war dance, carrying her gun and tomahawk." War Women also participated in the Eagle Dance, which commemorated previous victories. Athletic young men performed the actual dance, but in one part, old warriors and War Women related their exploits. These women sat apart from other women and children on ceremonial occasions and partook of food and drink not normally given to women.[11]

Lieutenant Henry Timberlake, who was stationed at Fort Loudoun near Nanye'hi's town of Chota in the 1750s, pointed out that while War Woman was the only title awarded to women, "it abundantly recompenses them, by the power they acquire by it, which is so great, that they can, by the wave of a swan's wing, deliver a wretch condemned by the council, and already tied to the stake." Nanye'hi, who by then was known as Nancy Ward because of her marriage to Bryant Ward, a white trader, exercised this power in 1776 when she rescued a white woman named Mrs. William Bean. Mrs. Bean lived in one of the illegal settlements along the Holston River in what is today northeastern Tennessee. The Cherokees captured her, took her to the town of Toquo, and bound her to the stake. They were about to ignite the tinder at her feet when Nancy Ward appeared and ordered her release. Nancy Ward took Mrs. Bean to her house and, according to an oral tradition, learned from her how to make butter. Ultimately Mrs. Bean was restored to her family. In 1781 Nancy Ward once again rescued prisoners—but this time she acted clandestinely. The Cherokees at Scitigi (Sitico) had imprisoned five white traders and intended to execute two of them before embarking on a raid against white frontier settlements. Instead of publicly demanding the freedom of the traders, Nancy Ward and several other women helped them escape and reach safety.[12]

Mercy was not the only factor that motivated War Women to spare condemned captives. Often they wanted to adopt the captives into their clans to replace members who had been killed in the incessant warfare of the eighteenth century. An adopted captive enjoyed all the rights and privileges of a person born into a clan, and the important decision of whether to accept a captive rested with the women of the clan. David Menzies, an English physician captured during the

Cherokee War of 1760, recounted the experience of being offered to and rejected by a clan:

> In proceeding to the town I understood that these Cherokees had in this expedition lost one of their head warriors, in a skirmish with some of our rangers; and that I was destined to be presented to that chief's mother and family in his room: At which I was overjoyed, as knowing that I thereby stood a chance of not only being secured from death and exempted from torture, but even of good usage and carresses. I perceived that I had overrated much my matter of consolation. . . . The mother fixt first her haggard bloodshot eyes upon me, then riveting them to the ground, gargled out my rejection and destruction.[13]

The warriors clearly favored Menzies' adoption; the chief's mother, however, prevailed. Menzies was subjected to torture but survived, and eventually secured his release.

War Women had an additional incentive to spare prisoners. European captives could be ransomed for a handsome sum, while native captives could be sold to white traders for use as slaves on plantations in the South and in the West Indies. Indeed, the Indian slave trade was a major enterprise throughout much of the eighteenth century involving, according to historian J. Leitch Wright, "tens of thousands" of war captives. As a result of the market for captives, competition for them developed in some towns. John Gerar William De Brahm, a British surveyor, observed the tactics used by some War Women:

> All prisoners must be delivered alive (without any Punishment) as her Slave, if she requires it, which is a Privilege no man can enjoy, not even their Emperor, Kings, or Warriors; there are but a few towns in which [there] is a War Woman; and if she can come near enough to the Prisoner as to put her hand upon him, and say, this is my Slave, the Warriors (tho' with the greatest Reluctancy) must deliver him up to Her, which to prevent they in a great hurry drive a Hatchet in the Prisoner's Head, before the War Woman can reach him; therefore the War Women use that Strategem to disguise themselves as Traders, and come in Company with them, as if out of Curiosity to see the Spectacle of the cruel War-dance.

Occasionally, an Indian woman did appear in Charleston with a prisoner to ransom or sell.[14]

Generally, however, War Women did not exercise their prerogative, but acquiesced to the people's desire for vengeance and condemned captives to torture. While there is no evidence that Nancy Ward actively engaged in torture, she did not rescue a boy who was about to be tortured along with Mrs. Bean, the white woman she had saved in 1776. Instead, she left the boy tied to the stake, where he was burned to death. Mooney recorded an oral tradition in which two women with snakes tattooed on their lips directed the other women to burn the feet of a captive Seneca war chief until they blistered. Then they put corn kernels under the burned skin, chased him with clubs, and ultimately beat him to death. A similar fate at the hands of the women awaited most captives. Usually they thrashed the prisoners, tied them to stakes, "larded their Skins with bits of Lightwood," and seared them with flaming torches. If victims collapsed from the pain, their tormentors threw water on them and gave them time to revive. Sometimes torture lasted for over twenty hours. Adair observed: "Not a soul, of whatever age or sex, manifests the least pity during the prisoner's tortures: the women sing with religious joy, all the while they are torturing the devoted victim, and peals of laughter resound through the crowded theatre—especially if he fears to die." Many victims, particularly Indian warriors, manifested no fear but bragged about martial deeds. When the women concluded that vengeance had been sufficiently exacted or the victim died, they took the scalp and dismembered the body.[15]

As appalling as such behavior is to us today, we must consider torture in its cultural context. Cherokees went to war for vengeance alone. They believed that relatives killed by an enemy could not go to the Darkening Land where spirits resided until their "crying blood" had been avenged. Indeed, kinfolk had a moral and sacred obligation to avenge "crying blood." Under normal conditions, only men had the opportunity to fulfill this obligation—on the warpath. Yet women grieved for their fallen kin as well and longed to participate in the freeing of their spirits. Consequently, the torture of captives brought back by warriors for this purpose was the only way in which women could satisfy their sacred duty.[16]

Occasionally women, including Nancy Ward, provided intelligence to people whom many Cherokee warriors considered enemies. Such activities, which we would consider treasonous, were possible because the Cherokees lacked a coercive centralized government and accorded individuals considerable autonomy. The British garrison at Fort Loudoun often relied on female spies, many of whom were married to soldiers. The commander, Raymond Demere, wrote Governor Henry Lyttleton of South Carolina that "intelligence from women amongst the Indians are always best." In 1756 the native woman employed to procure food for the garrison told Demere that the "Old War Woman" at Chota had confided in her about an Indian and French conspiracy against the English. After Cherokee warriors began a siege of the English fort, women continued to visit the garrison with both information and provisions. According to Tim-

berlake, the women laughed at the threats of the war chief who tried
to stop them, and told him "that if he killed them, their relations
would make his death atone for theirs."[17]

During the American Revolution, Nancy Ward supported the
cause of the new United States, a minority position among the
Cherokees who resented colonial encroachments on their land. In
1776 she warned the trader Isaac Thomas of a Cherokee plan to
attack settlements along the Holston River; he conveyed the message to the settlers in time for them to prepare for the attack. Four
years later, she once again warned white settlers of imminent Cherokee attack. For this reason, perhaps, United States officials received
Nancy Ward as a Cherokee emissary and diplomat. In 1781, when
Arthur Campbell led the Virginia militia into Cherokee territory,
burning several towns and capturing Chota, Nancy Ward called on
him. Campbell reported to Governor Thomas Jefferson of her visit:

> In the time the famous Indian woman Nancy Ward came to camp,
> she gave us various intelligence, and made an overture in behalf of
> some of the chiefs for peace; to which I then evaded giving an explicit
> answer, as I wished first to visit the vindictive part of the nation,
> mostly settled at Hiwassee and Chistowee: and to distress the whole
> as much as possible, by destroying their habitations and provisions.

Despite Nancy Ward's visit, Campbell burned Chota and moved on
to destroy other Cherokee villages. Yet she herself apparently was
accorded kinder treatment. Jefferson replied to Campbell's report:
"Nancy Ward seems rather to have taken refuge with you. In this
case her inclination ought to be followed as to what is done with
her."[18]

Nancy Ward was not alone in the role of female ambassador. In
1725 the Creeks trusted a Cherokee woman who had been taken
prisoner to represent them in treaty negotiations. She had been present during Creek council deliberations that centered on the mis-
taken belief that the Cherokees, rather than the "French Indians,"
had killed a number of Creek people and on the rumor that a joint
attack of the English and Cherokees was imminent. Fully apprised
of the Creek view, "Slave Woman" accompanied a Creek man, perhaps as a translator, to a Cherokee town to petition for peace. The
man fled in fear, but he left Slave Woman behind and "particularly
gave her in charge to talk about a peace."[19] Cherokee women also
represented their own people in negotiations with foreign powers. In
the 1750s a Cherokee woman traveled to Fort Toulouse, in what is
today Alabama, with French John, a captive whom the English suspected of espionage, to discuss the building of a French fort among
the Overhill towns. And the wife of the Mankiller of Tellico, who

had conspired with the French against the English, joined her husband in complaining to Demere at Fort Loudon about English treatment of the Indians.[20]

In negotiations, women may have met with women's councils among other native peoples. Women were almost always present at treaty conferences, but white male commissioners who were keeping records paid little attention to them except to complain about the additional expense of feeding them. Consequently, only indirect references to women's roles in diplomacy exist. In 1768, for example, Cherokee warriors negotiating with Iroquoian peoples at Johnson Hall in New York presented a wampum belt, used to symbolize and record agreements, that had been sent by Cherokee women to Iroquois women. Oconostota, a Cherokee war chief who was urging peace, relayed the women's message: "We know that they will hear us for it is they who undergo the pains of Childbirth and produce Men. Surely therefore they must feel Mothers pains for those killed in War, and be desirous to prevent it."[21]

Nancy Ward used similar language when she appeared in July 1781 at a treaty conference with United States commissioners held on the Long Island of the Holston in northeastern Tennessee. Because most Cherokees had allied with Britain in the American Revolution, the United States sought to exercise sovereignty over the trans-Appalachian region by forcing land cessions from its native inhabitants. In speaking at the conference, Nancy Ward reminded the commissioners that not all Cherokees had supported the British. She spoke eloquently for peace:

> You know that women are always looked upon as nothing; but we are your mothers; you are our sons. Our cry is all for peace; let it continue. This peace must last forever. Let your women's sons be ours; our sons be yours. Let your women hear our words.[22]

Her words had the desired effect, and the Cherokees ceded no land to the United States at the Long Island of the Holston. Her speech at Hopewell in 1785 echoed the same theme, but this time the Cherokees paid dearly for their alliance with the British during the American Revolution by losing thousands of acres of their national domain.

When Nancy Ward told the commissioners at the Long Island of the Holston that "women are always looked upon as nothing" she demonstrated considerable knowledge of Anglo-American attitudes toward her sex. She may have acquired this knowledge while she was married to the white trader Bryant Ward. Ward had taken up residence at Chota in the late 1750s, married the War Woman, and fathered one daughter, Elizabeth. At this time Nanye'hi anglicized her name, and subsequently was known as Nancy Ward. By the end of the decade, however, Bryant Ward had returned to his other family in South Carolina. Elizabeth remained with her mother, and Bryant Ward's desertion probably did not radically alter their lives.

Nancy Ward was only one of many Cherokee women who married white traders in the eighteenth century.[23] Traders sought native wives not only for companionship but also for the entree matrimony gave them into Cherokee society. Their wives acted as translators as well as tutors of the difficult Cherokee language. Furthermore, in dealing with a society dominated by kin networks, a wife belonging to a Cherokee clan was highly desirable. Marriage did not extend clan membership to a trader, of course, but his children inherited that affiliation from their mother. Since kinship—not race—determined who was a Cherokee, these children were truly a part of Cherokee society.

Unlike Bryant Ward, many traders remained with their native families throughout their lives and bequeathed to their children prosperous businesses, familiarity with Anglo-American ways, and fluency in English. By so doing, they wreaked social havoc on the Cherokees. Traditionally, Cherokees buried personal property with the deceased, but that, of course, was impractical with the entire inventory of a frontier trading post. Furthermore, children usually had acquired their fathers' materialistic values and had no intention of seeing their inheritance interred. By adopting their fathers' names and values, these children also began a reordering of kinship patterns, and paternity came to take precedence. In 1808 a council of Cherokee headmen (there is no evidence of women participating) formalized these trends by establishing a national police force to safeguard a person's possessions during life and "to give protection to children as heirs to their father's property, and to the widow's share."[24]

The importance of matrilineal clans waned. In 1810 a council representing the seven clans, but once again apparently including no women, abolished the practice of blood vengeance and surrendered to the Cherokee national government the responsibility to punish crime.[25] A class system began to replace the clans in ordering social relations as wealthy Anglo-Cherokees tended to marry whites or each other. Nancy Ward's daughter Elizabeth, for example, married Joseph Martin, the North Carolina agent to the Cherokees; their daughter Nannie married Michael Hildebrand, the son of a white miller and a Cherokee woman.[26]

The superior wealth of Anglo-Cherokees inspired envy in some of the native Cherokees, who began to imitate the descendants of traders by anglicizing their names, turning to trade and commercial agriculture, and bequeathing to their children the earthly rewards they managed to reap. Other Cherokees, less willing to alter traditional lifestyles, nevertheless treated highly acculturated Cherokees and Anglo-Cherokees with respect and deference. The ability of these people to interact easily with Anglo-Americans increasingly led the Cherokees to delegate political power to them. By 1830, a disproportionate number of Cherokee leaders descended from traders and/or possessed great wealth.[27]

Just as individual Cherokees began to adopt the values and lifestyles of Anglo-Americans, so the Cherokee Nation began to pattern itself after the United States. The near anarchy that had permitted Nancy Ward to warn colonists of Cherokee attacks in the American Revolution made the Nation vulnerable to the white people's insatiable hunger for land. Without a formal political structure and coercive power, a few individuals susceptible to threats and bribes could, and did, sell off much of the Cherokee homeland. Yet the political system that emerged had little room in it for Nancy Ward, the War Woman of Chota, and other women. The people who began to centralize political power in the Cherokee Nation were the male warriors, who could enforce national decisions, and the descendants of traders, who could deal more effectively with whites. With the defeat and pacification of a small band of Cherokees who had continued to wage war with the United States into the 1790s, the warriors' role declined—as did that of War Women—and the genetic and ideological heirs of traders gained ascendancy. For these people, women did not belong in the political arena. In 1818, Charles Hicks, who would become principal chief in the 1820s, described the most prominent men in the Nation as "those who have kept their women and children at home and in comfortable circumstances."[28]

These changes had the approval and encouragement of missionaries and United States agents who hoped to "civilize" the Cherokees. "Civilization" meant adopting the cultural norms of Anglo-American society—literacy in English, commercial agriculture, Christianity, republican government, and a patriarchal family structure. The "civilized" Cherokee John Ridge described what this meant for women: "They sew, they weave, they spin, they cook our meals and act well the duties assigned them by Nature as mothers." They clearly, in Ridge's view, did not go to war, speak in council, or negotiate treaties. Nancy Ward had become an anachronism.[29]

The final official pronouncement by the War Woman of Chota regarded a proposed sale of Cherokee land. In 1817, the United States sought a large land cession that would result in the removal of the Cherokees to land west of the Mississippi River.[30] Because of her advanced age, Nancy Ward was unable to attend the treaty confer-

ence, but she and twelve other women sent a message to the Cherokee National Council:

> The Cherokee ladys now being present at the meeting of the Chiefs
> and warriors in council have thought it their duties as mothers to
> address their beloved Chiefs and warriors now assembled.
>
> Our beloved children and head men of the Cherokee nation we
> address you warriors in council[. W]e have raised all of you on the
> land which we now have, which God gave us to inhabit and raise
> provisions[. W]e know that our country has once been extensive but
> by repeated sales has become circumscribed to a small tract and
> never have thought it our duty to interfere in the disposition of it till
> now, if a father or mother was to sell all their lands which they had to
> depend on[,] which their children had to raise their living on[,] which
> would be bad indeed and to be removed to another country[. W]e do
> not wish to go to an unknown country which we have understood
> some of our children wish to go over the Mississippi but this act of
> our children would be like destroying your mothers. Your mother and
> sisters ask and beg of you not to part with any more of our lands. . . .
>
> Nancy Ward to her children Warriors to take pity and listen to the
> talks of your sisters, although I am very old yet cannot but pity the
> situation in which you will hear of their minds. I have great many
> grand children which I wish them to do well on our land.[31]

Nancy Ward probably did not appear the next year when Cherokee
women pleaded with the Council, "our beloved children," to reject
the United States' proposal for allotment of land to individuals and
"to hold our country in common as hitherto."[32] She may very well,
however, have advised them on the subject.

The effect of these women's petitions is difficult to ascertain. In
1817 the Cherokees ceded tracts of land in Georgia, Alabama, and
Tennessee, and in 1819, they made a larger cession that included
Nancy Ward's town of Chota. Nevertheless, they rejected individual
allotments, retained common ownership of land, and strengthened
restrictions on the sale of improvements individuals had made to
the commonly held land. Furthermore, the Cherokee Nation gave
notice that it would negotiate no additional cessions—a resolution
so strongly supported that the United States ultimately had to turn
to a small unauthorized faction in order to obtain the removal treaty
from a minority group of Cherokee in 1835.

With the cession of her town, Nancy Ward moved south to the
Ocoee River valley, where she operated an inn along the federal road
that ran from Georgia to Nashville, Tennessee, through the Cherokee Nation. In 1822 the War Woman of Chota died, leaving behind a
Nation in which the status of women was suffering a precipitous

decline. Only five years after her death, the Cherokees enacted a new constitution that restricted the franchise to "free male citizens" and specified that only "a free Cherokee male" could sit in the General Council.[33]

Nancy Ward's life spanned the time in which the Cherokees abandoned a government in which women had a voice, an economy in which women's work was recognized as essential, not peripheral, and a definition of gender roles that did not subordinate one sex to the other. The society after which they patterned their new institutions relegated women to a secondary role, one which Nancy Ward probably found incomprehensible. Her life reminds us that such a subordinate position is not the natural order, that it is merely cultural, and that other cultures regard women in a different light than Western "civilization." And that is reason enough to remember the War Woman of Chota.

Notes

[1]*American State Papers*, Class 2: *Indian Affairs* (Washington, DC, 1832), 1: 41.

[2]Bernard Romans, *A Concise Natural History of East and West Florida* (New York, 1775), pp. 40–43; James Adair, *Adair's History of the American Indian*, ed. Samuel Cole Williams (Johnson City, TN, 1930), pp. 434–41.

[3]Biographies of Nancy Ward include Robert G. Adams, *Nancy Ward, Beautiful Woman of Two Worlds* (Chattanooga, TN, 1979); Pat Alderman, *Nancy Ward: Cherokee Chieftainess* (Johnson City, TN, 1978); J. P. Brown, "Nancy Ward, Little Owl's Cousin," *Flower and Feather* 13 (1957): 57–59; Annie Walker Burns, *Military and Genealogical Records of the Famous Indian Woman, Nancy Ward* (Washington, DC, 1957); Katherine Elizabeth Crane, "Nancy Ward" in *Dictionary of American Biography* (Washington, DC, 1936) 19: 433; Harold W. Felton, *Nancy Ward, Cherokee* (New York, 1975); Carolyn Thomas Foreman, *Indian Women Chiefs* (Muskogee, OK, 1954), pp. 72–86; Ben Harris McClary, "Nancy Ward: Last Beloved Woman of the Cherokees," *Tennessee Historical Quarterly* 21 (1962): 336–52, Norma Tucker, "Nancy Ward, Ghighau of the Cherokees," *Georgia Historical Quarterly* 53 (1969): 192–200. These range in quality from McClary's scholarly study to E. Sterling King's highly fictionalized *The Wild Rose of the Cherokee . . . or, Nancy Ward, The Pocahontas of the West* (Nashville, TN, 1895).

[4]The best study of the Cherokees' kinship system is John P. Reid, *A Law of Blood: Primitive Law of the Cherokee Nation* (New York, 1970).

[5]William Bartram, "Observations on the Creek and Cherokee Indians, 1789," *Transactions of the American Ethnological Society* 3 (1854): 66.

[6] Adair, *History*, pp. 105–15; Henry Timberlake, *Lieut. Henry Timberlake's Memoirs, 1756–1765*, ed. by Samuel Cole Williams (Johnson City, TN, 1927), pp. 64, 88.

[7] For a theoretical discussion of attitudes toward body fluids, see Mary Douglas, *Purity and Danger* (London, 1966).

[8] John Howard Payne Papers (Newberry Library, Chicago, Ill.), 3: 124, 4: 170; Diary of the Moravian Mission at Spring Place, 5 July 1807, trans. Carl C. Mauleshagen (typescript, Georgia Historical Commission, Department of Natural Resources, Atlanta, Ga.); James Mooney, "Myths of the Cherokee," *Nineteenth Annual Report of the American Bureau of Ethnology* (Washington, DC, 1900), p. 395.

[9] Bartram, "Observations," p. 32.

[10] Charles Hudson, *The Southeastern Indians* (Knoxville, TN, 1976), pp. 139–47.

[11] Mooney, "Myths," p. 395; Payne Papers, 6: 220; Alexander Longe, "A Small Postscript on the Ways and Manners of the Indians Called Cherokees," ed. David H. Corkran, *Southern Indian Studies* 21 (1969): 14, 16, 20, 22, 24.

[12] Timberlake, *Memoirs*, p. 94; John Haywood, *The Natural and Aboriginal History of Tennessee up to the First Settlements Therein by the White People in the Year 1768* (Jackson, TN, 1959, orig. ed. 1823), 278; William P. Palmer, ed., *Calendar of Virginia State Papers and Other Manuscripts, 1652–1781* (Richmond, 1875), 1: 446–47.

[13] David Menzies, "A True Relation of the Unheard-of Sufferings of David Menzies, Surgeon, among the Cherokees, and of His Surprising Deliverance," *Royal Magazine* (July 1761), p. 27.

[14] J. Leitch Wright, Jr., *The Only Land They Knew: The Tragic Story of the American Indians in the Old South* (New York, 1981), p. 148; John Gerar William De Brahm, *Report of the General Survey in the Southern District of North America*, ed. Louis De Vorsey (Columbia, SC, 1971), p. 109.

[15] Mooney, "Observations," pp. 360, 363; De Brahm, *General Survey*, p. 108; Adair, *History*, pp. 418–19.

[16] Adair, *History*, p. 155; Timberlake, *Memoirs*, p. 82.

[17] Timberlake, Memoirs, pp. 89–90.

[18] Samuel Cole Williams, *Tennessee during the Revolutionary War* (Rpt. Knoxville, 1974, orig. ed. 1944), pp. 36, 184; Palmer, 1: 435, Julian P. Boyd, ed., *The Papers of Thomas Jefferson* (Princeton, NJ, 1951), 4: 361.

[19] Newton D. Mereness, ed., *Travels in the American Colonies* (New York, 1916), pp. 120–21, 134–35.

[20] William L. McDowell, ed., *Documents Relating to Indian Affairs, 1754–1765* (Columbia, SC, 1970), pp. 201, 268.

[21] E. B. O'Callaghan and B. Fernow, eds., *Documents Relative to the Colonial History of the State of New York* (Albany, NY, 1849–51), 8: 43.

[22]Nathaniel Green Papers (Library of Congress, Washington, D.C.) quoted in Williams, p. 201.

[23]For the role of trade and traders in Cherokee society, see Verner W. Crane, *The Southern Frontier, 1670–1732* (Durham, NC, 1928); John P. Reid, *A Better Kind of Hatchet: Law, Trade and Diplomacy in the Cherokee Nation during the Early Years of European Contact* (University Park, PA, 1976); J. Leitch Wright, *The Only Land They Knew: The Tragic Story of American Indians in the Old South* (New York, 1981).

[24]*Laws of the Cherokee Nation: Adopted by the Council at Various Times, Printed for the Benefit of the Nation* (Tahlequah, Cherokee Nation, 1852), p. 3.

[25]Ibid., p. 4.

[26]Penelope Johnson Allen, "Leaves from the Family Tree," *Chattanooga Times* 12 August 1934.

[27]For the changes experienced by the Cherokees, see Henry T. Malone, *Cherokees of the Old South: A People in Transition* (Athens, GA, 1956); Willam G. McLoughlin, *Cherokee Renascence in the New Republic* (Princeton, NJ, 1986); McLoughlin, *Cherokees and Missionaries, 1789–1839* (New Haven, CT, 1984); Theda Perdue, *Slavery and the Evolution of Cherokee Society, 1540–1866* (Knoxville, TN, 1979).

[28]Ard Hoyt, Moody Hall, William Chamberlain, and D.S. Butrick to Samuel Worcester, 25 July 1818 (Papers of the American Board of Commissioners for Foreign Missions, Houghton Library, Harvard University, Cambridge, MA). For the effect of cultural changes on Cherokee women, see Mary E. Young, "Women, Civilization, and the Indian Question" in Mabel E. Deutrich and Virginia C. Purdy, eds., *Clio Was a Woman: Studies in the History of American Women* (Washington, DC, 1980); Perdue, "Southern Indians and the Cult of True Womanhood" in Walter J. Fraser, et al., eds., *The Web of Southern Social Relations: Women, Family, & Education* (Athens, GA, 1985).

[29]John Ridge to Albert Gallatin, 27 February 1826, Payne Papers.

[30]The removal policy is dealt with in Francis Paul Prucha, *American Indian Policy in the Formative Years: The Indian Trade and Intercourse Acts, 1790–1834* (Cambridge, MA, 1962); Ronald N. Satz, *American Indian Policy in the Jacksonian Era* (Lincoln, NE, 1975).

[31]Presidential Papers Microfilm: Andrew Jackson (Washington, DC, 1961), Series 1, Reel 22.

[32]Brainerd Journal, 30 June 1818 (American Board Papers).

[33]*Laws*, pp. 120–21.

PHILLIS WHEATLEY, NEGRO SERVANT to Mr JOHN WHEATLEY, of BOSTON.

Phillis Wheatley
(1753?–1784)

Charles Scruggs

Born in West Africa, the person to be named Phillis Wheatley was enslaved as a child and sold in Boston in 1761. Her purchaser, John Wheatley, intended her to be a domestic servant to help his wife Susanna. However, because Phillis showed great intellectual precocity, Susanna Wheatley educated her and fostered her talent. With the rest of the family, she became a member of Boston's Old South Church. Having demonstrated her poetic abilities, Phillis Wheatley was sent by her owners to England in 1773 to further her literary career. There, the most prominent evangelical woman in England, the Countess of Huntingdon (who was a friend of Susanna and Phillis through George Whitefield, one of the first and most popular evangelical Methodist preachers) sponsored the publication of Wheatley's poems. In 1773 she was manumitted in accordance with Susanna Wheatley's dying wish and then lived in the Wheatley household until John Wheatley died in 1778. Shortly thereafter, Wheatley married a free black man. She died a poor domestic servant in 1784.

Phillis Wheatley was born about 1753, in Senegal, West Africa. She was enslaved perhaps shortly before 1761. In that year a slave ship brought the Fulani child (whose African name is now lost) to Boston. White merchants in northern seaports had dramatically increased their importation of slaves during the first half of the eighteenth century. By the 1720s about one-fifth of Boston's families held slaves, and by 1742 about 8.5 percent of the population were slaves. African men frequently worked in the shipyards and on board ships while African women worked as domestic slaves.[1]

The young Fulani was purchased directly off the ship in Boston harbor by a prosperous merchant tailor named John Wheatley, to be the personal servant of his wife, Susanna. She was renamed and taught English in the Wheatley household and, as Phillis Wheatley, she would come to look on Susanna Wheatley as her adoptive and spiritual parent. After Susanna Wheatley's death when Phillis was twenty-one, Phillis said she felt "like one forsaken by her parent in a desolate wilderness," for Susanna Wheatley had given her both "uncommon tenderness for thirteen years" and above all "unwearied diligence to instruct me in the principles of the true Religion."[2]

As a child, Phillis soon demonstrated her extraordinary intellectual abilities. According to John Wheatley, "by only what she was taught in the family," which included the Wheatley's twin children, Mary and Nathaniel, "in Sixteen Months Time from her Arrival, [Phillis] attained the English Language, to such a Degree, as to read any [of] the most difficult Parts of the Sacred Writings, to the greatest Astonishment of all who heard her."[3] Like other well-educated persons of that era, she mastered Latin as well as English. By age thirteen she was writing poetry, publishing her first poem nine years after arriving from Africa.[4] English was now her private and public language, the cultural vehicle for her genius.

Phillis Wheatley became known in Boston as,

> a very Extraordinary female Slave, who had made some verses on our mutually dear deceased Friend [George Whitefield]: I visited her mistress, and found by conversing with the African she was no Imposter. . . .[5]

She was "extraordinary" not because of the quality of her verse but because, as a slave, an African, and a female, she made verses at all.

The writer of that "Extraordinary female Slave" letter was Thomas Wooldridge, well known to Susanna Wheatley because both were members of a transatlantic network of evangelicals inspired by the Great Awakening. Wooldridge's addressee was the Earl of Dartmouth, after whom Dartmouth College was named: its ostensible purpose was the evangelization of American Indians. We see from the letter that both Wooldridge and Dartmouth were close to the Rev. George Whitefield, perhaps the greatest preacher of the Great Awakening, the man who had originally converted Susanna Wheatley. We can assume that she, in turn, converted Phillis. These connections and Susanna's "principles of the true Religion" were reflected in the publication in 1770 of the Phillis Wheatley poem to which Wooldridge's letter refers, "An Elegaic Poem on the Death of the Celebrated Divine . . . George Whitefield." Whitefield and those inspired by him and his fellow itinerant preachers reached hundreds of thousands of the poor and enslaved, most in huge, outdoor camp meetings. When Wooldridge met "the African" she was already in correspondence with evangelicals on both sides of the Atlantic. Among them were Lady Huntingdon, as head of her "Connexion" a leading aristocratic sponsor of English evangelism and a good friend of Susanna Wheatley; and John Thornton, a rich English merchant at whose house in London would form the "Clapham sect," at the heart of the white component of English abolitionism.[6]

Phillis Wheatley visited England in 1773, where Susanna Wheatley believed that a volume of her poetry would stand a better chance of being published. Phillis had already published three poems in London and four in Boston, but had had proposals for a book of poems rejected in Boston. Susanna Wheatley then cultivated the support in London of the Countess of Huntingdon, who not only agreed that Phillis Wheatley might dedicate a volume of poems to her, but arranged to have a likeness of the author engraved for a frontispiece.

When Phillis Wheatley arrived in London, she was received there with more fanfare than she would ever receive in her lifetime in America. With the Lady Huntingdon as her patron, this humble young woman found herself courted and lionized by the city's literati. The former Lord Mayor of London presented her with a copy of John Milton's *Paradise Lost*, regarded as one of the greatest poems in the English language. And *Poems on Various Subjects* was actually published in England—primarily owing to Lady Huntingdon's efforts.[7]

Phillis Wheatley's public life was to reach a climax upon her presentation at the English royal court. But it was prevented by news from Wheatley's Boston home. Hearing of Susanna Wheatley's serious illness, Phillis left for America after only five weeks in England. Back in Boston, however, she was granted her freedom in December 1773—in her own words, "three months before the death of my dear mistress and at her desire, as well as [John Wheatley's] own humanity. . . ." It seems that the dying Susanna Wheatley was ensuring that Phillis would, indeed, be freed before she died. In the letter grieving her "parent's" death, Phillis noted the change in "the behavior of those who seem'd to respect me while under my mistresses [*sic*] patronage; . . . some of those have already put on a reserve. . . ."[8] She faced continuing racism. Her correspondent in this case, the evangelical John Thornton, advised Wheatley to return to Africa as a missionary, more specifically, by marrying one of two Rhode Island evangelized blacks named Bristol Yamma and John Quamine, neither of whom she had ever met.[9] It is crucial to recognize the historical meaning of Phillis Wheatley's reply to Thornton: "Upon my arrival [in Africa] how like a Barbarian shou'd I look to the natives; I can promise that my tongue shall be quiet, for a strong reason indeed, being an utter stranger to the Language of Anamaboe."[10] She had become "British and American." Returning to Africa would silence her.

She continued to live in the Wheatley household in Boston, a city dominated by the Revolution during the remainder of Phillis Wheatley's life. Responding to her "To His Excellency George Washington," published in Tom Paine's *Pennsylvania Magazine* (1776) when Washington was appointed commander in chief of the revolutionary armies, Washington invited Phillis Wheatley to his Cambridge headquarters. In March 1778, John Wheatley died, finally dissolving the secure circumstances under which Phillis Wheatley had lived since her arrival in America. The following month she married a free black shopkeeper, John Peters. They had three children (all of whom died young) before he left her life and the historical record. One of her last poems, "Liberty and Peace" (1784) celebrating the end of the American Revolution, was published under her married name. Phillis Wheatley was working as a servant in a cheap boardinghouse when she and her last remaining child died, on December 5, 1784. Her poetry was kept alive in the early nineteenth century by abolitionist publishers.[11]

Although we have learned a good deal in recent years about Phillis Wheatley's life and literary career, we have rarely attempted to discuss her poetry as poetry. A starting point is her reception in London. What was the reason for such lavish attention given to a lowly slave poet? The answer lies in England's fascination for poets who illustrated the principle of "natural genius." This principle can best be explained by the Latin aphorism, *poeta nascitur, non fit* ("a poet is born, and not made").[12] Although the idea of "natural genius" is ancient, it was given a new interpretation by the middle of the eighteenth century. This interpretation not only helps us to understand the English response to Phillis Wheatley, but it also enables us to see how she could use the idea of "natural genius" to her own poetical advantage.

The essayist Joseph Addison popularized the concept of "natural genius" in the eighteenth century. In 1711, in his very influential magazine, *The Spectator*, Addison had distinguished between two kinds of poetic genius. The first kind is those artists "who by the mere strength of natural parts, and without any assistance of art or learning, have produced works that were the delight of their own times and the wonder of posterity." The second kind is artists who "have formed themselves by rules and submitted the greatness of their natural talents to the corrections and restraints of art." Addison claims to make no disparaging comparison between the two types of genius, but he does admit that there is something "nobly wild, and extravagant in . . . natural geniuses that is infinitely more beautiful than all the turn and polishing of what the French call a *bel esprit*, by which they would express a genius refined by conversation, reflection, and the reading of the most polite authors."[13] As Addison defined the term, "natural genius" implied an elitist view of the poet—some are born with this divine talent, others are not— for he never imagined that the idea of "natural genius" could be applied to a working-class poet.

Nevertheless, at mid-century this concept was given a distinctly democratic twist. Some members of the English aristocracy became convinced that among the poor were to be found "mute, inglorious Miltons," who if only given the chance would burst forth in glorious song.[14] Thus poets were seized upon because they were "unlettered," and in the thirty-five or so years before Phillis Wheatley began to write in the late 1760s, we find numerous examples of bards from the lower classes who were patronized by people of position. For example, Joseph Spence sponsored Stephen Duck, the "Thresher-Poet"; Lord Lyttelton encouraged James Woodhouse, the "Shoemaker-Poet"; Lord Chesterfield helped Henry Jones, the "Bricklayer-Poet"; and in little more than a decade after Phillis Wheatley's death, Hannah More sponsored Ann Yearsley, the poet known as Lactilla, the "Milkmaid-Poet."[15]

Given this atmosphere, it is understandable that Lady Huntingdon became excited over the poetry of a young slave woman.[16] To Lady Huntingdon, Phillis Wheatley was another example of "natural genius" among the impoverished classes. Furthermore, Lady Huntingdon knew that others would respond to this new manifestation of the "Unlettered Muse" and that a picture of the author as the frontispiece of *Poems on Various Subjects* would call attention to the author's humble station.

The advertisement for Phillis Wheatley's book also emphasized the author's "natural genius." This notice appeared in the *London Chronicle* (September 9–11, 11–14) and in the *Morning Post and Advertiser* (September 13 and 18), and it included a testimonial from people "distinguished for their learning" who "unanimously expressed their approbation of her genius, and their amazement at the gifts with which infinite Wisdom has furnished her." The language of the advertisement implies that Phillis Wheatley and Africa were inseparably linked in the minds of the eighteenth-century English readers:

> The Book here proposed for publication displays perhaps one of the greatest instances of pure, unassisted genius, that the world ever produced. The Author is a native of Africa, and left not that dark part of the habitable system, till she was eight years old. She is now no more than nineteen, and many of the poems were penned before she arrived at near that age.
>
> They were wrote upon a variety of interesting subjects, and in a stile rather to be expected from those who . . . have had the happiness of a liberal education, than from one born in the wilds of Africa.[17]

Phillis Wheatley is not praised because she expressed her naked, unadorned self; she is praised because, deprived of a "liberal education," she intuitively knows the adornments of art.

The tradition of "natural genius" continues well into the nineteenth century and is the basis of Margaretta Odell's short biography of the African poet. A strange mixture of fact and fancy, Odell's *Memoir* (1834) is our major source of information about Phillis Wheatley's life, and the myth which Odell expounds has its roots in eighteenth-century England. We learn, for instance, that as a young girl, Phillis Wheatley took to poetry as naturally as ducks take to water. Although people encouraged her to read and write, "nothing was forced upon her, nothing was suggested, or placed before her as a lure; her literary efforts were altogether the natural workings of her own mind." Also, she never had "any grammatical instructor, or knowledge of the structure or idiom of the English language, except which she imbibed from a perusal of the best English writers, and from mingling in polite circles. . . ." Furthermore, she was visited by visions in the night which awakened her and which she wrote down as poems. The next morning, she could not remember these dreams which had inspired her to write poetry.[18]

The extent to which Phillis Wheatley believed she was a "natural genius" is difficult to determine, but she did skillfully employ this public image of herself in her poetry. The appearance of the idea of "natural genius" in her poems presented a familiar paradox, as her age would have instantly recognized. In a poetical correspondence with Lieutenant Rochfort of His Majesty's Navy, Phillis Wheatley modestly disclaims the use of artifice, at the same time that she artfully defines the kind of poet she is and hopes to be.

Phillis Wheatley had written a poem, addressed to Rochfort, in which she had praised the sailor's martial valor, and Rochfort responded by sending her a poem of his own. In "The Answer," Rochfort eulogizes Phillis Wheatley by glorifying the country of her birth. Africa is depicted as a "happy land" where "shady forests . . . scarce know a bound." Here there are

> The artless grottos, and the soft retreats;
> "At once the lover and the muse's seats."
> Where nature taught, (tho strange it is to tell,)
> Her flowing pencil Europe to excell. (84)

In these lines, Rochfort romanticizes Africa. Primitivistic and picturesque, this Africa is as unreal as the "dark continent" of the advertisement to *Poems on Various Subjects*. Rochfort sees Africa as the cause of Phillis Wheatley's power as a poet; the simple "artless" land has given birth to an "artless" poet. In later lines, he celebrates "Wheatley's song" as having "seraphic fire" and an "art, which art could ne'er acquire."

When Phillis Wheatley wrote a poetic reply to this poem, she employed the same motifs which Rochfort had used. She refers to Africa as a luxuriant "Eden." Then she humbly says of Rochfort's flattery:

> The generous plaudit 'tis not mine to claim,
> A muse untutor'd, and unknown to fame. (86)

She laments further that her "pen . . . Can never rival, never equal thine," but she will nevertheless continue to study the best authors to improve her talent. She illustrates this thought by soaring into poetic flight:

> Then fix the humble Afric muse's seat
> At British Homer's and Sir Isaac's feet *
> Those bards whose fame in deathless strains arise
> Creation's boast, and fav'rites of the skies. (86)

It is easy to see that Rochfort and Phillis Wheatley are playing an elaborate game in these poems, with the assumptions on both sides well understood. Rochfort tells her that she is an "artless" poet, and she modestly agrees, only to prove his thesis that her "untutored" muse has the capacity for true "seraphic fire." She is the "artless" poet as wise *ingénue*. It is worth noting that in the above passage,

---

*The "British Homer" is the poet Alexander Pope, who translated Homer; "Sir Isaac" is the scientist and astronomer Sir Isaac Newton.

Phillis Wheatley says that she will worship at the shrines of Pope
and Newton, two of the greatest "bards" of the age.

What Phillis Wheatley learned from Alexander Pope, her favorite
author, was an ability to transform her real self into an imagined
self, a *persona*, that functioned as a means to a precise end, rhetorical persuasion. Instead of being a liability, this imagined self became
a poetic asset. Often it was used as the cornerstone of an argument
which she was building in a poem, and since the imagined self was
based upon assumptions about race and "natural genius" that she
and her age understood, the poem was convincing to the people who
read it. Whatever her real feelings, it was her imagined self that she
showed to the world. Whatever the disadvantages, her imagined self
made her eloquent in places where she might have been simply
maudlin.

Let us look more closely at a poem in which Phillis Wheatley uses
her imagined self for rhetorical purposes. In "To The Right Hon-
ourable William, Earl of Dartmouth, His Majesty's Principal Secretary of State for North America," she congratulates Dartmouth on
his new political post and pleads with him to protect and preserve
the rights of Americans, vis-à-vis England, in the New World. To
reinforce her point, she makes an analogy between America's situation and her own:

> I, young in life, by seeming cruel fate
> Was snatch'd from *Afric's* fancy'd happy seat:
> What pangs excruciating must molest,
> What sorrows labour in my parent's breast?
> Steel'd was that soul and by no misery mov'd
> That from a father seiz'd his babe belov'd:
> Such, such my case. And can I then but pray
> Others may never feel tyrannic sway? (34)

These lines have been alternately praised and blamed for their sincerity or lack of sincerity. As we know from Dr. Johnson's dictionary
(1775), although the word "fancy" can be a synonym for "delusion",
it can also be a synonym for the "imagination" which, in Johnson's
words, "forms to itself representations of things, persons, or scenes
of being." In this definition, "fancy" is that part of the mind that
makes images, ones that in turn have their origin in sense experience. Phillis Wheatley's "Afric's fancy'd happy seat" might be "the
happy seat" which other poets have pictured Africa to be—either
from seeing it themselves or from seeing it in their imaginations. We
know that Phillis Wheatley was aware of the primitivistic tradition
in eighteenth-century England that often conceived of Africa as a

fruitful paradise.[19] Not only did she use this idea in her poem to Rochfort, but we also know that in her poem "To Imagination" she used "fancy" and "imagination" interchangeably and that both words were placed in the context of the mind's ability to perceive a truth beyond one's own immediate experience.

Thus, the entire passage above might be read as follows:

> I, Phillis Wheatley, now a Christian slave, was once taken from my native land, Africa, which others besides myself have recognized as a Golden World. Not only did it cause my father much grief but also it has given me an understanding of the word "freedom." Fortunately for me, everything worked out for the best, for now I am a Christian (the "fate" is only "seeming cruel"), but others like myself, the Americans of these colonies, are being threatened by political tyranny.

In this poem, Phillis Wheatley has artfully used the pathos of her own past to persuade Dartmouth to assuage the wrongs done to the Americans by the British. This is neither the poetry of self-expression nor the poetry of cold elegance; rather it is the poetry of argument and rhetorical persuasion. As such, this poem is reminiscent—not in excellence but in intention—of some of the great poems of the Restoration and eighteenth century: John Dryden's "Absalom and Achitophel," and Alexander Pope's "An Essay on Man," and "An Epistle to Dr. Arbuthnot."

"To the University of Cambridge, in New England" also illustrates Phillis Wheatley's ability to manipulate an imagined self for the sake of rhetorical persuasion. This poem is addressed to the students at Harvard who are urged by this young African slave to mend their profligate ways. To underscore her didactic theme, Phillis Wheatley describes the world from which she came:

> 'Twas not long since I left my native shore
> The land of errors, and *Egyptian* gloom:
> Father of mercy, 'twas thy gracious hand
> Brought me in safety from those dark abodes. (5)

This is a different picture of Africa from the one of happy primitives; it is an Africa without Christianity and without civilization. Although this portrait is not flattering to her native land, it is rhetorically useful; it creates an ironic contrast between her lot and that of the Harvard students. The latter are Christians by birth, and because they have the privileges of class, they are offered a knowledge of the highest civilization that human beings have attained. Yet they are abusing this god-given gift, one that has been denied to members of Phillis Wheatley's race. A lowly African must remind them that they too, like all people, may be destroyed by sin:

Ye blooming plants of human race devine
An *Ethiop* tells you 'tis your greatest foe;
Its transient sweetness turns to endless pain,
And in immense perdition sinks the soul. (6)

As an "Ethiop," that is, an African, Phillis Wheatley is exploiting a situation here that is quite familiar to her audience. In this instance, the simple savage *knows* more than the sophisticated Harvard students.

In another well-known poem, "On Being Brought from Africa to America," we see a similar rhetorical strategy. Phillis Wheatley begins by celebrating God's mercy in bringing her from her "Pagan land" to the New World: "Once I redemption neither sought nor knew." Nevertheless, she is aware that some Christians in America "view our sable race with scornful eye." These Americans see the "Negro's" color as "diabolic," and thus Phillis Wheatley reminds them in the last two lines of the poem:

Remember, *Christians, Negroes*, black as *Cain*,
May be refin'd, and join th' angelic train. (7)

As Phillis Wheatley said in one of her letters, God "was no respecter of Persons."[20] Although the Negro appears to be Cain to white Americans,[21] he is not Cain in Christ's eyes. The italicized words not only emphasize the falsehood of the analogy but they also serve as a reminder that all human beings—including whites—need to be "refined" before they "join th' angelic train."

The quiet irony of these last two lines seems to echo Pope's "lo, the poor Indian" passage in "An Essay on Man." In Pope's poem, civilized man thinks himself superior to the simple savage; yet it is the savage's simplicity that serves as a satiric comment upon the actual behavior of those people who call themselves "Christians." For the "poor Indian," heaven is a place where "No fiends torment, no Christians thirst for Gold." By placing her imagined self in ironic juxtaposition to the "Christians" who would view her as "diabolic," Phillis Wheatley is making the same satiric point.

Pope was not the only one to teach her how to use a *persona* to rhetorical advantage. One poem recently discovered in manuscript indicates that Phillis Wheatley was probably aware of John Dryden's poetry. "To Deism" is similar to Dryden's "Religio Laici" in both theme and technique; both authors use the *persona* of the "layperson" to attack the web-spinning sophistry of Deism. In the eighteenth century, Deism was called "natural religion" because it assumed that human reason was sufficient to discover the intricate workings of God's universe. The world, in other words, was like a clock, and one need only understand the mechanism to understand the clockmaker. Thus, Christianity is not mysterious and there is no need for revelation to make God known to humankind.

Phillis Wheatley appears in "To Deism" as an unlettered African who nevertheless knows the fundamental truths of Christianity. Her antagonist, a Deist, is out to disprove the doctrines of revelation and the trinity, and like John Dryden, Phillis Wheatley cannot hide her indignation at such folly:

> Must Ethiopians be imploy'd for you
> [I] greatly rejoice if any good I do
> I ask O unbeliever satan's child
> Has not thy savior been to[o] meek [&] mild. . . .[22]

Phillis Wheatley weighs God's mercy against the Deist's reason and finds the latter light indeed; the Deist rejects the very attribute of God, His infinite mercy, that for his sake he ought to hope exists. For if the Savior had not been "meek [&] mild," He would have already damned the Deist to endless perdition for his impudence. Again like John Dryden, Phillis Wheatley suggests that only the direct, simple truth will cut through the tissue of the complicated reasoning that has so entrapped the Deist.

Phillis Wheatley's mastery of poetic technique, such as her ability to shape a *persona* for rhetorical purposes, shows her to be a more artful poet than we have previously recognized. At times she eloquently wrote in the "sublime" mode which so fascinated her age. As a religious poet, she found the "sublime" a perfect vehicle for expressing transcendent emotions. As an artist, she responded to the secular theories of the "sublime," a kind of poetry which tried to be grandiloquent rather than clear, astonishing in its effects rather than logical. In this verse, whether sacred or profane, Milton and the Old Testament were influences upon her—but so was Alexander Pope.

We are told by Margaretta Odell that Phillis Wheatley specifically admired "Pope's Homer."[23] This fact is significant, for Pope's preface to *The Iliad* and translation of it helped to create the critical opinion in the eighteenth century that Homer was the master of "sublimity."[24] The "sublime" reached the zenith of its popularity around the same time that Phillis Wheatley began writing poetry.[25] In "To Maecenas," Wheatley describes herself as a humble poet who wishes to soar in exalted flight. Homer, she says, is her model, but she laments that she cannot "paint" with his power. Homer makes lightning "blaze across the vaulted skies," and causes the thunder to shake "the heavenly plains," and as she reads his lines: "A deep-felt horror thrills through my veins." She too would fly like both Homer and Virgil but complains:

. . . here I sit, and mourn a grov'ling mind,
That fain would mount, and ride upon the wind. (3)

Not only is there an oblique reference to the Old Testament in the
last line, but she is also remembering two lines from Pope's "An
Essay on Man":

Nor God alone in the still Calm we find;
He mounts the Storm, and *walks upon the wind*.[26]

Phillis Wheatley identifies herself with Pope because as the translator of Homer and as the author of "An Essay on Man," Pope is a poet
who has already excelled in the "sublime" mode; in these two
works, he has, as it were, mounted "the storm" and walked "upon
the wind." To the pious young slave poet, for instance, "An Essay on
Man" would be an example of the highest kind of "sublimity," for
Pope's poems contain passages which grandly describe the vast, mysterious, awe-inspiring universe of God's creation.[27]

The "sublime" takes various forms in Phillis Wheatley's poetry.
One of the instruments enabling one to reach the sublime was "terror." In "Goliath of Gath," she is consciously creating an epic character who terrifies us through our inability to imagine him as finite.
In "On Imagination," she celebrates the imagination's capacity to
seize upon what our senses cannot hold, the vast immensity of the
universe. In "Ode to Neptune" and "To a Lady on Her Remarkable
Preservation in an Hurricane in North Carolina," she is concerned
with the "natural sublime," the fact that some objects in nature
such as storms and hurricanes fill us with terror because of their
uncontrollable power. In "Niobe in Distress for Her Children Slain
by Apollo," Phillis Wheatley is domesticating a mythological figure
by treating Niobe as a distressed mother. Not only is the poet's
portrait contemporary in that Niobe is a favorite figure in the "Age
of Sensibility," but Phillis Wheatley is also illustrating an aesthetic
commonplace of the period: pathos is a branch of the "sublime."

If we examine two of her "sublime" poems, we shall see just how
thoroughly Phillis Wheatley knew the taste of her age. In "Goliath
of Gath," for instance, she illustrates aesthetician Edmund Burke's
famous dictum in *The Sublime and the Beautiful* (1757) that "to
make anything very terrible, obscurity seems in general to be necessary."[28] Burke's point is that if a character is going to affect our
imaginations with ideas of terror and power, the artist must not
draw him or her too precisely. Hence, Phillis Wheatley describes
Goliath as a "monster" stalking "the terror of the field" as he comes
forth to meet the Hebrews. She mentions his "fierce deportment"
and "gigantic frame," but never descends to particulars when she

refers to his physical characteristics. Rather, she obliquely depicts Goliath by focusing upon his armor and weapons:

A brazen helmet on his head was plac'd,
A coat of mail his form terrific grac'd,
The greaves his legs, the targe his shoulders prest:
Dreadful in arms high-tow'ring o'er the rest
A spear he proudly wav'd, whose iron head,
Strange to relate, six hundred shekels weigh'd;
He strode along, and shook the ample field,
While *Phoebus* blaz'd refulgent on his shield:
Through *Jacob's* race a chilling horror ran. . . . (14)

Like Achilles in Book 22 of Homer's *The Iliad* and Sat in Book 1 of Milton's *Paradise Lost*, Goliath is terrifying because our sensory perceptions fail to contain him. If she had not read Edmund Burke, she at least knew about his psychological theory of the "sublime."

Goliath is meant to frighten us (like storms and hurricanes in nature), but the imagination in "To Imagination" is meant to bring us to an emotional state of religious awe. Following poet Mark Akenside's lead ("The Pleasures of the Imagination" [1744]), Phillis Wheatley sees the infinite soul of a human being as a microcosm of God's infinite universe; only the imagination can capture a sense of that infinity:

Imagination! who can sing thy force?
Or who describe the swiftness of thy course?
Soaring through air to find the bright abode,
Th' empyreal palace of the thund'ring God,
We on thy pinions can surpass the wind,
And leave the rolling universe behind:
From star to star the mental optics rove,
Measure the skies, and range the realms above.
There in one view we grasp the mighty whole,
Or with new worlds amaze th' unbounded soul. (30)

The imagination is a kind of mental eyesight ("optics") which allows us to penetrate the finite world and discover, to use Marjorie Nicolson's phrase, "the aesthetics of the infinite."[29] In this context, it is no wonder that Phillis Wheatley referred to Sir Isaac Newton as one of the greatest "bards" of the age, for Newton's theories about the universe expanded God's world at the same time that they explained it.

Although eighteenth-century England saw Phillis Wheatley as a "natural genius," she had larger plans for herself. She aspired to be an artist in the manner of Homer, Milton, and Pope. If we still complain that she failed as a poet because she did not express, with sufficient vehemence, her suffering black self, then we might do well to listen to Ralph Ellison, a contemporary black writer, who has argued against "unrelieved suffering" as the only basis of Afro-American art:

> ... there is also an American Negro tradition which teaches one ... to master and contain pain. It is a tradition which abhors as obscene any trading on one's own anguish for gain and sympathy; which springs not from a desire to deny the harshness of existence but from a will to deal with it as men at their best have always done. It takes fortitude to be a man and no less to be an artist. Perhaps it takes even more if the black man would be an artist.[30]

Phillis Wheatley could be called the founding mother of this tradition which Ellison describes, for the eighteenth century provided her with the tools to transmute her pain into art. She saw herself as a *poeta*, a maker of poems, and not as a suffering black slave who happened to be a poet.

Notes

[1]Gary Nash, *The Urban Crucible: Social Change, Political Consciousness, and the Origins of the American Revolution* (Cambridge, MA: Harvard University Press, 1979), 445.

[2]Phillis Wheatley to John Thornton, 30, Oct. 1774, quoted in James A. Rawley, "The World of Phillis Wheatley," *New England Quarterly* 50 (1977), 666–77; 669.

[3]Quoted in Terence Collins, "Phillis Wheatley: The Dark Side of the Poetry," *Phylon* 36 (1975), 78–88; 78.

[4]In 1966, Julian Mason published a modern critical edition of Phillis Wheatley's poetry, including a biographical sketch and critical introduction. Since then several new letters and poems have been found. Two essays in particular have provided us with biographical information that Mason seemed to have missed: James R. Rawley, "World of Phillis Wheatley," *New England Quarterly*, 50 (1977), 666–77; and William H. Robinson, "Phillis Wheatley in London," *College Language Association Journal*, 21 (1977), 187–201. Rawley's article also includes a list of recent discoveries in the Phillis Wheatley canon, and *PMLA* bibliographies from 1970 to the present show that our interest in her has not diminished. Specific references to Phillis Wheatley's poetry are to Mason's edition, *The Poems of Phillis Wheatley* (Chapel Hill: North Carolina Press, 1966), and will appear in the text.

[5]Thomas Wooldridge to the Earl of Dartmouth, 24, Nov. 1772, quoted in Rawley, "World of Phillis Wheatley, p. 670.

[6]Rawley's "World of Phillis Wheatley," describes these connections.

[7]We know that Phillis Wheatley first tried to get her book published in Boston in 1772. See Muktar Ali Isani, "The First Proposed Edition of *Poems on Various Subjects* and the Phillis Wheatley Canon," *American Literature*, 49 (1977), p. 98. The project mysteriously failed. An American edition of her poems was not published until 1789, five years after her death (Rawley, p. 677).

[8]Phillis Wheatley to John Thornton, 29, Mar. 1774, quoted in Rawley, "World of Phillis Wheatley," p. 673.

[9]Rawley, "World of Phillis Wheatley," p. 674.

[10]30, Oct. 1774, in Rawley "World of Phillis Wheatley," p. 674.

[11]Saunders Redding, "Phillis Wheatley," *Notable American Women, 1607–1950*, 3 vols. (Cambridge, MA: Belknap Press, 1971), 3: 573–74; 574.

[12]See Jefferson Carter, "The Unlettered Muse: The Uneducated Poets and the Concept of Natural Genius in Eighteenth-Century England" (Diss. University of Arizona 1972), pp. 6, 7. Although Carter does not discuss Phillis Wheatley, I am using his ideas when describing the eighteenth century's interest in "natural genius" and the "unlettered" poets.

[13]Scott Elledge, *Eighteenth-Century Critical Essays* (Ithaca: Cornell University Press, 1961), I, 27–29.

[14]Carter, "Unlettered Muse" p. 103.

[15]Ibid., pp. 69–238.

[16]According to Susanna Wheatley, when Phillis Wheatley's poems were first read to the Countess of Huntingdon, the latter would interrupt by saying, "Is not this, or that very fine? Do read another." See Kenneth Silverman, "Four New Letters by Phillis Wheatley," *Early American Literature*, 8 (1973–74), p. 269.

[17]As quoted in Robinson's "Phillis Wheatley in London," p. 97.

[18]*Memoir and Poems of Phillis Wheatley, A Native African and A Slave* (1838; facs. rpt. Miami: Mnemosyne, 1969), pp. 18, 20. The *Memoir* was published anonymously in 1834.

[19]See Wylie Sypher, *Guinea's Captive Kings: British Anti-Slavery Literature of the XVIIIth Century* (1942; rpt. New York: Farrar, Straus, 1969), pp. 103–55. Sypher notes that the African as "Noble Savage" had strong roots in eighteenth-century English culture; whereas Winthrop Jordan points out that this tradition fell on barren soil in America, *White over Black: American Attitudes toward the Negro, 1550–1812* (1968; rpt. Baltimore: Penguin, 1969), p. 27.

[20]See Silverman, "Four New Letters," p. 265. Also, see Acts 10:34.

[21]That the Negro's black skin is the mark worn by Cain seems to be a predominantly American idea. See Jordan, *White over Black*, pp. 42, 416.

[22]Phil Lapsansky, "Deism: An Unpublished Poem by Phillis Wheatley," *New England Quarterly*, 50 (1977), 519. Lapsansky does not mention the rather obvious connection to Dryden's poem.

[23]*Memoir*, p. 20.

[24]See Pope's "Preface to the Translation of *The Iliad*" and his "Postscript to the Translation of *The Odyssey*" in *Eighteenth-Century Critical Essays*, I, 257–78, 291–300. Pope especially emphasized the "sublimity" and daring "invention" of *The Iliad*.

[25]Samuel H. Monk, *The Sublime: A Study of Critical Theories in Eighteenth-Century England* (1935; rpt. Ann Arbor: University of Michigan Press, 1960), pp. 101–33.

[26]"An Essay on Man," II, 11. 109–10. Also, see Psalms 104:3.

[27]For example, "An Essay on Man," I, 11. 22–32; I, 11. 247–58.

[28]Edmund Burke, *A Philosophical Inquiry into . . . the Sublime and Beautiful*, in *Eighteenth-Century Poetry and Prose* (1939; rpt. New York: Ronald Press, 1956), p. 1166.

[29]Marjorie Nicolson, *Mountain Gloom and Mountain Glory: The Development of the Aesthetics of the Infinite* (Ithaca: Cornell University Press, 1959). In *Newton Demands the Muse: Newton's "Optics" and the Eighteenth-Century Poets* (Princeton: Princeton University Press, 1946), Nicolson makes a connection between Newton's *Optics* and the poetry of the imagination which became popular in the 1740s. Phillis Wheatley's reference to "mental optics" may be another illustration of the impact of Newton's treatise on the poetry of the eighteenth century.

[30]Ralph Ellison, *Shadow and Act* (1953; rpt. New York, Random House, 1966), p. 119. Also, see Henry-Louis Gates, "Dis and Dat: Dialect and the Descent," in *Afro-American Literature: The Reconstruction of Instruction* (New York: MLA, 1979), pp. 88–119. Gates's fascinating essay focuses upon the relationship of the African "mask" to Afro-American poetry. He does not discuss Phillis Wheatley's poetry, but some of the implications of his essay have relevance to her art. Perhaps Phillis Wheatley's poetical *persona* has its roots in African culture as well as in the artistic practices of eighteenth-century England.

Mercy Otis Warren
(1728–1814)

Marianne B. Geiger

Born in Barnstable, Massachusetts, on September 14, 1728, Mercy Otis Warren was not formally schooled, despite the middle-class trappings of her family. She learned from her brother James's tutors and was relatively well educated by the time of her marriage in November 1754 to James Warren, who became a leader within Massachusetts Revolutionary circles. The couple had five sons.

Warren's roles as wife and mother did not satisfy her during an age of explosive ideas and radical transformations, and she became one of a generation of prolific American political writers, publishing three satiric plays, although like many of her male contemporaries she published under a pen name. Despite their pseudonymous publication, her works became known as a product of her prolific wit. Warren also, at age seventy-six, distinguished herself as a historian when she published, under her own name, a three-volume history of the American Revolution. Her history was one of the first accounts written by an American, and is widely recognized as a classic eighteenth-century interpretation of the era. Warren died in Plymouth in 1814.

Mercy Otis Warren was born into a politically active family, married into a politically active family, and raised sons who in their maturity held appointive federal office. Although she was interested in politics all her life, her participation in politics was circumscribed, for women in the eighteenth century were not permitted to participate directly in public life. Nevertheless, Warren made her voice heard in public political discourse, decade after decade, through her writing, by her cultivation of a "salon," and through an extensive correspondence with men active in political life. Warren also cultivated a wide circle of female correspondents, including women like herself with close ties to political leaders. Through their correspondence, these women shared and shaped each others' political understanding and implicitly that of their husbands and sons, and perhaps even their daughters.

As Linda Kerber has observed, "the newly created republic made little room for [women] as political beings." Republicanism, in the Anglo-American meaning of the word, was the advocacy of representative self-government by a "people," which meant in effect, men. Men who qualified for participation in such government possessed land or held it in nondependent tenure, which also entitled them to bear arms. Republican government was intended to allow the expression of personal virtue through "civic" and public participation. Republican men excluded women from political rights and required them to be "submissive to men . . . as loving wives, prudent mothers, and mistress of families, faithful friends and good Christians."[1]

Mercy Otis Warren departed from this limited definition by becoming a woman who was clearly and publicly a political being. However, she also served as an exemplar for the ideal of the "republican mother," a woman who served her country politically by educating her sons to lead lives of lofty republican virtue, putting the good of the state ahead of their own personal good.

Warren's life followed conventional lines, as she played the roles of daughter, wife, and mother, until she was in her mid-forties. Her brother, James Otis, had led the resistance to the British Parliament's new program for dealing with the colonies, thundering, "Taxation without representation is tyranny." Mercy Otis Warren had shared all his early education as a child, and ardently shared his political views as an adult. Her letters reveal a literary talent comparable to his, and when James Otis fell ill, a victim of a disease akin to manic depression, Mercy Otis Warren, encouraged by her husband James Warren and his friends, particularly John Adams, used her talents to promote the patriotic cause in his place. Her views were well regarded because she clearly articulated a political philosophy that her friends, men on the brink of revolution, believed in. In addition, her flair for vivid expression compelled assent and, at times, delight.

Warren could not act in the political realm for herself, but she could, and did, speak both for herself, for her family, and for the thousands who shared their political convictions. Warren's political credo, exemplified by her brother James Otis's opposition to British authority in the 1760s, was labeled the "Real Whig," or "Country," ideology. It held that republicanism was the best form of government, that those who were ruled must participate in the choice of those who were to rule. Rulers must frequently rotate out of their offices in order to participate anew in the life of ordinary people. The tendency to undue ambition and avarice in officials must be controlled through the practice of civic virtue, the placing of the good of the whole people before one's individual good. These Real Whigs, or republicans, were characteristically suspicious of the motives of those in power and always concerned about the independence both of electors and of members of representative assemblies.[2]

Mercy Otis was born in Barnstable in Cape Cod, Massachusetts, in 1728, the first daughter and third child of thirteen. The Otises were descendants of farmers from Glastonbury, England, who had come to New England in the 1630s. Mercy's father, James Otis, Sr., was a third son and sixth child of a branch of the family that had settled on the Great Salt Marshes at Barnstable. Fiercely ambitious, but without the Harvard education given his two elder brothers, James Otis, Sr., combined farming, storekeeping, merchant-trading, and the practice of provincial law to make himelf a leading citizen of Massachusetts. He was always known as "Colonel Otis" because of his office in the Barnstable County militia.

The Otis children received their early education from their uncle Jonathan Russell, minister of the Barnstable church, who enjoyed young James and Mercy's quick intelligence, and fostered in them his love for the works of William Shakespeare and Alexander Pope. The cadences of Pope and of Shakespeare reverberate in all the published work of both James and Mercy.

After graduation from Harvard in 1743, James did postgraduate work in literature for two years, spending a great deal of time at home in Barnstable while writing a manual of Latin prosody. His sister Mercy's obvious skill in using formal techniques of versification and classical drama reflect familiarity with the works her brother James was studying at this time.

James Otis was one of the few revolutionaries to express dissatisfaction with the political status of women in his time. In his 1764 pamphlet, *The Rights of the British Colonies Asserted and Proved*, speculating on the origins of government, James Otis said, "May there not be as many original compacts as there are men and women born or to be born? Are not women born as free as men? Would it not be infamous to assert the ladies are all slaves by nature?"[3] The man whose education had begun at the side of Mercy Otis Warren could never acquiesce to his age's denigration of women's intellectual capacities. His sister was to justify his faith in women's abilities when she carried on his political work after he no longer could.

James Otis studied for the Massachusetts Bar under one of its leading members, Jeremiah Gridley. Once admitted, James became his father's envoy in seeking colony-wide office. The elder Otis hoped to be named to the next vacant seat on the Superior Court. But when there was a vacancy, a new royal governor, Francis Bernard, gave the Court's chief justiceship to Thomas Hutchinson (a descendant of Anne Hutchinson), a man who already had more than his share of colonial offices. The elder Otis's bitterness grew, flowering into a great resentment of Hutchinson and of all his extensive family. The Colonel imbued his children with his resentment: James's most vivid speeches and Mercy's most vivid writings referred to the Hutchinsons, always in searing negatives.[4]

Mercy Otis married James Warren of Plymouth, a gentleman farmer and merchant, in November 1754. In the impressive Warren house at North and Main Streets in Plymouth, Mercy gave birth to five sons between 1757 and 1766. James Warren succeeded his father as sheriff of Plymouth County and, in 1766, was elected to the General Court, serving often as Speaker.

John Adams, a longtime admirer of James Otis's political oratory, became a close friend and political ally of James Warren; he and his wife Abigail also developed strong bonds with Mercy Otis Warren. The families exchanged visits, and many letters. Abigail and Mercy in their letters mixed politics, literature, and musings about the dilemmas of bringing up children in the comfortable manner of people whose minds are in deep sympathy. The Adamses encouraged Warren's literary and political interests. Abigail Adams warmly admired the literary gifts of the woman fifteen years her senior, assuring her, "I love characters drawn by your pen."[5]

Abigail Adams thought Warren had a particular wisdom in divining political motivations, praising her as one "who have so thoroughly looked thro the Deeds of Men, and Develloped the Dark designs of a Rapatio [Thomas Hutchinson] soul."[6]

In the early 1770s, encouraged by both John and Abigail Adams and, as time went on, by popular approval, Warren anonymously published a series of three satirical plays in pamphlet form, denouncing a thinly disguised Thomas Hutchinson. Since anonymous satirical publications were a common vehicle for eighteenth-century political expression, Warren could manuever within customary boundaries to gain a political voice without revealing her identity as a woman.

The first of Warren's plays, *The Adulateur*, was published in the *Boston Gazette* in the spring of 1773. It centers around the villain Rapatio, obviously Thomas Hutchinson, planning revenge for the wreck of his house during the 1765 Stamp Act riots. *The Defeat*, which appeared a few months later, satirizes Hutchinson's perceived sacrifice of virtue for political advancement.[7] The third play, *The Group*, mocks the men who accepted places on the new, gubernatorially appointed, council established by the hated 1774 Massachusetts Government Act.

The plays make no attempt at plot or character development. Warren's villains are consciously evil. They proudly face the audience and recite their ignoble motives, the acquisition of power and money. The good men are virtuous beyond compare; the people's good is their only motive. There are no women in the trilogy: these plays deal with the public arena, from which women were excluded.

It is touching to see how Warren continually has James Otis, usually called "Brutus" and described as "The First Patriot," act in the plays the noble part he was unable to take in real life because of his increasing mental deterioration. His speeches in the play resound with the most high-flown patriotic rhetoric:

> I spring from men, who fought, who bled
>   for freedom:
> From men, who in the conflict laugh'd at danger:
> Struggl'd like patriots, and through seas of
>   blood,
> Waded to conquests.—I'll not disgrace them.[8]

Mercy Otis Warren was not alone as a woman interested in writing as a political person. Her brother James, and other American patriots, had during the late 1760s and early 1770s corresponded with Catharine Macaulay, a British historian whose work, critical of the seventeenth-century Stuart monarchy, was more widely popular in America than in Britain. Macaulay also wrote political pamphlets deploring the actions of the current British government and expressing sympathy for the American cause. At the suggestion of John Adams, Mercy Otis Warren began to correspond with Macaulay. Warren and Macaulay exchanged letters on political topics for the next two decades, until Macaulay's death in 1791.[9]

During the 1770s, James Warren became ever more active in the revolutionary cause. His service gave Warren access to the information she was to use in the great work of her life, the *History of the Rise, Progress, and Termination of the American Revolution*. A leader in the Massachusetts General Court since 1766, James Warren served as president of the Massachusetts Provincial Congress in 1775. After George Washington was appointed commander in chief of the Continental army, Warren assumed the post of paymaster.

Mercy Warren frequently visited her husband at army headquarters at Watertown, and there she began to write what she thought of as her "Memoir," a description of the exciting revolutionary activity that swirled around her. She sent personality descriptions, which she called "characters," to John Adams in Philadelphia. Warren was later to use these for some of the most appreciated pages of her *History* of the American Revolution.

James Warren continued to serve as John Adam's eyes and ears in Massachusetts while Adams spent years in Philadelphia at the Continental Congress. Through their extensive correspondence with Adams, the Warrens became familiar with all the ramifications of political and military developments in the rest of the states. The correspondence continued during the years Adams served in diplomatic posts in Europe.

The years after the American victory at Yorktown were difficult for Mercy and James Warren. Despite his consistent preference for asserting himself in state rather than national politics, James Warren was not politically successful in Massachusetts during these years. Elections were most often won by John Hancock and men allied with him. The Warrens and the Adamses regarded Hancock as an intellectual lightweight and a political opportunist who lacked the stern virtues proper to one who aspired to govern in a republican state. They thought he flattered people too much and spent too much of his own fortune on lavish entertainments designed to build political support, behavior anathema to committed republicans.

James Warren recognized that Plymouth was too isolated a location on which to build a firm political base, and decided to become more a part of the ongoing political life of the state by moving closer to Boston. In an exquisite irony, in 1780 the Warrens purchased Milton Hill, the former home of their archenemy, the now deceased Thomas Hutchinson. Ten miles south of Boston, the beautiful estate was meant to be the headquarters for the Warrens and their political dynasty.

Catharine Macaulay came to the United States in 1784, staying in the Boston vicinity for the winter. She spent several days with the Warrens at Milton Hill, and Mercy Warren wrote a series of letters to introduce Macaulay to political leaders in New York and Philadelphia, as Macaulay and her young second husband William Graham undertook a tour of the new United States. After Macaulay spent ten days with George and Martha Washington at Mount Vernon, she decided that she would not, after all, write a history of the American Revolution. On the eve of embarking for Europe in 1785, she wrote to Warren to tell her so, leaving the field clear for her American friend.

None of the five Warren sons showed the flair for politics their Otis forebears had demonstrated. The eldest, James Warren, Jr., who had lost a leg as a result of service on the *Alliance* during a revolutionary war naval battle, spent most of the decade following the war coming to terms with his disability. He revealed a tendency to melancholy similar to that of his uncle James Otis. James Otis himself died in 1783, dramatically, when struck by a bolt of lightning. The Warrens' second son, Charles, stricken with that scourge of the age, tuberculosis, spent part of the decade searching for health, dying in Lisbon in 1785. Their third son, the mercurial Winslow, hoped to become a successful merchant, but succeeded only in amassing large debts both in the United States and Europe. After being imprisoned for debt, he joined the army, only to be killed in an Indian attack in the Ohio country in 1791, while serving under the ever-luckless General Arthur St. Clair. The fifth son, George, became a landowner and merchant in the Maine region; he died in 1801, at age thirty-five. Henry, the fourth son, settled on the Plymouth farm, the one son to marry and have children.

Finding neither the political nor economic rewards they had anticipated, deeply saddened by their sons' lack of worldly success, the Warrens put Milton Hill up for sale and returned to their Plymouth house in 1786. Mercy Warren's brothers Joseph and Samuel Alleyne Otis underwent bankruptcy in this decade, because of their misreading of the turbulent trade patterns that followed resumption of trade with Great Britain after the Treaty of Paris in 1783. Regretting the Otis and Warren misfortunes, John Adams declared, "I dont believe there is one Family upon Earth to which the United States are so indebted for their Preservation from Thraldom," adding, "There was scarcely any family in New England had such Prospects of Opulence and Power . . . they have sacrificed them all."[10]

The economic hardships endured by the Otis brothers reflected patterns throughout Massachusetts. A group of people led by Daniel Shays attempted to force the courts in the western part of the state to remain closed, so that no more bankruptcies could be declared. This lawlessness lent urgency to the interstate meeting called for Philadelphia in 1787 to consider ways to strengthen the Articles of Confederation that bound the states together. Although young Henry Warren was among those who marched to suppress the Shaysites, James and Mercy Warren were not convinced that a new instrument of central government was needed. Because of this

Antifederalist opposition to the resulting Constitution that created a stronger central government, James Warren was not elected to represent Plymouth at the state ratifying convention. However, Mercy Otis Warren wrote antiratification speeches for some who were elected, making her words heard even though her husband's voice was silenced.

When the Constitution was narrowly approved in Massachusetts, Warren wrote a nineteen-page pamphlet, again anonymously, to dissuade New York delegates from approving the Constitution in their convention. She began by imagining the "slavery" that would occur under the Constitution, "when the inhabitants of the Eastern States are dragging out a miserable existence, *only* on the gleanings of their fields; . . . languishing in hopeless poverty" because they had had to send "the flower of their crop, and the rich produce of their farms" to "the *Federal City.*"[11]

Warren pointed out that there was no provision for freedom of conscience or of the press; there were "no well defined limits of the Judiciary Powers, they seem to be left as a boundless ocean."[12] She objected to the lack of provision for rotation in office, saying, "By this neglect we lose the advantage of that check to the overbearing insolence of office, which . . . keeps the mind of man in equilibrio, and teaches him the feelings of the governed."[13] Warren knew that after approval by Massachusetts, ratification by the required nine states was likely. "But if after all," she concludes, "on a dispassionate and fair discussion, the people generally give their voice for a voluntary dereliction of their privileges, let every individual who chooses the active scenes of life, strive to support the peace and unanimity of his country."[14]

In 1790, Mercy Warren for the first time published under her own name, dedicating her volume, *Poems, Dramatic and Miscellaneous,* to President George Washington. Warren, who had suffered the deaths of three of the sons for whom she had hoped so much, did not publish anything else for the next fifteen years. She did, however, work on her "Memoir" about the Revolution, writing to Washington, General Benjamin Lincoln, the commander of the revolutionary forces in the South, and John Adams to gather documents.

However, James and Mercy Warren felt themselves increasingly separate from political developments in the nation's capital. They saw in Alexander Hamilton's financial program the beginnings of the victory of the money power and the fostering of political and financial corruption that had triumphed in 1760s Britain, forcing the American Revolution. Further, the Warrens disapproved of Jay's Treaty with Great Britain, which was designed to resolve commerce and navigation issues as well as violations of the Treaty of Paris. They viewed it as an unseemly capitulation of the new United States to its former enemy. The Warrens considered themselves the true republicans, and dismissed their Federalist opponents as "monarchists."

Ardent Republicans, believers in the Democratic-Republican principles of Thomas Jefferson and James Madison, the Warrens in the 1790s found themselves increasingly out of sympathy with the man in the presidency, first with George Washington and then with their old friend John Adams.

But after an easy victory at the polls (sometimes referred to as the "Revolution of 1800") placed Thomas Jefferson in office, Mercy Otis Warren thought the country was ready at last to read a truthful, unbiased republican account of the American Revolution. She worked feverishly, with her son James serving as her scribe, compiling, arranging, and rewriting the materials gathered over three decades. Late in 1805, she published a three-volume account of the *History of the Rise, Progress, and Termination of the American Revolution. Interspersed with Biographical, Political and Moral Observations.* Mercy Warren was seventy-six years old; this book was the first overtly political publication she had ever signed with her own name.

Warren admitted in the introduction that "There are certain appropriate duties assigned to each sex."[15] Men not only fight the battles, they also write the battle accounts, attempting "in the nervous style of manly eloquence, to describe the blood-stained field, and relate the story of slaughtered armies." Yet she defended her historical work by pointing out that everyone feels "a concern for the welfare of society." Women, the hearthkeepers, suffer if deprived of liberty, since "every domestic enjoyment depends on the unimpaired possession of civil and religious liberty."[16]

Warren outlined her qualifications for writing: a brother and a husband deeply involved in the early days of the conflict, continuing relationships with such political leaders as John Adams and such military leaders as General Benjamin Lincoln. She maintained, "Connected by nature, friendship, and every social tie, with many of the first patriots and most influential characters on the continent . . . I had the best information."[17]

Warren made clear at the outset that she would carefully present the character of the people responsible for events, since the writer and the reader of history must have "a just knowledge of character, to investigate the sources of action."[18] Warren here expressed her strong belief, typical of the majority of eighteenth-century historians, that people make history, that what happens in the world happens because people plan, even plot, for it to happen. By the time Warren published, sophisticated historical explanation had abandoned this interpretive stance, taking greater account of the role of the contingent in human affairs. But at the time Warren wrote, this more skeptical viewpoint was not yet influential in America.

People are the key to events, Warren said, and ambition is the key to an understanding of people's character. Ambition, "the love of distinction," is "a noble principle," she maintained, "when kept under the control of reason."[19]

Warren paired ambition with avarice, saying that these are the "primary sources of corruption" from which "have arisen all the rapine and confusion, the depredation and ruin, that have spread distress over the face of the earth from the days of Nimrod to Cesar [*sic*] and from Cesar to an arbitrary prince of the house of Brunswick."[20]

Thinking morally, wanting to bring her readers to a sense of possible doom if the ideals of the Revolution were compromised, Warren used the language of the New England jeremiad, language that had reverberated in her ears and in her heart from earliest memory. She rejected the notion of inevitable progress. It would be all too easy for the fragile new republic to slip under the yoke of some foreign power, to decline into slavery. Warren sought, through the *History*, to avert this by presenting a stirring and truthful story of the sufferings that had brought Americans to their present happy republic.

Considering her own family's political eclipse, Warren observed that "virtue and talents do not always hold their rank in the public esteem. Malice, intrigue, envy . . . frequently cast a shade over the most meritorious characters." She was convinced that "Fortune [good luck] . . . established the reputation of her favorites," leaving posterity to regard them with an admiration "which perhaps they never earned."[21]

Calling her brother James "the celebrated Mr. Otis," and "the first martyr to American freedom," she said "truth will enrol his name among the distinguished who have expired on the 'blood-stained theatre of human action.' " Warren described her brother as almost an angel of light, possessed of "independent principles, comprehensive genius, strong mind, retentive memory and great penetration" with "extensive professional knowledge."[22]

In the first, most vivid volume of the *History*, James Otis is the hero, Thomas Hutchinson the villain. Warren had first treated this conflict in her 1770s satires: the dramatic struggle between the forces of light (the Otises and their allies) and of darkness (Hutchinson and his clan) shaped her presentation in the *History*. The malevolent, almost satanic figure of Thomas Hutchinson stalks through all Warren's political work, both the pamphlet-plays and the *History*. Accusingly, she said: "Few ages have produced a more fit instrument for the purposes of a corrupt court. He was dark, intriguing, insinuating, haughty and ambitious, while the extreme of avarice marked each feature of his character."[23]

Warren set up a tension between Hutchinson and James Otis, one the personification of evil, the other the impassioned advocate of the right and the true. She blamed Hutchinson for "instigating . . . the innovating spirit of the British ministry." This "prostituter of power, nurtured in the lap of America, and bound by every tie of honor and gratitude," had "for some time" encouraged the British minister to "interrupt. . . the tranquility of the province."[24]

Warren's second and third volumes are a more conventional chronological narrative account of the course of the Revolution and its aftermath. Because of her and her husband's extensive correspondence with John Adams, her accounts of revolutionary diplomacy are particularly detailed and authoritative. Warren's descriptions of battles are well organized and dramatic; the playwright's flair for scene-setting and for choosing the right incident are abundantly in evidence.

Reading Warren's account of the Constitutional Convention, one would never know how vehement had been her objections to its work. True to her stated purpose, Warren in the *History* did all she could to foster loyalty and love for the new American republic for which she and her family had longed. Mercy Otis Warren wanted to teach the new country's citizens how to live as the kind of free people her brother James Otis had idealized; criticisms of the instrument of government could have no place in her lesson.

Warren had praise in her history for everyone except Thomas Hutchinson. Even her old enemy John Hancock was let off lightly. She deleted a reference to him under her old nickname for him of "the state baby" (so called because his gout necessitated assistance in walking) and buried her unflattering assessment of his capacities and actions in an endnote.[25]

It was then with some shock that Warren in the summer of 1807 received a letter from a furious John Adams protesting her treatment of his career. About Adams's presidency, Warren had merely said she would treat "summarily" the administration of George Washington's "immediate successor." She did point out that "the heart of the annalist may sometimes be hurt by political deviations which the pen of the historian is obliged to record."[26] She conceded that "Mr. Adams was undoubtedly a statesman of penetration and ability; but his prejudices and his passions were sometimes too strong for his sagacity and judgment."[27]

Enraged and deeply hurt, Adams in a series of fourteen tempestuous letters proceeded to demonstrate the truth of Warren's judgment. He accused her of writing to the taste of the nineteenth century, meaning to the taste of Jeffersonian Republicans. Not intimidated by the eminence her old friend had achieved, Warren replied with asperity, reminding him that her work had been mainly written before he had become president. Further, she taunted him that he himself had often urged her to write the history of the Revolution. In exasperation, Warren criticized Adams for "feelings so deficient in the benign and heavenly spirit of friendship," saying his concluding lines "cap the climax of rancor, indecency, and vulgarism."[28] No answer came from Adams.

Mercy Otis Warren retired from the political lists at age seventy-eight. Her eyesight had long been failing; with the death of James Warren in 1808 much of the zest for partisan battle left her. With her pen she had fought for the principles her brother James trumpeted to the world. She had lived to see those principles triumph. There seemed no battle that needed to be, or could be, fought by a woman of her age, in isolated Plymouth.

In 1812, after a five-year estrangement because of their differences over the *History*, Warren was reconciled with John and Abigail Adams, through the good offices of Elbridge Gerry, a prominent figure throughout the Revolution, and at this time governor of Massachusetts. The old revolutionaries exchanged visits, choosing to remember what united rather than what had divided them. It is not recorded, but surely present at the Adamses' visit to Plymouth was young Marcia Warren, Mercy's eldest granddaughter, named in honor of the "republican" pseudonym her grandmother had used in writing to the Adamses when they and the Warrens and the American Revolution were young.[29]

Mercy Warren lived on into the second administration of James Madison, enduring another war with Great Britain, the War of 1812. Her son Henry was deeply embroiled in conflicts with the Plymouth townspeople during the war, since, as Collector of the Port of Plymouth he was a Madison appointee, and "Mr. Madison's War" was ruining the town's commerce. However, it does not appear Mercy Warren kept any papers to help write a history of that war.

Warren died on October 19, 1814, a month after her eighty-sixth birthday, in the Plymouth house at the corner of North and Main Streets. As an articulate, impassioned member of a political family, she had had her say on wars, revolutions, and republics long before, and what she said had made a difference. Through her pen, Warren achieved something unique: her political satires of the 1770s, her extensive correspondence with American and British political figures, her publishing a *History* written from the unique point of view of a woman and a Jeffersonian Republican were the means Mercy Otis Warren used to move the politics of her time and place.

Notes

[1]Linda Kerber, *Women of the Republic: Intellect and Ideology in Revolutionary America* (Chapel Hill: University of North Carolina Press for the Institute of Early American History and Culture at Williamsburg, 1980), 11, 27–32.

Some of Warren's letters are transcribed in the manuscript Mercy Warren Letter Book held at the Massachusetts Historical Society. But since these transcriptions were done in the nineteenth century, in various hands, none of which is Warren's, they must be used cautiously when drawing conclusions about Warren's intellectual development. The original letter-copies used to make the transcriptions appear to have been lost.

[2]For an examination of the context and significance of these ideas in the period of the American Revolution, see Bernard Bailyn, *The Ideological Origins of the American Revolution* (Cambridge, MA: Belknap Press of Harvard University Press, 1967), and Gordon Wood, *The Creation of the American Republic* (New York: W. W. Norton, 1972). The content of the ideas is provocatively examined in Edmund S. Morgan, *Inventing the People: The Rise of Popular Sovereignty in England and America* (New York: W. W. Norton, 1988).

[3]James Otis, *The Rights of the British Colonies Asserted and Proved*, Boston, 1764. Reprinted in Bernard Bailyn, ed., *Pamphlets of the American Revolution, 1750–1776* (Cambridge, MA: Belknap Press of Harvard University Press, 1965), 1: 420.

[4]Thomas Hutchinson to Israel Williams, 21 Jan. 1761, Mass. His. Soc., Williams MSS, II, 155. Cited in Douglass Adair and John A. Schutz, eds., *Peter Oliver's Origin and Progress of the American Rebellion* (Stanford, CA: Stanford University Press, 1967), p. 28, n. 3.

[5]Abigail Adams to Mercy Warren, 13 Apr. 1776, in Lyman Butterfield, ed., *Adams Family Correspondence* (Cambridge, MA: Belknap Press of Harvard University Press, 1963), 1: 378.

[6]Abigail Adams to Mercy Otis Warren, 5 Dec. 1773, in *Warren-Adams Letters: Being Chiefly a Correspondence among John Adams, Samuel Adams, and James Warren*. Massachusetts Historical Society *Collections*, 72 (1917). Reprint ed. New York: AMS Press, 1972, vol. 1: 18–19.

[7]An identification key to the characters is in a fragment of *The Defeat* in the Mercy Warren Papers at the Massachusetts Historical Society. Rapatio is Thomas Hutchinson; Limpet is Andrew Oliver; Rusticus is James Warren; Hortensius is John Adams; Brutus is James Otis.

[8][Mercy Otis Warren], *The Adulateur*, act I, sc. i. Benjamin Franklin V, ed., *The Plays and Poems of Mercy Otis Warren: Facsimile Reproductions*. (Delmar, NY: Scholars' Facsimiles & Reprints, 1980), p. 6.

[9]This series of letters is placed first in the compilation known as the Mercy Warren Letter Book, suggesting that Warren, or whoever compiled it, considered this correspondence the most important of Warren's life.

Warren wrote an introduction for the 1791 American edition of Macaulay's pamphlet attacking Edmund Burke's *Reflections on the Revolution in France.*

[10]John Adams to Thomas Jefferson, 13 Dec. 1785, in Lester J. Cappon, ed., *The Adams-Jefferson Letters* (Chapel Hill: University of North Carolina Press for the Institute of Early American History and Culture at Williamsburg, 1959), p. 107.

[11][Mercy Otis Warren] *Observations on the New Constitution, and on the Federal and State Conventions, By a Columbian Patriot.* (Chicago: Quadrangle Books, 1962. Reprint of New York 1788 ed. Bound with [Richard Henry Lee?] *An Additional Number of Letters From the Federal Farmer to the Republican . . .*), 1.

[12][Warren], *Observations*, p. 7.

[13][Warren], *Observations*, p. 9.

[14][Warren], *Observations*, p. 19.

[15]Mercy Otis Warren, *History of the Rise, Progress, and Termination of the American Revolution. Interspersed with Biographical, Political and Moral Observations.* 3 vols. (Boston, 1805. Reprint: New York: AMS, 1970) 1: iv. Hereafter, MOW *History.*

[16]MOW *History* 1: iii.

[17]MOW *History* 1: i.

[18]MOW *History* 1: 1.

[19]MOW *History* 1: 1.

[20]MOW *History* 1: 2.

[21]MOW *History* 2: 247.

[22]MOW *History* 1: 85.

[23]MOW *History* 1: 79.

[24]MOW *History* 2: 37.

[25]See MOW *History* 1: 430, note 13.

[26]MOW *History* 3: 391.

[27]MOW *History* 3: 393.

[28]Mercy Otis Warren to John Adams, 27 Aug. 1807, in Charles F. Adams, ed., *Correspondence between John Adams and Mercy Warren, Collections of the Massachusetts Historical Society,* Vol. 4, 5th series, Boston, 1878. [Reprint ed.: New York: Arno Pres, 1972], p. 490.

[29]Warren left her copy of Catharine Macaulay's *Letters on Education* to this granddaughter, whom she hoped would see in her lifetime the implementation of the new kind of women's education Macaulay advocated.

PART III

The Flowering of Antebellum Culture

The year 1800 marked not only the opening of a new century but also the beginning of major transformations in women's lives. In the wake of the American Revolution, political leaders celebrated the crucial role mothers might play in the growth of the new nation. The importance of women's roles in the new nation was stressed by statesmen who wanted the "production of children" recognized as vital to national prosperity. Within the new regime, "republican mothers" were encouraged to rear "liberty-loving sons."

As a result, the initial impetus for the reform and improvement of women's education stemmed directly from women's roles as educators of their own children. Colonial parents welcomed the replacement of dame schools, which taught ornamental arts such as dancing and embroidery, with more rigorous academies to provide young women with "classic English educations." These new curriculums included geography, history, and other more intellectually demanding subjects. Though these changes were not intended specifically to enhance the opportunities available for women to improve their status, they did enrich the intellectual climate for daughters of the upper and middle classes. Many young women, afforded improved training, became educators themselves; they founded and taught in academies up and down the eastern seaboard.

A transition during this era that had an even more widespread and immediate effect upon women was the development of centralized manufacturing or the "Waltham system." This shift in the production of an enormous range of goods from the individual household to the factory dramatically sharpened the division of women's and men's spheres. Women were now identified more exclusively with the home or private domain, where their duties included maintenance of family stability, protection of traditional values, and advancement of children's welfare. The public or male sphere included all other realms outside the household, including politics, law and business. Within this new framework of separate spheres, "work" was assigned a new meaning. With the expansion of manufacturing outside the home, household production, the core of the agrarian colonial economy, declined in economic influence. As domestic labor in the household became "women's work," its status declined relative to wage-paying work in the public realm. Thus while in early nineteenth-century America, society accorded women an enhanced social status as the moral leaders and protectors of their families, their economic roles were accorded less value. This exchange was not satisfying to those women unfulfilled by their images as republican mothers. In the ferment of reform during the 1830s, '40s and '50s, many women forged new movements to reshape their image as moral leaders to their own advantage.

Though the factory system made firmer the ideology of republican motherhood and the division of men and women into separate spheres, economic necessity did draw a small but significant number of women out of the private domain and into the public world. As the West attracted legions of men, many of the young women left behind flocked to factories to supply the workforce for the textile industry. Yankee fathers welcomed their daughters' opportunities to earn wages, as most sent a portion of their income back to their families. Thousands of young women in New England and the middle-Atlantic states abandoned family farms and became "mill girls."

Women's lives in these factory towns were still governed by extreme paternalism. Factory owners required that women live in company-sponsored boarding houses, attend church regularly, and maintain a curfew. Moreover, both their fathers and their bosses expected that women would be wage earners for only a short time, until they married. This was the pattern during the first part of the century; however, by the 1830s, many women who saw their work in the factory as more than temporary began to organize to protect their interests. As late as 1850, despite the increase in immigrant workers and the fact that less than ten percent of American women earned wages outside the home, women were the majority of textile operators. Work as labor organizers gave women such as Harriet Hanson Robinson of the Lowell Cotton Mills their first experiences as reformers. Robinson and others raised public consciousness about women's roles and encouraged active participation in the women's rights movements and other reform campaigns.

The expansion of industrial markets may have drawn only a minority of women into production, but it had a dramatic effect on all women as consumers, and affected patterns of domesticity for all classes. Literacy and consumerism stimulated an explosion of magazines, advertising enterprises and, eventually, the invention of "domestic science." Although many of these enterprises would develop later in the century, the seeds for this revolution were sown during the pre-Civil War era.

Because of the popularity of academies, New England women like Maria Weston Chapman and her sisters, Anne, Deborah and Caroline, received the kind of intellectual foundation which allowed them to cultivate literary and reform pursuits. Many sought careers as teachers—Catharine Beecher promoted reform and women's education throughout her lifetime, and Chapman taught before marriage and her antislavery career. Education allowed women of all classes to expand their horizons.

In order to maintain the integrity and stability of their families, many women felt compelled to extend their concerns to the evils of the world outside the household, including drunkenness, licentiousness, and impiety. Through religious and reform institutions, women attacked those elements in the public sphere that provided a threat to the security of the family. Though such attempts might have undermined male authority, they were, as a logical consequence of female preoccupation with moral reform, an extension of concerns of the private sphere into the public domain. Evangelical Christianity and reform movements spurred many women into action—actions based on religious and moral principles, which could and often did lead women out of the home and into the wider world.

One of the most powerful movements of the era, antislavery, attracted thousands of women. Prominent in the abolitionist movement were the Grimké sisters, Sarah and Angelina, who abandoned their home in South Carolina to practice their faith as Quakers in a more receptive New England climate. The Grimkés joined a thriving network of women abolitionists, including Lucretia Mott, Abigail Kelley, and Lydia Maria Child. African-American members of the network such as Maria Stewart and Sarah Parker Remond formed separate societies for black women, as well as working within the larger movement.

Slavery took its toll on both men and women. However, the exploitation of female slaves was extraordinary. With the abolition of the external slave trade in 1807, the only way plantation owners could increase their slave labor force was by reproduction among the current slave population. The fertility rate for slave women exceeded that of white women, North and South which contributed to the phenomenal growth of the slave population. (This was at a time when the slave infant mortality rate has been calculated as high as 25 percent.) Many masters treated slaves as valuable stock to be bred and, perhaps, even sold for profit. Despite their reproductive values, female slaves were integrated into almost all aspects of agricultural production on the plantation. Pregnancy and nursing did not exempt women from work in the fields during hoeing and harvest. Then, after a hard day in the fields, women returned to slave cabins where they were expected to fulfill their domestic labors as wives and mothers.

It is testimony to the strength of these African-American women that crucial elements of their culture and values were preserved. Slave mothers instilled a sense of family pride and cultural tradition into children. Many preserved and passed on aspects of African culture (language, medicinal practices, rituals) despite the massive campaign of white slaveowners to indoctrinate slaves against their own cultural heritage. Not only did slave women resist their masters' intellectual coercion, many resisted the sexual harrassment, sexual coercion and rape exploitative masters practiced from the colonial period onward. Slave mothers could rarely gain protection or legal freedom for their children, but they struggled to impart to them a sense of self and heritage that might help sons and daughters escape the rigid confines slavery and racism attempted to impose. The efforts of slave mothers struck a chord with women abolitionists. Again and again, white abolitionist women posed their appeals on the common ground of motherhood and sisterhood, but bonds of common decency emerged.

Antislavery was but one of a whole range of charitable endeavors and reforms. Others included the improvement of living conditions of immigrants and the urban poor, fighting alcoholism (the Daughters of Temperance), opposing prostitution (Mary Magdalene societies), and ameliorating the conditions of convicts and the inmates of lunatic asylums. Margaret Fuller worked on behalf of female convicts at Rikers Island, New York. Dorothea Dix, the most famous reformer of conditions in asylums, began her career as a teacher in Boston. In 1841 she began ministering to the insane when she was asked to conduct Sunday school in a local prison and discovered felons and disturbed persons mixed together irrespective of age, sex, and mental capabilities. Through her campaign efforts, over thirty mental hospitals were established in over 15 different states. Despite her repeated bouts of bad health which included tuberculosis, she was a vigorous champion of the rights of those unable to fight for better conditions.

All of these reform activities could be made to square with women's "primary function" as a maternal nurturer, guardian of those who needed special care. At the same time, such involvements allowed women the opportunity for a more public life, for the explorations of new capacities (from politicking within organizations to fundraising) and, above all perhaps, for a new sense of group awareness.

Women armed with education and intellectual curiosity could and did launch other pioneering efforts for reform. Sarah Josepha Hale edited *Godey's Lady Book*, one of a score of successful magazines aimed at a burgeoning female readership. Designed to inform and entertain ladies, the antebellum literary magazine addressed a range of issues designed to inform and entertain ladies, including domestic and moral reform, hygiene, leisure and recreation, health, religion and most subjects except electoral politics. They linked a wide female readership to the efforts of a small vanguard of reformers. Another female entrepreneur, Lydia Pinkham, mass-marketed home remedies, notably her "Vegetable compound." She saw her work as contributing to health reform and addressed herself specifically to "female complaints" in a way that the new male medical specialists could not. The segregation of women into this "domestic sphere" resulted ironically in female captains of newly-created industries.

As women began to establish their own literary and critical voice, male critics began to carp at "scribbling women," as Nathaniel Hawthorne called the prolific female writers who were his contemporaries. Catharine Maria Sedgwick, Caroline Gilman, Lydia Maria Child, Caroline Hentz, Lydia Sigourney, and the most popular of them all, Emma D.E.N. Southworth (whose novels were issued in forty-two volumes in 1877), found fame by appealing to female audiences through a range of literary forms, most notably the novel. (Ironically, the most brilliant and talented woman writer of this generation did not even have an audience, as poet Emily Dickinson was a recluse who did not publish any of her verse during her lifetime—1830–1886.)

Most women writers imbued their work with themes of female sacrifice, maternal stoicism, and the three "p"s: purity, propriety and piety. Some pushed beyond the limits of the sentimental novel and incorporated powerful messages about domestic politics that celebrated women's capacities for sustaining family relationships. Tyrannical fathers and husbands were favorite targets for these novelists. Indeed, the "male sphere" was ridiculed in many novels as being a world bankrupt of enduring worth and abundant in greed and selfishness. Most familiar of all such books was *Uncle Tom's Cabin*, published in 1852 by Harriet Beecher Stowe, Catharine Beecher's sister. A work of abolitionist propaganda, the novel illuminated the hypocrisy of politicians and the evils of human bondage, especially in its heartwrenching descriptions of slavecatching. Stowe's novel branded slavery as a product of the ruthless greed honored in the male-dominated public sphere. Her audience and influence reached far beyond American women. The novel was widely read in Europe and heavily criticized by slaveowners in the South. Abraham Lincoln, referring to the Civil War and acknowledging the power and popularity of Stowe's attack on slavery addressed her during their meeting in 1863 as "the little lady who made this big war."

As early as the 1830s, many women transferred their influence beyond social and moral reforms to the growing movement in women's rights. Scottish immigrant Frances Wright, founder of a Utopian community in 1825 in Nashoba, Tennessee, moved to New York to co-edit *The Free Enquirer* with social reformer Robert Dale Owen in 1828. They advocated, among other changes, property rights for married women and the practice of birth control. They also contributed to the formation of the New York Workingmen's Party in 1829. Wright boldly involved herself in the world of male politics which women like Stowe addressed only indirectly. She was part of the early group of activists and writers of her day committed to women's rights. Women of the New York Female Reform Society established a respected forum for their views, *The Advocate*, in the 1830s. The journal attracted over 16,000 subscribers and continued well into the 1850s. Sarah Grimké published *The Equality of the Sexes* in 1838, one of the most important early works to call for women's legal rights. Margaret Fuller's *Woman in the Nineteenth Century* (1845) was another ground-breaking feminist work. These developments signalled the stimulation of a feminist sensibility which initiated a series of political conventions at mid-century, beginning at Seneca Falls, New York in 1848.

Many outstanding women during the first half of the nineteenth century battled for the cause of those less fortunate and in doing so articulated their own individuality. Many sought to increase their authority and independence beyond the confines of "woman's sphere" and the household, while others eventually challenged altogether the notion of separate spheres and pursued leadership positions in reform movements. Maria Weston Chapman and abolitionist women crusaded on behalf of slaves, especially women subjected to sexual exploitation and mothers deprived of their children. Catharine Beecher and her disciples sought to transform the lot of the isolated farmers' daughters scattered across the countryside. Margaret Fuller fought for autonomy on behalf of her sex. The energies of these pioneers contributed to enormous changes within American society as a whole and women's role within this dynamic era.

Maria Weston Chapman
(1806–1885)

Catherine Clinton

Born into an affluent Massachusetts family, Maria Weston Chapman was educated in local ladies' academies and in England before she became a school principal. After her marriage to Henry Grafton Chapman, a Boston merchant, she left her position to fulfill the role of wife and mother. Adopting the Chapman family's antislavery stance as her own, Maria Weston Chapman became an influential abolitionist in addition to rearing six children and serving as wife—and nurse—to her invalid husband until his death.

Allying herself with William Lloyd Garrison and his followers, Chapman organized the Boston Female Anti-Slavery Society in 1832 to complement Garrison's all-male New England Anti-Slavery Society. Although she was a forceful personality, she never developed a platform speaking style and was content to wield influence from behind the scenes or with her pen. Chapman spent over thirty years as organizer, fundraiser, and valued executive for several antislavery groups, and as writer and editor of various abolitionist journals. She was especially active during the split in the movement in 1839 that involved dissent concerning women's roles, among other issues, but her advocacy for women's equal participation was never extended beyond the antislavery movement to political feminism. With the end of slavery following the Civil War, Chapman retired from public life, devoting herself to her children and their business interests. She also focused her energies on writing, and produced a biography of Harriet Martineau, the famed English reformer and chronicler of American society, as well as her own autobiographical writing. Chapman died in Weymouth in 1885.

A wealth of letters and papers from Maria Weston Chapman to noted abolitionist William Lloyd Garrison and his followers attest to Chapman's invaluable contributions to the crusade against slavery. The abolitionists, like many other social and political reformers, had leaders who functioned exclusively within the organizational fold. Although this left them prey to historical neglect, their political impact was not diminished.[1] The platform personalities played a major role in antislavery leadership, but were by no means the sole parties determining abolitionist policy and productivity. Maria Weston Chapman was a member of the less visible but not less influential leadership who, as she herself put it, spent their time "in the trenches, filling up on the way for others to mount the break."[2]

Maria Weston Chapman was born July 25, 1806, in Weymouth, Massachusetts, the eldest of Warren and Anne Bates Weston's six children. She grew up on her parents' farm and attended local schools until her teens, when she was sent to England to live with a maternal uncle, Joshua Bates. Her years abroad acquainted Maria Weston with a highly cultivated circle of people concerned with political as well as cultural affairs. From them, she acquired a cosmopolitan polish and a taste for reform that shaped her future—she later credited this experience with starting her on her activist career. Upon her return to America, she maintained similar ties with political thinkers. When she returned to Massachusetts in 1828, she served as the first "lady principal" of Ebenezer Bailey's Young Ladies' High School in Boston, wanting more to her life than the traditional roles of wife and mother expected of her.

Within a year of her return to Boston, Maria Weston fell in love with Henry Grafton Chapman, a wealthy Brahmin merchant. Although little is known of their romance and courtship—no letters have survived from this early period—the two probably met through their common affiliation with William Ellery Channing's Unitarian Church. They were married on October 6, 1830. Maria Weston Chapman discontinued her work as principal to embark on what she believed at the time was an even more challenging career, abolition.

The Chapman family were abolitionist sympathizers; Henry himself was an ardent Garrisonian. By marrying into the Chapman family, Maria Weston became firmly ensconced within the Boston antislavery circle. She chose to become a follower of the outspoken Garrison instead of a disciple of Channing, whose Unitarian church advocated a conservative approach to abolition, because, as she wrote: "I have never been cured by a busy, battling controversial laborious lifetime of the very great imperfection of inability to wait patiently, even for greater satisfaction."[3] Her political zeal was further nurtured by her rebellious personal style: "It is we who are against the world. But then, . . . it is the only comfort of our lives—this being in the opposition."[4] Chapman saw her antislavery work as a "mission," believing herself neither saint not martyr, merely an instrument of God.

Chapman devoted herself to the antislavery cause with a religious fervor. Believing in the absolute existence of a right and wrong path, she felt antislavery was her only choice. She often described her mission in highly emotive terms ("our views are larger and our souls steadier than those of man"), yet her rhetoric of self-glorification was restrained for its day. When she was praised by a friend as a martyr to the cause, Chapman replied, "I can't say I have made any sacrifices. I have had my choice."[5] In another piece of correspondence Chapman answered the accusation that abolitionists were not the saints they pretended to be: "We deeply feel that the reformer ought to be perfect, but when would reform begin if it were to wait till there were perfect reformers?"[6]

Chapman was acutely aware of many of her imperfections as well as her contradictions. She was firm in her opposition to slavery and able to defend herself in public, but in private she suffered extreme anxiety about her shortcomings. Her doubts about her career plagued her throughout her life. In a letter to a friend, she listed her sins: "How heretical, harsh, fanatical, moon-struck, unsexed I am. I hate much."[7] The terms in which she expressed her doubts are as intriguing as her sense of guilt about her faults. The controversy that her career provoked in Chapman was reflected in her internal conflict. This dilemma proved an unending struggle for Chapman. The personal and political riddles of her role as a female activist mystified Chapman herself and continue to puzzle the social historian.

The issue of slavery divided the upper-classes north of the Mason-Dixon line during the antebellum era. In response, the abolitionists developed their own society and hierarchy within that society.[8] Chapman sensed no loss of status through her association with antislavery: "We were possessors of great social influence before we were abolitionists. Now let us use it—for we have never lost it."[9] Content to form their own social spheres, many aristocratic abolitionists considered any social ostracism a minor element in the scheme of their lives; this was certainly the case with Chapman.

Her abolitionist accomplishments were achieved in the context of a more traditional domestic life than most of her female colleagues. She was married, unlike Sallie Holley. She was a mother, unlike Lydia Maria Child. She did not limit her antislavery activity with the birth of her children, unlike Angelina Grimké Weld (who also drafted her sister Sarah as domestic companion during her confinement). Maria Weston Chapman's participation in the movement far outweighed her husband's abolitionist contribution, unlike Abby Kelley Foster's compared to her husband Stephen's. Managing a household, bearing four children and raising three (one daughter died in infancy) while nursing her consumptive husband (Henry contracted tuberculosis in 1834), Maria Weston Chapman created for herself one of the most productive careers of the movement.

On October 14, 1832, Chapman joined with several other women to form the Boston Female Anti-Slavery Society, an organization inspired by the formation of the all-male New England Anti-Slavery Society earlier in the year. Both groups rejected gradual emancipation and African colonization, measures endorsed by more conservative antislavery organizations, arguing for more immediate action through moral persuasion that slavery is wrong. The Boston women held weekly meetings, conducted prayer vigils, circulated antislavery petitions, and distributed Garrison's popular weekly journal, the *Liberator*. Their work expanded the antislavery realm incalculably.

In 1834 Chapman organized the first of what was to become an annual event, the antislavery fair. The first fair netted $1,000 through the sale of gift items and handcrafted goods contributed by sympathizers. Through the years "antislavery friends" throughout the country and abroad (principally England and France) shipped tons of material to Boston for the fairs. Maria Chapman tirelessly solicited monetary or material contributions for these antislavery fairs which became well attended and effective both as fundraisers and as propaganda. By the 1850s the annual profit averaged $4,000, providing funds desperately needed by the near-bankrupt antislavery operation. Thus, this activity cannot be dismissed as "mere" charity work; Chapman's ingenuity often saved the Garrisonians from financial ruin.

In 1835 Chapman assumed the first of what was to become a series of concurrently held antislavery leadership positions. She became corresponding secretary of the Boston Female Anti-Slavery Society, and in 1836 began writing its annual reports. During the twenty-seven years of her executive career (1835–1862), she displayed enviable stamina, serving fourteen terms on the business committee of the Massachusetts Anti-Slavery Society, thirteen years as a member of the American Anti-Slavery Society Executive Board, and throughout the 1830s and 1840s on the Central Committee of the Boston Female Anti-Slavery Society. In addition, Chapman continued to organize the annual bazaars.

In 1839 Chapman initiated a new antislavery fundraiser, the *Liberty Bell*, a collection of abolitionist writings. Her pet project, this gift book with a golden bell on the cover was conceived and edited by Chapman to raise desperately needed money. Chapman solicited contributions from antislavery sympathizers throughout the world: political writers Harriet Martineau (who was a close personal friend of Chapman's) and Alexis de Tocqueville, feminists Fredrika Bremer and Margaret Fuller, and poets Elizabeth Barrett Browning, Henry Wadsworth Longfellow, and James Russell Lowell. The collection of poetry and prose by "Friends of Freedom" was in great demand and continued in popularity until its final issue in 1858. The annual subscription revenue greatly augmented the abolitionist treasury. Chapman hardly wrote a letter to a literary personage without requesting some short article as a donation. Although it was but one of her many activities, she reminded a friend: "Don't forget the Bell, it is a trifle, but it does much good."[10] Not only did this volume net profit, but it promoted the message of abolitionism in a sugar-coated format.

Chapman, unlike most influential abolitionists, was unwilling to take to the public platform. In 1835 when a mob threatened violence during an interracial abolitionist meeting in Boston and the mayor ordered immediate dispersal, Chapman replied: "If this is the last bulwark of freedom, we may as well die here as anywhere." (At length, the group adjourned to the Chapman home.) This oft-quoted phrase is the only public remark with which Chapman has been associated. Although many of her female contemporaries—Angelina Grimké, Abby Kelley Foster, and Lucretia Mott, to name but a few— were known for their stirring abolitionist lectures, Chapman was not comfortable with public speaking. In private or on paper she was articulate and persuasive. She did not shy away from oration for reasons of propriety; in fact, Chapman openly attacked criticisms of "promiscuous audiences" and women lecturers. She simply suffered from a form of stage fright.

She did deliver one public speech, at the Women's Anti-Slavery Convention in Philadelphia in 1838. Her performance was widely acclaimed, and she was lauded as a dynamic speaker. Unfortunately for her speaking career, she suffered a complete breakdown on the train returning to Boston. Her husband's illness and the strains of an overactive schedule contributed to her collapse, but the breakdown apparently was triggered by the unnerving experience of speaking at the convention.[11] She was removed from the train and placed in a convalescent home in Stonington, Connecticut. During her hospitalization, friends and family alike feared she would never recover, so severe had been her mental collapse. Yet after a few months rest, Chapman emerged to resume her former activities with an increased commitment. She refused to reduce her work load after her return, nor would she elaborate on the causes of the breakdown or the reasons for recovery. She tried to erase this episode from her record through a regimen of strenuous antislavery activity. However, Chapman never again took the podium after her Philadelphia experience, instead confining herself to her primary talents as fundraiser, editor, and essayist.

Following her recovery from her breakdown, Chapman began to produce reform literature at a phenomenal rate. After launching the *Liberty Bell*, yet while continuing her executive and secretarial posts as well as managing the annual fairs, Chapman organized a pacifist group, the New England Non-Resistance Society with Garrison. (Non-resistance was tantamount to withdrawal from all institutions deemed to operate by way of force.) She became its corresponding secretary and assistant editor of its periodical, the *Non-Resistant*, from 1839 to 1842. Chapman next collected manuscripts and published an antislavery songbook in 1839 titled *Songs of the Free*. In 1840 she initiated and financed a new abolitionist paper in New York as an attempt to strengthen the American Anti-Slavery Society, which had undergone severe damage during an organizational split.

The new journal, the *National Anti-Slavery Standard*, had a shaky start with Nathanial P. Rogers as temporary editor and Chapman advising by post. Chapman had gained a working knowledge of journalism through her association with the *Liberator* and the *Non-Resistant*. When Garrison had been away on tour or during one of his frequent illnesses, Chapman had been drafted to compose editorials, solicit articles, rewrite copy, and even do layouts for the *Liberator*. In 1841 Lydia Maria Child became editor of the *Standard*, proceeding to fashion the weekly into a "family paper." This doubled the circulation of the *Standard*, but the Garrisonians were not pleased with Child's political moderation, as the *Standard* under her direction did not feature controversial abolitionist news and avoided inflammatory issues. The Boston radical clique withdrew their support. In 1843 David Child succeeded his wife as editor, but he, too, failed to reflect the political sensibilities of the sponsoring organizers, and in 1844 was replaced by an editorial board consisting of Edmund Quincy, Sydney Howard Gay, and Maria Weston Chapman.[12]

Chapman's involvement with the paper became all-consuming, for at this point in her career, her work was especially important to her. In 1841 she had accompanied her invalid husband to Haiti, a trip undertaken to benefit his waning health. While in the Caribbean she had not only continued her efforts for the Boston fair, but had worked for the Philanthropic Society of Porto Plate, a West Indian auxiliary of the American Anti-Slavery Society.[13] Upon his return to the United States, Henry Chapman's health failed rapidly and he died in 1842. Caroline Weston, Maria's sister, reported Henry's deathbed words to his wife: "I leave you to the Cause."[14] Rather than retire into a prolonged mourning, Maria Chapman took her husband's words to heart. She allowed only the responsibilities of rearing her children to temper her abandoning herself to abolitionism.

From 1844 to 1848 Chapman contributed a ceaseless stream of articles and advice to the *Standard's* New York headquarters. Her letters to Gay are full of suggestions for layout, subscription drives, and editorial policy. She wrote to a female abolitionist: "I am hard at work. What I do makes no show, and only I tell you that you may not feel deserted and alone . . . . I average five columns a week for the *Standard*, so the rest of the days to do writing to stir up people's minds about the fair."[15]

Under the direction of Gay, Chapman, and Quincy, the *Standard* declined in popularity, but Chapman reveled in the unpopularity, confiding to Gay:

> E. M. Davis pays us the highest possible compliment—quite takes away Garrison's crown—says the *Standard* is the most despised of any of the papers. If we had not passed the age of caring for honours it is enough to make us vain.[16]

At a low point, when Gay feared the *Standard* was failing to accomplish its propagandistic purpose because of declining subscriptions, Chapman counseled: "The existence of the *Standard* is a proof to the eyes of the nation that the highest morality does yet *live* in this nation. I do know that fact is torment enough for the satisfied."[17] She saw the abolitionist journals as essential to the cause.[18] The antislavery press was Chapman's foremost effort among her many concerns.

Even at a peak of her editorial reign, Chapman did not lessen her organizational efforts. She was a prime mover in the 1839 power coup within the Boston Female Anti-Slavery Society, during which Garrisonian forces ousted more moderate leadership. Throughout abolitionist infighting Chapman was a ferocious warrior, always involved in one debate or another. Most of her arguments, however, were published as anonymous editorials and she refrained from personalizations. Thus when asked to publish a rebuttal to an article by Harriet Beecher Stowe that Chapman composed for personal correspondence, Chapman refused:

> I would have nothing controversial rise between her and me at this juncture. You know how good I think controversy is at the right time that like somebody, I forget who, in Bunyan, I can "fight till the swordhilt cleaves to my hand as if they were one piece." I have no abstract dislike of controversy—quite the contrary.[19]

Chapman felt that personal exchanges should not be aired in public, urging abolitionists to present a united front. Of proslavery critics, she commented, "It is their policy to represent the abolitionists as broken up into parties. This is not the case. There are in our ranks diversities of opinion, but there are not divisions of hearts."[20]

Yet in her correspondence she lashed out at "diversities of opinion" that took their toll during the 1840s and 1850s. For instance, she bemoaned the actions of Gerrit Smith, "who has formally merged the Liberty Party in free soilism which is the natural form of imperfect devotedness and waning convictions."[21] Of James Buffam's defection, she is only a little more sympathetic: "*Who* leads the procession and *where* is it going—and what have they got in their pockets? Dear good Buffam! I pity him, I do. What is an honest man in the hands of knaves?"[22] Over the years she grew bitter about those who broke from the ranks, and about her own embattled position. In 1852 she lashed out indignantly:

> When you see a quarrel, it is not about words, but about base personal betrayal and treason to the cause and abandonment of its principles— all trying to conceal themselves under the cloak of love of the cause. Think how hard it must be to stand upright in such a current of iniquity as this and not swim with it.[23]

While she witnessed others drifting away from the "one true path," Chapman stood steadfast, pledging her unwavering support of Garrison: "It is my freedom to keep my faith unbroken."[24] Her unfailing assistance was a source of comfort to the much maligned *Liberator* editor. Garrison expressed his gratitude in a letter dated 1848: "We have a few suggestive creative, executive minds and such is yours in an eminent degree. . . . How immensely indebted I am to you for counsel, encouragement, commendation and support."[25]

Chapman, however, did not blindly follow Garrison through the years. She trusted him implicitly on matters of principle and philosophy, although she often found his methods "soft-hearted." In turn, Garrison never questioned Chapman's actions, recognizing that her motives were as he considered his own, above reproach. During the long years of their association Garrison constantly consulted Chapman on a variety of issues. (Due to their proximity, they rarely communicated by letter; thus, only a minimum of documentary evidence concerning their relationship exists.) One antislavery crusader held that Garrison was entirely ruled by Chapman.[26] Although an obvious overstatement, Chapman's influence should not be underestimated. Perhaps Garrison himself best summed up their relationship in a letter to her:

How could the *Liberator* have been sustained . . . without your power-ful cooperation? Where would have been the Boston Female Anti-Slavery Society? How could the Massachusetts and American Anti-Slavery Society have put forth such exertions, independently of your own! The National Bazaar—what does it not owe you! Your position and influence have been preeminently valuable.[27]

There was one instance in their long years of friendship when Chapman, impatient with what she felt to be Garrison's incompe-tence, took matters into her own hands. When Frederick Douglass was on a lecture tour of England, Chapman became convinced of his treachery to the cause. She confided to Harriet Beecher Stowe:

> We shall be obliged, I think (we the American Anti-Slavery Society, I mean) to withdraw our recommendation of Frederick Douglass in Great Britain as promptly as we gave it—since by means of it he is enabled to use money to tell falsehoods to raise more money to tell more falsehoods, all under the false pretense of serving a cause he has not the slightest interest in but as it serves his selfish purposes. He changes his politics and his tactics exactly like a base white man. And we have been, I fear, weak on account of his color.[28]

This tirade was brought about by Douglass's purchase of his free-dom, against the express wishes—for tactical purposes—of the Bos-ton antislavery clique.[29] Chapman drummed up opposition to Doug-lass among her colleagues. Her harassment of Douglass prompted him to warn Chapman in 1846: "If you wish to drive me from the Anti-Slavery Society, put me under overseership and the work is done. Set someone to watch me—for evil—and let them be so simple-minded as to inform me of the office and the last blow is struck."[30]

Although an "overseer" never materialized, Chapman launched a series of attacks upon Douglass in her private correspondence. Doug-lass's campaign to sell his autobiography and his neglect of his fam-ily for the sake of more "refined" companionship elicited severe criticism. Chapman wrote a confidante: "As for F. Douglass, he is like Harry Wind 'fighting for his own hand'—and he will always take the course that most promotes his own interest."[31]

The controversy centered on Douglass's independence from the Boston power base and was aggravated by his association with the "refined" Julia Griffiths, his white female assistant who returned with him to the United States following his British tour. In 1847 Douglass initiated and edited the *North Star*, an abolitionist paper based in Rochester, New York. While Garrison was content merely to scold Douglass for his "impulsiveness," the rest of the abolition-ist community was livid. Chapman expressed herself in public with restraint, wishing Douglass well on his new endeavor for the cause, but in private she was enraged:

> The measure of his crimes is full. It is high time we took away his character. He *never had any* but what we gave him, we were all [unintelligible] into thinking he was capable of having one by his cunning artfulness. Our committee say—"what can one expect better of a slave" true—but it does not absolve us from the duty of exposing him—to my judgement.[32]

The Douglass episode demonstrates some of Chapman's "contradictions": self-righteousness, stubbornness, the power of her influence, and racist attitudes.[33] She felt it was *her* duty to expose Douglass (within the realm of the organization) for what she felt him to be and to drive him from the movement, even against Garrison's expressed wishes to the contrary. She accomplished this task with little regret.

In the midst of her career and at the height of her influence, Chapman chose to leave America. She believed her life had been transformed by her education abroad, and she was determined that her children should profit from a similar advantage. Colleagues were shocked at her apparent "abandonment of the cause" just at the time the Mexican War was fanning the flames of the debate over slavery. Chapman was convinced her trip to Europe would not eliminate but merely reduce her antislavery activity. With her three children and her sister Caroline, Chapman sailed in the summer of 1848. During her seven years abroad she tirelessly continued her campaign, raising enormous sums of money in London and Paris. Although Chapman left the annual bazaar in the able hands of her sisters Anne and Deborah, she fired off a continuous stream of postal directives to supervise their activities. The *Liberty Bell* continued under her editorship, and Chapman wrote articles for the antislavery press as a foreign correspondent.

Upon her return in 1855, she resumed her old executive duties, regaining her former power. As an example of renewed strength, in 1858 she singlehandedly forced discontinuance of the fairs. In Europe she had witnessed the success of antislavery salons—some of which she herself organized—galas staged for cultural edification rather than commercial sales. Patrons invited to attend the galas pledged donations to the cause. Chapman thought the bazaar had become an outmoded event, and wanted to replace it with an annual salon. The antislavery women of Boston who had worked for years with Chapman and her sisters were enraged, not only because of her cancellation of the fairs, but because of Chapman's callous dismissal of their objections. With minimal assistance, Chapman organized her "Subscription Anniversary" in an atmosphere of thinly veiled hostility. In spite of antagonism, the benefit netted a profit of $5,700—$1,200 more than the most lucrative of fairs. Chapman's critics were silenced. When there was money to be had for antislavery, Chapman exerted her iron will to gain it.

Her domineering manner provoked severe criticism from other sources as well. Fellow abolitionist John Greenleaf Whittier called her Garrison's "evil genius."[34] Branded the "Lady Macbeth" of the movement, Chapman's inflexible personality kept her from compromise on many matters. She argued it was a "necessity for walking right over a good many things and persons that have not sense of good feeling to do their best for good order."[35] Her willfulness was certainly a response to the requirements of leadership. It is significant to note that most of her enemies within the movement were men—her sex as much as her methods sparked many attacks upon her.

Her coolness gave her an aura of detachment that many abolitionists believed was a reflection of "aristocratic disdain." She was labeled a blueblood and a snob by some of her critics. Yet Chapman never expressed any of these characteristics in her correspondence; to the contrary, she believed that antislavery affiliation was a great and positive leveler.[36] Raised as an aristocrat and married into a Brahmin family, Chapman struggled to repress her inherent snobbery for the good of the cause. Her success in doing so was praised by colleague Abby Kelley Foster:

> So far as I have been able to learn the minds of the abolitionists, M. W. Chapman is the person to bear up our banner, boldly and gallantly, and at the same time with all due hum'ty to *all* persons whatever may have been their different degrees of progress, if they are sound at heart.[37]

In spite of Chapman's public endorsement of antislavery solidarity, a stance she believed was the most tactically advantageous to the cause, she privately advocated individualism. She wrote to a coworker: "I can never make myself responsible for any man's language, nor do I wish any man to be responsible for mine."[38] Her sense of independence often undermined the representative nature of the abolitionist movement. Her individualism was in direct conflict with her collectivist politics, a contradiction she failed to resolve throughout her career.

Chapman was an ardent critic of the government. The murder of abolitionist editor Elijah Lovejoy at the hands of a mob proved a catalytic experience for her and many other abolitionists, and after his death she declared: "There is no law for us."[39] Her political sensibilities hardened. In 1837, she wrote:

I fear when I see the strength of slavery *here* [Boston] and how the institutions of the South are interwoven with our own free ones—not openly indeed, but like the roots of a giant tree, *beneath the soil*—I fear that abolition will be resisted by the South to her own destruction and by the North until the last possible day of grace.[40]

And in 1861, Chapman concluded: "Civil war . . . is not so bad as slavery."[41] Early in her political career she had rejected the Constitution as "a compact by which the South bound herself to the North on the condition that the North should guarantee the existence of slavery in perpetuity,"[42] in favor of the Declaration of Independence which she saw as "an expression of the abstract opinions of the framers of the Constitution."[43] To Chapman the political aims of the abolitionist movement were a "renovation" of the Constitution and a restoration of democratic principles. Although opposed to war on principle, she saw the conflict as irrepressible.[44] When the Civil War broke out, Chapman was hopeful for "the Cause."

By the surrender of the Confederacy five years later, Chapman was jubilant, confiding to Garrison: "I believe we are of the number (smaller than I had hoped) who can really rejoice with the slaves at the downfall of the system."[45] At the close of the war she retired from the abolitionist ranks, rationalizing:

> There is no need for me now—I mean in any strenuous absorbing sense—for I draw with the millions the stones of reconstruction though we were alone in the duty of demolition. . . . Quiet hard work now is better than anything else. I cannot be too glad that I had an experience of life, anterior to our anti-slavery life so that I did not get so bent to battle in the days when battle was *sina qua non*, that I am unable to fulfill the duties of victory.[46]

Chapman radically misjudged the power of the law and the South's commitment to Reconstruction. She mistakenly believed the emancipated slaves would be guaranteed equality through political necessity.[47]

By war's end, Chapman was weary of her activist career. Although her work had been freely chosen as a rewarding vocation, her letters amply document the strenuous aspects of a quarter century of abolitionism. She described her working conditions to a friend: "Any excuse, the haste in which I *always* write, surrounded by children getting their lessons, Board meeting in full sail, of laughing girls in full sail—young men singing and snapping their fingers at the universe and a stream of people passing through all the while."[48] Her schedule was no less hectic:

I have been all summer driven hither and thither with matters per-
taining to death and shall probably be all winter driven still more
furiously by affairs of life. So that it seems to matter of life and death
with me all the time. . . . [T]he Fair gets every instant of my life with
the mortifying reflection that if I were only on a level with a cat and
had nine lives, I could carry on the work with geometrically propor-
tional results.[49]

Chapman having but one life, and although well spent on a worthy
cause, was to reflect regretfully in 1866:

My public work in life did not come to me as I should have planned
for it to come. I should have given my earlier life to my children
wholly, I suppose, if I had been laying a plan at the outset and have
wrought for public good in later life. But it was not to be so.[50]

Like many mothers who worked outside the home, she would suffer
guilt and anguish over the tension between family commitment and
the demands of a career.

Following the war, Chapman spent several years in the New York
home of her son, Henry, occupying herself with his business concerns before retiring permanently to Boston. In 1877 she edited a
memorial edition of Harriet Martineau's autobiography. Chapman
died in Weymouth in 1885 at age seventy-nine.

Maria Weston Chapman's abolitionism stemmed from her complex view of self and society. Her strong religious beliefs dictated for
her a rigid path to "right" behavior. She believed her individual
freedom was to do the greatest good for society and she pegged slavery as the ultimate evil. Just as her convictions led her to divide the
world into good and evil, private and public, temporal and spiritual,
so her sense of duality dictated masculine and feminine spheres. She
believed men and women were identical in a spiritual realm—
rendering their souls and intellects equal, yet Chapman maintained
that the sexes were, by necessity, separate and distinct in a temporal
realm.

Because she believed antislavery to be a matter of conscience,
Chapman championed the equal participation of women in the
movement:

Women, whose efforts for the cause could not be hindered by men
were more valuable auxiliaries than the men whose dignity forbade
them to be fellow laborers with women.[51]

She even welcomed the opportunity for women to demonstrate their
"God-given" talents, claiming "in situations of peril and difficulty,
they [men] have looked for aid to women superior to themselves in

ability."[52] Yet she never channeled her energies into any women's rights activity. She greeted Margaret Fuller's *Women in the Nineteenth Century* with tepid approval, praising the author's "general feeling that a woman's duties like a man's are to her country, her race and her religion: as well as to her personal ties and to her home."[53] Her conservative response to any feminist doctrine continued throughout her career. It is especially ironic that on the opening day of the first women's rights convention in Seneca Falls, New York, while one of her poems was being read to the delegates, Chapman sailed for Europe with her family. Despite her singlemindedness, her involvement with non-resistance demonstrated an interest in reform outside the antislavery umbrella. Her lack of enthusiasm for women's rights must be judged a disapproval of feminist organization rather than indifference to it.

Maria Weston Chapman, like many women of her generation and those of her milieu who followed, was not attracted to feminism. Feminists sought political equality, and Chapman would have none of it. Women who did not ally themselves with the women's rights movement have been properly termed "nonfeminist." But to leave the matter at that is to rob ourselves of clearer understanding of both the era and those women challenging established social roles.

Barbara Welter's work illuminates the popular alternative to political feminism in the antebellum era with the cult of domesticity.[54] Ann Douglas's sophisticated and provocative treatment of Victorian America sheds light on a concurrent if not overlapping phenomenon, the cult of sentimentality.[55] Another less prominent but nonetheless significant group of women developed what might be called a "cult of influence."[56]

This particular group drew its ideological tenets from a variety of texts ranging from Mary Astell's *Serious Proposal to the Ladies for Advancement of Their True and Greatest Interest* (1694) to Daniel Defoe's *Essay on Projects* (1698) and most significantly from the works of the "high priestess" of influence, Hannah More: *Essays on Various Subjects* (1777), *Sacred Dramas* (1782), *Estimate of the Religion and the Practical World* (1790), *Structures on the Modern System of Female Education* (1799).

Just as the intellectual origins of political feminism stemmed from European political thought, American domestic feminism also drew from British sources. The split between domestic and political feminism was as wide a gulf in the United States as it was in England. Kathryn Kish Sklar illustrates this dichotomy by contrasting the leadership styles of Angelina Grimké and Catharine Beecher in her biography of Beecher. An even more striking counterpoint is found by comparing Catharine Beecher and Margaret Fuller. These two women were essentially American counterparts of a pair of influential British activists, Hannah More and Mary Wollstonecraft. Whereas More and Beecher were both conservative theorists who spent their lives unmarried and committed to educating women and writing texts of domestic feminism, both Wollstonecraft and Fuller committed themselves to radical political causes, experimented with marriage and childbearing, and wrote major influential works of political feminism.

Much has been written about the colorful figures of Fuller and Wollstonecraft, who both suffered premature and tragic deaths. Beecher and More led less melodramatic lives, but had no less an impact on the culture. While the works of Fuller and Wollstonecraft enjoy notoriety and popularity during the twentieth century and Beecher and More suffer relative obscurity, the opposite was true in antebellum Anglo-America. Beecher, More, and other promoters of women's moral superiority and domestic priority triumphed during the middle of the nineteenth century. Their ideology of influence challenged and in a very real sense crippled political feminism. The cult of influence, built on a blue-stocking model, created an intellectual alternative to political feminism for the female elite.

These particular nonfeminists believed that although women were intellectually equal, if not morally superior to men, the world was divided into two spheres (the public and the private) as well as into two sexes. The female sex, being restricted to the private sphere, was in no way inferior to the male sex who occupied the public arena. The believers in the cult of influence wished to enlarge the female domain by redefining the domestic sphere.[57] Their employment of enlightenment theory and in many cases republican ideology[58] bolstered their arguments for a program of social redistribution of responsibility—without tampering with traditional authority. Yet their philosophy in no way endangered either sex segregation of social spheres or by extension, male domination in political and economic realms. Feminists, by contrast, presented a triple threat: they demanded equal political rights, an end to male domination in economic matters, and a fundamental restructuring of society.[59]

The concept of "influence," much like "virtue," has undergone considerable change since the eighteenth century. Influence was perhaps as crucial to social change in antebellum America as "media" is to cultural transformation in the present day. Women sought influence through education, through religion, and lastly, through reform. Their struggle for influence was essentially a bid for power, yet their challenge was for themselves as an elite minority, not for women as a whole. And these women failed to take into consideration that their gains of influence might result in influence's immediate social and political devaluation.

Maria Weston Chapman spent the most productive part of her adult life fighting for freedom, against slavery. Her struggle for influence generated a very real impact in her lifetime. Although she expressed explicitly feminist ideas with her support of female orators and her contempt for men who objected to women's participation in the antislavery movement, Chapman also endorsed separate (but equal) abolitionist societies for women and refused to join with female colleagues in their political organization for women's rights. She resisted the intellectual shift from fighting white's enslavement of blacks to battling men's domination over women. Her career as an activist was fraught with conflict. Whereas she was often attacked in antifeminist terms, as an "aggressive" and "domineering" woman, Chapman was unable to embrace feminism and deflect male criticism. She took derision personally, and to heart; her self-doubts created waves of emotional unrest. While she could function smoothly and effectively within the private realm of the antislavery circles, the instant she took a more public abolitionist role, such as orator, Chapman collapsed. She was not loathe to make her antislavery views public, as her politics were well known in print, but Chapman's conflict concerning woman's roles in society was perhaps the crucial factor in her breakdown. Although she recovered to resume an even more dynamic role in abolitionist activities, Chapman never again ventured into the public arena. Her experimental attempt at "mounting the break," rather than "filling in the trenches," was disastrous. She firmly settled on the principle of separate spheres for men and women, in both her personal and political philosophy.

Conflict, so much a part of the abolitionist struggle within and without, plagued Chapman's personal life as well as her career. She was committed to antislavery, indeed it was her husband's dying wish that she continue her abolitionist crusade. Yet motherhood proved an emotional and ideological stumbling block. In 1848 Chapman left the United States to further her children's education, in spite of her colleagues' scorn that she was "abandoning the Cause." Chapman countered that motherhood was necessarily her primary concern. In later years she expressed guilt over time not spent with her children during her antislavery career, and her "lament of the working mother" was quite moving. Indeed Chapman endorsed a woman's duty to her conscience, and the moral necessity of antislavery activity, yet when this abolitionism interfered with domestic and maternal roles, as it was bound to do on a long range if not daily basis, problems were inevitable. The conflict between nonfeminist principles and social activism produced a constant and critical dilemma for Maria Weston Chapman, a dilemma which remained unsolved throughout her lifetime, even though she managed to fulfill both her domestic and activist roles.

Maria Weston Chapman alone does not demand a more complex rendering of the feminist context. Many women of her generation—Catharine Beecher, Catharine Sedgwick, and Fanny Kemble to name but a few—constituted a discernible opposition to the women's rights movement yet maintained an important alternative to the anti-intellectualism of the majority of nonfeminists. These women merit more careful attention as they have too long been condemned to the lower historical depths of "minor figures." Chapman and many other women of her day made significant contributions within their context of femininity, outside the bounds of feminism, carving out for themselves creative and above all influential careers.

Notes

[1] There is no biography of Maria Weston Chapman. A majority of antislavery literature deals little if at all with the remarkable accomplishments of her career. The work of Alma Lutz (*Crusade for Freedom*) and William and Jane Pease (*Bound with Them in Chains*), and Blanche Hersch (*Slavery of Sex*) treat Chapman.

[2] Letter of Maria Weston Chapman (MWC), n.d., n.a., Gay Collection, Columbia University Library.

[3] MWC, March 1853, Weston Collection, Boston Public Library.

[4] MWC to Estlin, March 1852, Estlin Collection, Boston Public Library.

[5] MWC, n.d., 1855, Weston Collections, Boston Public Library.

[6] MWC, n.d., 1852, Boston Public Library.

[7] MWC, March, 1853, Weston Collection, Boston Public Library.

[8] MWC, 8 March, 1873, Jay Collection, Columbia University Library.

[9] MWC, n.d., 1855, Weston Collection, Boston Public Library.

[10] MWC, n.d., n.a., Weston Collection, Boston Public Library.

[11] The trauma of the burning of Independence Hall during the convention had an effect on Chapman's mental state, in addition to her public speaking ordeal.

[12] Much of what is known about Chapman's political views is to be found in the remains of her correspondence with coeditor Gay. Chapman had the utmost respect for her colleague, not only for his journalistic abilities, but

also for his abolitionist commitment. Gay went on to edit the *New York Tribune* during the Civil War years, where his antislavery sympathies made him an effective propagandist for the abolitionist crusade. Gay, like Chapman, suffers from historical neglect despite the significance of his contributions and the availability of manuscripts.

[13]In a January 1841 letter to Garrison, Chapman requested 1,000 extra copies of the *Liberator* for distribution.

[14]Caroline Weston, 23 Feburary, n.a., Harriet Beecher Stowe Collection, Schlesinger Library, Radcliffe College.

[15]MWC quoted in Alma Lutz, *Crusade for Freedom: Women of the Anti-Slavery Movement*, 1968, p. 201.

[16]MWC, 8 Septemeber 1845, Gay Collection, Columbia University Library.

[17]MWC, n.d., n.a., Gay Collection, Columbia University Library.

[18]MWC to Estlin, n.d., n.a., Estlin Collection, Boston Public Library.

[19]MWC, March 1853, Weston Collection, Boston Public Library.

[20]MWC, n.d., n.a., Weston Collection, Boston Public Library.

[21]MWC, September 1852, Weston Collection, Boston Public Library.

[22]MWC to William Lloyd Garrison, 4 August 1843, William Lloyd Garrison Collection, Boston Public Library.

[23]MWC to Estlin, n.d., 1852, Estlin Collection, Boston Public Library.

[24]MWC to WLG, 4 August 1843, William Lloyd Garrison Collection, Boston Collection, Boston Public Library.

[25]WLG to MWC, quoted in W. P. and F. J. Garrison, *William Lloyd Garrison*, New York, 1885–1889, 3, p. 229.

[26]Deborah Weston to Anne Weston, 16 April, n.a., Weston Collection, Boston Public Library.

[27]WLG to MWC quoted in W. P. and F. J. Garrison, *op. cit.*, p. 229.

[28]MWC to Harriet Beecher Stowe, 1845, Stowe Collection, Schlesinger Library, Radcliffe College.

[29]Chapman's reaction is particularly insensitive. In spite of his "interference" with the tactics of the Boston abolitionist clique, it is reprehensible for Chapman to accuse Douglass of not having the "slightest interest" in antislavery.

[30]Frederick Douglass to MWC, 29 March 1846, Weston Collection, Boston Public Library.

[31]MWC, n.d., n.a., Weston Collection, Boston Public Library.

[32]MWC, n.d., 1855, Weston Collection, Boston Public Library.

[33]Although much of her criticism of Douglass is tinged with racism, it is notable that Chapman consistently endorsed the campaign to allow racial intermarriage in Massachusetts and she gave her unfailing support to black abolitionist Charles Redmond.

[34]Whittier quoted in Alma Lutz, *Crusade for Freedom*, 1968, p. 191.

[35]MWC, 13 September, n.a., Weston Collection, Boston Public Library.

[36]MWC, n.d., 1852, Weston Collection, Boston Public Library.

[37]Foster quoted in William and Jane Pease, *Bound with Them in Chains: A Biographical History of the Anti-Slavery Movement*, 1972, p. 56.

[38]MWC, n.d., 1852, Weston Collection, Boston Public Library.

[39]MWC, n.d., 1837, Weston Collection, Boston Public Library.

[40]*Ibid.*

[41]MWC, n.d., 1861, Weston Collection, Boston Public Library.

[42]MWC, 10 December 1853, Weston Collection, Boston Public Library.

[43]MWC, n.d., n.a., Weston Collection, Boston Public Library.

[44]MWC to WLG, n.d., n.a., William Lloyd Garrison Collection, Boston Public Library.

[45]MWC to WLG, n.d., 1861, William Lloyd Garrison Collection, Boston Public Library.

[46]MWC to WLG, n.d., 1863, William Lloyd Garrison Collection, Boston Public Library.

[47]MWC, n.d., n.a., Weston Collection, Boston Public Library.

[48]MWC, 13 September n.a., Weston Collection, Boston Public Library.

[49]MWC to Sydney Howard Gay, 7 November 1847, Gay Collection, Columbia University Library.

[50]MWC, February 1866, Weston Collection, Boston Public Library.

[51]MWC, *Right and Wrong*, 1838, 1, p. 12.

[52]15 April 1848, *Liberator*.

[53]20 March 1845, *National Anti-Slavery Standard.*

[54]See Barbara Welter, *Dimity Convictions: The American Woman in the Ninteeenth Century*, 1976.

[55]See Ann Douglas, *The Feminization of American Culture*, 1977.

[56]These upper-class women sought access to intellectual circles, armed with classical educations and democratic ideologies. They were the American equivalent of the blue-stockings in England. Their challenge to male domination was cosmetic rather than fundamental, but nonetheless significant. These women proposed tokenism not unlike W. E. B. Dubois' "talented tenth" strategy to undermine white male establishment a century later.

[57]See Marlene Stein Wortman, "Domesticating the Nineteenth Century City," *Prospects: An Annual of American Cultural Studies*, Vol. 3, Fall 1977, pp. 531–72.

[58]Linda Kerber, "The Republican Mother: Women and the Enlightenment, An American Perspective," *American Quarterly*, Vol. 27, Summer, 1976.

[59]Not all feminists during the nineteenth century embodied the "triple threat." But those men and women who joined together under the banner of women's rights are my primary concern. Although each and every individual might not have supported radical reform and a movement by its organizational nature restricts itself to a limited program of demands, the actual binding together for feminism is a defining principle. Collective action both reflects and initiates consciousness while undermining domination.

Catharine Beecher
(1800–1878)

Kathryn Kish Sklar

*Catharine Esther Beecher was born September 6, 1800, in East
Hampton, Long Island, New York, the eldest of the eight children of Lyman and Roxanna Foote Beecher. Her father, a Congregational preacher, was a leader of the Second Great Awakening,
the resurgence of religious revivals in the nineteenth century.
Briefly attending Sarah Pierce's school in Litchfield, Connecticut, Beecher began teaching in New London in 1821. She challenged the harsher doctrines of her father's Calvinism in two
publications:* Letters on the Difficulties of Religion *(1836) and*
Common Sense Applied to Religion *(1857). With her sister,
Mary, Beecher founded the Hartford Female Seminary in 1823.
In 1837 Beecher published* An Essay on Slavery and Abolition,
with Reference to the Duty of American Females, *chastising
noted abolitionist Angelina Grimké for leaving what Beecher
called "her appropriate sphere" in order to speak publicly
against slavery. Beecher believed women should only exert
themselves within their domestic spheres. However, as the following portrait demonstrates, Beecher advocated a kind of "domestic feminism" within the home. Beecher believed that
within the separate sphere of the household, middle-class
women could assert their domestic authority by making responsible decisions, thus gaining control over immediate circumstances. Moreover, she claimed that women at home had vital
social importance. On that basis, she worked for improvement
in women's education. After 1837 Beecher traveled incessantly,
lobbying, fundraising, and organizing for the training of women
as teachers, especially in the West. She wrote many books devoted to the practical education of women, supplementing her
extraordinarily influential* A Treatise on Domestic Economy for
the Use of Young Ladies at Home and School *(1841). An ex-*

panded version of her Treatise, *American Woman's Home (1869) was written in collaboration with her sister, author Harriet Beecher Stowe. Catharine Beecher died in Elmira, New York, in 1878.*

Catharine Beecher was primarily known in her own time for *A Treatise on Domestic Economy*, first published in 1841. Considered historically significant today, the *Treatise* is also a document of importance in the history of nineteenth-century feminism. Printed at the dawn of a new era in American publishing, Catharine's *Treatise* was among the first books to be distributed by the modern methods established between 1830 and 1860.[1] Reprinted annually from 1841 to 1856,[2] the *Treatise* enjoyed its hegemony in American domestic affairs during the same years in which book marketing became more responsive to popular demand and feminism flowered into a political movement.

Initially printed by a small Boston firm that distributed most of its publications locally over its own counter, the *Treatise* was purchased immediately by Harper and Brothers, who distributed it through the new system whereby publishers abandoned their own retail efforts and specialized in supplying a network of booksellers with volumes on consignment. Bookstores sprang up whenever urban populations were forming during this period. They served the regional hinterland as well as their own communities. During the 1840s and 1850s, Catharine's *Treatise* was carried by trains and boats to established provincial centers such as Hartford and Albany, as well as to newer cities like Rochester and Buffalo, and through the Ohio Valley to Cincinnati, Louisville, and St. Louis, and across the northern Great Lakes route to Cleveland, Detroit, and Milwaukee.[3]

This new system printed larger editions, distributed them more widely, and made possible the development of specialized reading constituencies, the largest of which was middle class and female. Although no exact measurement has been taken of the proportion of books and magazines aimed at female readers during the mid-nineteenth century, these readers and the women authors who addressed them were a well established feature of the American literary landscape by 1840. More than one-third of the American novels published before 1820 were written by women and it is well known that women dominated the literary marketplace by mid-century.[4] The times were therefore propitious for female authorship, and Catharine was one of hundreds of women who found domestic writing a profitable enterprise.

The biographical context in which the *Treatise* was written was not, however, nearly so promising as the literary one. If one were to graph the contours of Catharine Beecher's career from the time she founded the Hartford Female Seminary in 1823 until her quasi-retirement in the late 1850s, . . . he would note that the *Treatise* was written during the career nadir that followed her emigration with her father, Lyman, to Cincinnati in 1832 and the career low that preceded her national prominence in women's education during the 1850s. The West was more an arena of struggle than achievement for the Beecher family in the 1830s, and Catharine's experience was no exception.[5] Determined to increase her sphere of influence from the local parameters she had known at Hartford, she founded the Western Female Institute in Cincinnati in 1833, but she saved her own energies for prospective work in the larger national arena and refused to direct the school herself. Yet with the exception of her 1835 speech to the American Lyceum in New York on *The Education of Female Teachers*, her efforts to reach a national audience proved futile. By the time her local school failed for lack of enrollment in 1837, Catharine's career was foundering without an economic base or a support constituency.

In the spring of 1838, therefore, it was not surprising that she turned to the female literary constituency that her sister, Harriet, had already begun to tap as a lucrative source of self-support. Writing her friend, Lydia Sigourney, Catharine asked advice as to what magazines she should write for. Her purpose, she said, was "to make myself known, and as popular as I can with all classes of readers. I need not tell you that this may be aimed at without any craving for fame or notoriety, but as one means of increasing the sphere of usefulness."[6]

Yet Catharine Beecher's forays into the literary arena and away from her field of education were less successful than Harriet's example had led her to hope, and during that year she earned only one-tenth what Harriet did—far from enough to relieve her financial dependence on Lyman and worlds away from the substantial income that had allowed her to rent her own house at Hartford a decade earlier.

In a mood of personal pessimism and professional disarray, Catharine consoled herself during 1839 with technical religious writings and with the belief that "good must be done for its own sake and not for any gain or profit that may come from it."[7] In that year and the next, during which she wrote *A Treatise on Domestic Economy*, Catharine came close to the role occupied by her aunt, Esther Beecher—that is, an unmarried female dependent who contributed her labor to the household in exchange for room and board. It was from this dead end in her career that Catharine produced the work establishing her national reputation and her historical significance.

Catharine's relative failure to support herself during these years must have made her admire all the more Harriet's ability to earn autonomous space for herself within her own household. This achievement was accomplished even though Harriet bore three children during her first two years of marriage. Harriet bore twins nine months after she married Calvin Stowe, and she was pregnant again a few months afterwards. Catharine described Harriet's plight to their sister, Mary Beecher Perkins, in 1837.

> Harriet has one baby put out for the winter, the other at home, and number three will be here the middle of January. Poor thing, she bears up wonderfully well, and I hope will live through this first tug of matrimonial warfare, and then she says she shall not have any more *children, she knows for certain* for one while. Though how she found this out I cannot say, but she seems quite confident about it.[8]

Harriet's "matrimonial warfare" was, it seems, only part of her effort to control the circumstances of her life as a married woman rather than be controlled by them. In a letter to Mary Dutton in 1838 Harriet described her new domestic regime.

> I have about three hours per day in writing, and if you see my name coming out everywhere you may be sure of one thing, that I *do it for the pay.* I have determined not to be a mere domestic slave without even the leisure to excel in my duties. I mean to have money enough to have my house kept in the best manner and yet to have time for reflection and that preparation for the education of my children which every mother needs. I have every prospect of succeeding in this plan.[9]

Harriet's determination "not to be a mere domestic slave" and her successful implementation of a systematic plan to avoid sinking to such a condition makes her the unsung heroine of Catharine's *Treatise*. For Catharine's book was written for women with Harriet's double view of the potential of the nineteenth-century domestic arena: that it could increase as well as decrease the autonomy women experienced within it.

Catharine's *Treatise* was a response to the circumstances in which mid-nineteenth-century middle class American women found themselves. The transfer of economic production from family-sized units to units of larger scale profoundly disrupted traditional patterns of domestic life. Children, whose labor had once been necessary to sustain the family economy, now served no such direct economic purpose. Native white fertility rates fell throughout the nineteenth century, reflecting the demographic transition from high birth and death rates to low birth and death rates that every industrializing European nation was experiencing during this time. Even as motherhood was praised as life's most desirable state, more women were experiencing fewer births than ever before, and the number of spinsters tripled.[10] With this long term decline in fertility came a more rapid decline in household-made goods. By 1860 the ease with which a woman could contribute to her family's support while raising children at the same time was considerably reduced compared to 1800 when much of the gross national product was produced in family units.[11] The dispersion of the traditional work of the household outward into specialized work arenas—whether in Lowell mills or in common schools—created new work for single women outside the home, but this shift cast the work status of married women within the home into doubt. Housewives were left with a collection of preindustrial tasks and skills seemingly disassociated from the modern world around them.

Catharine's response to this historical situation was to emphasize the modernity of women's domestic responsibilities. She treated motherhood and childbearing as the production of the new democracy's most valued commodity—the good citizen. She described the entirety of women's work within the household in industrial terms. She emphasized the need for women as individuals to exercise responsible decision-making power over the circumstances of their lives. Concerned throughout the *Treatise* with enhancing both the theoretical and practical value of women's work, Catharine's goal was to link the female work sphere in a positive way with the currents transforming it. As such, her book was an ideological as well as a practical achievement. The function of ideology, Clifford Geertz has written, is to "make an autonomous politics possible by providing the authoritative concepts that render it meaningful, the suasive images by means of which it can be sensibly grasped."[12]

Catharine Beecher's *Treatise* created an autonomous politics through the use of concepts and images related to democracy and to modern work forms. It will be seen that this politics, though based in the home and founded on motherhood, was both behaviorally and conceptually congenial to nineteenth-century feminism because it promoted autonomous or self-motivated behavior. Catharine analyzed the domestic arena so as to make clear its internal constraints and its social resources, creating a vocabulary and a methodology by which nineteenth-century women could assess their needs and assert their interests.

No concept was more central to the *Treatise* than that of democracy. The first chapter, entitled "The Peculiar Responsibilities of American Women," was a paean to the potential of democratic individualism—with a warning that only women could make it work.

> The success of democratic institutions, as is conceded by all, depends upon the intellectual and moral character of the mass of the people. If they are intelligent and virtuous, democracy is a blessing; but if they are ignorant and wicked, it is only a curse. . . . It is equally conceded, that the formation of the moral and intellectual character of the young is committed mainly to the female hand.[13]

Describing traditional female responsibilities as political or social responsibilities, Catharine depicted women as an elite[14] who had special access to moral resources because they themselves were engaged in the production of a valuable resource—namely, the "character of the mass of the people."

Her book was an effort to give women a sense of their social mission and to describe appropriate means for carrying it out. Women needed a proper sense of mission, Catharine believed, in order to perform their work successfully.

> The mind is so made, as to be elevated and cheered by a sense of far-reaching influence and usefulness. A woman, who feels that she is a cipher, and that it makes little difference how she performs her duties, has far less to sustain and invigorate her, than one, who truly estimates the importance of her station.[15]

The dramatic tension of Catharine's *Treatise* arose from the contrast she drew between the importance of work "committed mainly to the female hand" and the lack of resources available to most women for the successful performance of their work. The value and effectiveness of women's lives were seriously undermined, Catharine said, because, unlike men, women received no specialized training for their work. Such training was needed, she implied, because the modern world confronted women with experience incongruent with traditional patterns of behavior and belief. What once seemed inevitable now was problematic. As Catharine wrote: "Many a reflecting young woman is looking to her future prospects, with very different feelings and hopes from those which Providence designed."[16] She dramatized the distance modern society had placed between biological design and actual experience with vivid personal testimony.

> The writer has repeatedly heard mothers say, that they had wept tears of bitterness over their infant daughters, at the thought of the sufferings which they were destined to undergo; while they cherished the decided wish, that these daughters should never marry.[17]

Catharine's answer to these grave circumstances was to advise women to approach the female life cycle as a work cycle and prepare for it as a man would prepare for a vocation. She urged her readers to "systematize" as much of domestic life as possible and gain control of their lives by gaining control of their work. To begin a system, she suggested that her readers compose a list of all their "religious, intellectual, social, and domestic" duties[18] and use time as the basic standard by which they measured their priorities.

> Let a calculation be made, whether there be time enough, in the day or the week, for all these duties. If there be not, let the least important be sticken from the list, as not being duties, and which must be omitted.[19]

This assessment of female responsibilities was a long way from traditional prescriptions. It was pragmatic rather than dogmatic, time-oriented rather than task-oriented. Above all, it was individuated and designed to enhance autonomous female decision-making in the domestic arena. For Catharine Beecher the most important fact in a woman's life was not whether she was moral or pious but whether she controlled her life circumstances or they controlled her. This distinction was basic to her *Treatise.*

> Without attempting any such systematic employment of time, and carrying it out, so far as they can control circumstances, most women are rather driven along, by the daily occurrences of life, so that, instead of being the intelligent regulators of their own time, they are the mere sport of circumstances. There is nothing, which so distinctly marks the difference between weak and strong minds, as the fact, whether they control circumstances, or circumstances control them.[20]

Not passive submission to their biological identity, nor fetching dependency on their husbands, but active control of their immediate life circumstances was the model Catharine held out to her readers.

Catharine collected the data for her *Treatise* from the extensive travels that replaced her steady employment during the 1830s. Traveling for her health, for pleasure, and for the cause of education, she routinely inquired about local household practices. The breadth of her inquiry and her sharp eye for detail were recorded by Edward King when she visited his family in Chillicothe in 1835. "She asked more questions than one could answer in a day," King wrote to his daughter.

> Why the fields were so square! Why there were not better houses! Why the current ran where it did! Whose property was this and that! She asked innumerable questions about the house, how long it had

been built, why the walls were so thick, when everybody slept, why Lizzy slept in that room, whether mother managed her farm, whether she gave orders to the men, whether labor was difficult to procure, what was the price of help, why this fence was built and that.[21]

Catharine incorporated the conclusions drawn from such inquiries into thirty-seven chapters of about eleven pages each. Each chapter was laced with examples of real life experience, making her book more intimate and immediate than it would otherwise have been and providing behavioral evidence to show that her ideas were workable. Four of her chapters were devoted to theoretical considerations of women's work. Seven major chapters were devoted to health, five to interpersonal topics such as "On Preservation of a Good Temper in a Housekeeper," and four to explicitly economic considerations such as that "On Habits of System and Order." Only three were devoted to the care of the dependent young and the ill. Nearly half the book, seventeen chapters, was devoted to house construction, furnishing, and grounds, together with specific receipts and designs. Whatever the topic, "systematization" was the answer and wherever true system was employed, autonomous female responsibility was expanded.

In her chapter "On Economy of Time and Expenses," for example, after establishing the general principle that "care be taken to know the amount of income and of current expenses, so that the proper relative proportion be preserved,"[22] Catharine acknowledged that many women could not balance income with expenditures because their husbands were "business-men" who had trouble predicting their incomes, or because the expenses of the family were "more under the control of the man than of the woman."[23] Asserting, nevertheless, that "every woman is bound to do as much as is in her power, to accomplish a systematic mode of expenditure, and the regulation of it by Christian principles,"[24] Catharine related several anecdotes drawn from real life showing how women could effectively control their household finances.

> [One woman] whose husband is engaged in a business, which he thinks makes it impossible for him to know what his yearly income will be, took this method. She kept an account of all her disbursements, for one year. This she submitted to her husband, and obtained his consent, that the same sum should be under her control, the coming year, for similar purposes, with the understanding, that she might modify future apportionments, in any way her judgement and conscience might approve.[25]

In this case, as in others throughout the *Treatise*, Catharine used real life experience to show that true systematization and the assertion of female control went hand in hand.

In keeping with her view of domestic life as an arena of work and responsibility for women, Catharine persistently discredited unproductive leisure. Women should "subtract from [their] domestic employments, all the time, given to pursuits which are of no use, except as they gratify a taste for ornament,"[26] she wrote. Intellectual improvement, benevolent activity, and religious reflection all had a place within Catharine's work system, but unproductive leisured activities such as "dressing, visiting, evening parties, and stimulating amusements"[27] came in for severe criticism as unhealthy, selfish, and ultimately degrading. When women of the wealthier classes "are called to the responsibilities and trials of domestic life, their constitution fails, and their whole existence is rendered a burden,"[28] Catharine wrote. She attributed this widespread malaise to insufficient familiarity with manual labor. Modern attitudes no longer held labor to be "the badge of a lower class,"[29] Catharine said, and she recommended that mothers of all classes "make it their first aim to secure a strong and healthful constitution for their daughters, by active domestic employments."[30]

Discrediting the unproductive use of the leisure that middle class women increasingly found at their disposal, Catharine also discouraged its traditional corollary: the employment of domestic servants. "Awkward," "ignorant," and "careless" were her typical characterizations of hired domestic labor, although she encouraged her readers to pay their servants a living wage and to sympathize with their life circumstances.[31]

Treating the domestic sphere as a specialized segment of modern society, Catharine rejected the notion that women were naturally equipped to perform their complex duties. Skills and training were as necessary for them as for men. To meet this need she advocated the creation of endowed institutions of learning for women, and she urged her readers to support this cause.

Are not the most responsible of all duties committed to the charge of woman? Is it not her profession to take care of mind, body, and soul? and that, too, at the most critical of all periods of existence? And is it not as much a matter of public concern, that she should be properly qualified for her duties, as that ministers, lawyers, and physicians, should be prepared for theirs? And is it not as important, to endow institutions which shall make a superior education accessible to all classes,—for females, as for the other sex?[32]

Called by their society to serve others, Catharine concluded that women were first required to serve themselves through education—specifically through an education in the basics of independent decision-making. Since their duties as mothers and housekeepers required them to exercise "quickness of perception, steadiness of purpose, regularity of system, and perseverence in action," Catharine urged that women be trained in "the formation of habits of investigation, of correct reasoning, of persevering attention, of regular system, of accurate analysis, and of vigorous mental action."[33] Catharine's call for a superior education for females of all classes was the keystone to her domestic politics. Because women's work was equal in value to men's, women had a right to equal access to the educational resources of their society. Catharine's fullest statement of her domestic politics came thirty years after her *Treatise*, but it deserves full quotation here as an extension of the ideas contained in the *Treatise*.

> We agree . . . that women's happiness and usefulness are equal in value to those of man's, and, consequently, that, she has a right to equal advantages for securing them. We agree also that woman, even in our own age and country, has never been allowed such equal advantages, and that multiplied wrongs and suffering have resulted from this injustice. Finally, we agree that it is the right and the duty of every woman to employ the power of organization and agitation, in order to gain those advantages which are given to the one sex, and unjustly withheld from the other.[34]

Although based on motherhood and located in the home, Catharine's domestic politics was designed to consolidate rather than erode the links between women and their society.

Catharine's politics did more than idealize the value of women's domestic responsibilities—it identified them as socially-derived, hence meriting commensurate social reward. The popularity of her *Treatise* has long been thought to lie in the fact that in it her readers found a formula for understanding their social context as well as their personal responsibilities, but the modern cast she gave to female responsibilities has not been fully appreciated for the modern potential it gave to female social participation. The importance of the close link Catharine established between female responsibilities and adequate means of carrying out these responsibilities can be seen in an anthropological essay written by William Graham Sumner in 1909.

> In all societies usages which were devised to cherish and pet women become restraints on their liberty and independence, for when they

are treated as unequal to the risks and tasks of life by men who take care of them, the next stage is that men treat them as inferior and contemptible and will not grant them dignity and respect. When they escape responsibility they lose liberty.[35]

For Catharine Beecher the definition of women's responsibilities led directly to an assertion of their "right to equal advantages." For her women were not passive bystanders, imprisoned in their biology, but social actors capable of independently assessing their own responsibilities and asserting their own rights.

What overall sense can be made of the domestic politics of Catharine's *Treatise* both with the development of her own thought and the development of nineteenth-century feminism? Within her own thought the *Treatise* constituted a dramatic break with the evangelical tradition that had informed her earlier writings on women. In *An Essay on Slavery and Abolitionism* (1837) she had argued against Angelina and Sarah Grimké's example of female activism by invoking divine law and its immutable deference to male authority.

It is the grand feature of the Divine economy, that there should be different stations of superiority and subordination, and it is impossible to annihilate this beneficent and immutable law . . . Heaven has appointed to one sex the superior, and to the other the subordinate station.[36]

Yet in her own life Catharine had found this "Divine economy" more restraining than liberating, and in her next breath she added an important loophole to it.

While woman holds a subordinate relation in society to the other sex, it is not because it was designed that her duties or her influence should be any the less important, or all-pervading.[37]

Sometime between 1837 and 1841, Catharine read Alexis de Tocqueville's *Democracy in America* and found there the principle that could extricate her from the confusion of a divinely decreed sexual hierarchy. In Tocqueville she found an alternative and more functional explanation for gender distinctions. She quoted him in her *Treatise*.

Americans have applied to the sexes the great principle of political economy, which governs the manufactories of our age, by carefully dividing the duties of man from those of woman, in order that the great work of society may be the better carried on.[38]

In his study, *The Division of Labor in Society*, Emile Durkheim said that the modern era had one categorical imperative: "*Make yourself usefully fulfill a determinate function.*"[39] Obeying this modern im-

perative in her *Treatise,* Catharine escaped the strictures of perennial female inferiority and thereby moved from the margin to the
mainstream of nineteenth-century feminism.

She published other volumes on domestic life, including her *Letters to the People on Health and Happiness* (1855) and her *American
Woman's Home* (1869), essentially an expansion of the *Treatise* but
with Harriet as co-author. Neither of these books was reprinted for
more than two years, whereas the *Treatise* was reissued annually for
a decade and a half. The proceeds from its sale supported the second
phase of Catharine's career during which she founded and directed
the American Woman's Educational Association and nurtured the
growth of educational institutions for women throughout the East
and West. She traveled widely during the 1840s and 1850s, and from
Boston to Burlington, Iowa, she was welcomed, in the words of the
Iowa State Gazette in 1848, as one "whose name has long since
become a household divinity."[40]

Catharine's reputation as a domestic commentator smoothed her
path as an educator, but the last year that the *Treatise* was reprinted
was also her last year of active work in behalf of women's education.
In 1857 she returned once again to religious writings, seeking to
clarify further her place in the Beecher theological pantheon.

It makes a certain amount of sense that American women in the
antebellum period should have taken their domestic directives from a
woman not herself embroiled in the day-to-day reality of family life.
Her view from the sidelines gave her greater perspective on the historical forces transforming the family and, thus, on the effect of those
transformations on women. Catharine's contribution to these transformations was to idealize not the ascriptive qualities of submission,
delicacy, and weakness that had been attributed to women by those,
who in Sumner's words, wished "to cherish and pet" them but to
idealize the achieved qualities of "correct reasoning," "accurate
analysis," and "vigorous mental action"—exactly those qualities she
herself exercised as a single woman seeking to support herself.

A considerable amount of excellent scholarship has recently been
devoted to nineteenth-century feminism, and its findings uphold
Aileen Kraditor's 1968 definition of feminism as essentially the assertion of female autonomy.

> What the feminists have wanted has added up to something more
> fundamental than any specific set of rights or the sum total of all the
> rights men have had. This fundamental something can perhaps be
> designated by the term "autonomy." Whether a feminist's demand
> has been for all the rights men have had, or for some but not all the
> rights men have had, or for some men have *not* had, the grievance

behind the demand has always seemed to be that women have been regarded not as people but as female relatives of people.[41]

The basic message of Catharine Beecher's *Treatise* is that women should regard themselves as people as well as "female relatives of people"—as people who try to assert autonomous control over their immediate life circumstances and act as self-motivating individuals.

A hypothesis about nineteenth-century feminism may account for the autonomous politics seen in Catharine Beecher's *Treatise*. This hypothesis proposes that nineteenth-century feminism continues along a spectrum called the assertion of female autonomy. This spectrum begins with the assertion of female sexual autonomy and ends with the assertion of female civil autonomy. In between there is room for a wide variety of feminist expressions, one of which might be called the assertion of female domestic autonomy. Harriet Beecher Stowe, Catharine Beecher, and Isabella Beecher Hooker[42] seem to exemplify three variations of feminist expression. The hypothesis further proposes that these three merge into and grow out of one another, that they constitute a continuum rather than divergent paths.

To test this hypothesis one must return to the letter that Catharine wrote to Mary about Harriet in 1838. There Harriet vowed "not [to] have any more *children, . . . for certain* for one while." How general was such a vow among Harriet's contemporaries and, thus, among the readers of Catharine's *Treatise*? How was such a vow implemented? It is by pursuing these questions that one can see even more clearly why Catharine's *Treatise* deserves a place in the history of nineteenth-century feminism.

Although Catharine expressed surprise at Harriet's vow and pretended ignorance as to the means Harriet might use in implementing it, recent studies, particularly Daniel Scott Smith's 1972 article, "Family Limitation, Sexual Control, and Domestic Feminism in Victorian America," have shown that nineteenth-century sexual ideas facilitated the female control of family planning that Harriet's remarks implied.[43] Caught in the grips of the demographic transition from high birth and death rates to low birth and death rates, Victorian society valued the control and limitations of sexuality and, seeing women as the best representatives of such a policy, gave them considerable social and ideological support for asserting control over their own bodies and limiting their husband's traditional right of sexual access. Elizabeth Cady Stanton and other suffragists attacked the legal base of this traditional right, but most women, like Harriet Beecher Stowe, fought this battle in the domestic rather than the public arena. The sexual ideas that accompanied the nineteenth-century fertility decline meant that the biological imperatives of the past were broken in a climate that encouraged the exercise of female sexual autonomy. Thus behavior and ideology conspired to promote an arena of female autonomy that did not previously exist. From 1830 and 1880 the number of children under five years of age per one thousand women of childbearing age declined by a third.[44] Adopting Smith's hypothesis that "the wife significantly controlled family planning in the 19th century,"[45] one can conclude that Harriet's vow of 1838 was typical of a large number of her contemporaries.

The way Harriet implemented this vow was also typical. Quantitative studies have shown that the American fertility decline, like fertility decline elsewhere, was achieved by two means: first, by longer intervals between births during the early and middle childbearing years; and second, by a dramatic reduction of births in the late childbearing years.[46] Harriet's experience followed this pattern. While she bore three children during the first two years of her marriage, she bore only two during the next five years and then maintained a six-year interval between the birth of her fifth and sixth children. Roxana Beecher, in contrast to her daughter, did not exhibit such fertility control and bore children regularly every other year until her death in 1816 at the age of forty-one. Thus Harriet, like most nineteeth-century women did effectively limit her fertility, and with increasing maturity, she became increasingly successful at it.

Such a resolve did not inevitably lead Harriet or her contemporaries into gradually greater personal autonomy but, frequently, to its contrary—invalidism. Since the only reliable contraceptive techniques—coitus interruptus and abstinence—involved direct intervention with sexual behavior and, thus, the overt exercise of personal choice, such methods overtly violated the traditional and still strongly held belief that family limitation was ungodly and unnatural. By adopting invalidism rather than autonomy as a strategy for managing the dilemmas posed by the nineteenth-century female life cycle, women could justify their desire for sexual abstinence without seeming to have made a personal choice in the matter. Harriet adopted this strategy when she spent months at a time away from her husband, Calvin, at the Brattleboro Water Cure in the mid-1840s.

In her *Treatise* Catharine addressed the strategy of invalidism as though it were her primary behavioral and ideological opponent. Her volume was filled with the personal testimony of those whose constitutions failed when they were "called to the responsibilities and trials of domestic life," and whose whole lives were subsequently rendered a burden to themselves and their families. She acknowledged invalidism as a characteristic shared to some extent by almost all middle class women.

> A perfectly healthy woman, especially a perfectly healthy mother is so unfrequent in some of the wealthier classes, that those who are so may be regarded as the exceptions, and not as the general rule.[47]

Although she did not hint at the conscious or self-motivated origin of this general ill health, demographic evidence does show that native born women were growing more healthy rather than less healthy during the nineteenth century. The percentage of women who had children but died before the age of fifty-five decreased from twelve percent in 1830 to eight percent in 1880.[48] Although this topic has not been studied systematically, it does seem as though this slight decrease in female mortality during and after the childbearing years of the life cycle was the result of the sharp decrease in contemporary fertility rates, which fell by a third from 1830 to 1880. For many nineteenth-century women, therefore, invalidism may paradoxically have been a means by which they lived longer lives and enjoyed good health. An unwell woman was a sexually abstemious woman.

Catharine addressed women who pursued this strategy sympathetically but firmly. Not challenging the traditional premise on which invalidism was based—that the female constitution was by nature weak and flawed—she, nevertheless, urged her readers to see their health as susceptible to the same kind of control they could exercise over other aspects of their domestic life. Complete with anatomical drawings, the *Treatise* presented a full discussion of most of the body's physiological processes.

> There is no really efficacious mode of preparing a woman to take a *rational* care of the health of a family, except by communicating that knowledge, in regard to the construction of the body, and the laws of health, which is the basis of the medical profession.[49]

Her many chapters on health urged women to discard fashionable practices that contributed to their enfeeblement—tightly laced corsets and the lack of physical exercise. She urged women to choose health, to choose to exercise personal choice in their lives, and to move from forms of dependency to forms of self-assertion as a life strategy. For women posed with the choice between continued dependency through invalidism or overt assertion of their decision-making power over their own lives, the *Treatise* offered a total strategy for autonomous growth, a behavioral blueprint and ideological support for their self-determination in the domestic arena. This is the importance of her *Treatise*, and this is the reason it belongs on the scale of nineteenth-century feminism somewhere in between the assertion of sexual autonomy and the assertion of civil autonomy.

Harriet Beecher Stowe, Catharine Beecher, and Isabella Beecher Hooker all sought in various ways to enlarge the arena in which they acted as self-determining agents. Each of these daughters of Lyman Beecher also explored themes in her own writing relating to domestic life and female influence. Anne Farnam has shown how Isabella moved from the assertion of domestic autonomy to the assertion of civil autonomy.[50] Catharine Beecher aided nineteenth-century women toward autonomous personal growth. Her version of domesticity can be seen as congruent with, not in opposition to, the basic thrust of nineteenth-century feminism.

Notes

[1] W. S. Tryon, "Book Distribution in Mid-Nineteenth Century America," *Papers of the Bibliographic Society of America*, Vol. 41 (3rd Quarter, 1947), pp. 210–230.

[2] For a full discussion of the printing history of *A Treatise on Domestic Economy* see Kathryn Kish Sklar, *Catharine Beecher: A Study in American Domesticity* (New Haven: Yale University Press, 1973), p. 305.

[3] "Book Distribution," p. 219.

[4] For the best discussion of the domestic novel and female authors see Herbert Ross Brown, *The Sentimental Novel in America, 1789–1860* (Durham: Duke University Press, 1940), pp. 281–322. See also Carl Bode, *The Anatomy of American Popular Culture, 1840–1861* (Berkeley: University of California Press, 1959), pp. 169–188.

[5] For a discussion of Catharine Beecher's experience in Cincinnati in the 1830s see *Catharine Beecher*, pp. 107–150.

[6] Letter, Catharine Beecher to Lydia Huntley Sigourney, 1838 April 24, The Connecticut Historical Society, Hartford.

[7] Letter, Catharine Beecher to Mary Dutton, 1839 February 13, Mary Dutton—Beecher Letters, Yale University, New Haven.

[8] Letter, Catharine Beecher to Mary Beecher Perkins, 1837 Fall, Beecher—Stowe Collection, Radcliffe College, Cambridge.

[9] Letter, Harriet Beecher Stowe to Mary Dutton, 1838 December 13, Mary Dutton—Beecher Letters, Yale University, New Haven.

[10] Wilson H. Grabill, Clyde V. Kiser, and Pascal K. Whelpton, "A Long View," *The American Family in Social-Historical Perspective*, ed. Michael Gordon (New York: St. Martin's Press, 1937), pp. 374–396, especially p. 387.

[11]Rolla M. Tryon, *Household Manufacturers in the United States, 1640–1860: A Study in Industrial History* (Chicago: University of Chicago Press, 1917), pp. 242–303.

[12]Clifford Geertz, "Ideology as a Cultural System," *Ideology and Its Discontents,* ed. David Apter (New York: Free Press of Glencoe, 1964), p. 63. For a discussion of autonomous politics see pp. 47–75.

[13]Catharine Beecher, *A Treatise on Domestic Economy,* rev. ed. (Boston: Thomas H. Webb & Co., 1842), pp. 36–37.

[14]For a discussion of strategic elites see Suzanne Keller, *Beyond the Ruling Class: Strategic Elites in Modern Society* (New York: Random House, 1963), pp. 30–38, 134–145.

[15]*Treatise,* pp. 150–151.

[16]*Treatise,* p. 43.

[17]*Treatise,* pp. 42–43.

[18]*Treatise,* pp. 157–158.

[19]*Treatise,* p. 166.

[20]*Treatise,* p. 160.

[21]Letter, Edward King to Sarah King, 1834 December 24, King Family Papers, Cincinnati Historical Society, Cincinnati.

[22]*Treatise,* p. 186.

[23]*Treatise,* p. 186.

[24]*Treatise,* p. 186.

[25]*Treatise,* p. 187.

[26]*Treatise,* p. 161.

[27]*Treatise,* p. 45.

[28]*Treatise,* p. 42.

[29]*Treatise,* p. 147.

[30]*Treatise,* p. 50.

[31]*Treatise,* pp. 204–208.

[32]*Treatise,* p. 52.

[33]*Treatise,* p. 56.

[34]Catharine Beecher, *Woman's Profession as Mother and Educator, with Views in Opposition to Woman Suffrage* (Philadelphia: Geo. Maclean, 1872), p. 4.

[35]William Graham Sumner, "The Status of Women," *War and Other Essays,* ed. Albert Keller (New York: AMS Press, 1970), p. 71. Reprint of 1911 original.

[36]Catharine Beecher, *An Essay on Slavery and Abolitionism, with Reference to the Duty of American Females* (Philadelphia: Henry Perkins, 1837), pp. 98–99.

[37]*An Essay on Slavery,* pp. 99–100.

[38]*Treatise*, p. 28.

[39]Emile Durkheim, *The Division of Labor in Society* (New York: The Macmillan Co., 1933), p. 43.

[40]*Iowa State Gazette*, March 29, 1848.

[41]Aileen Kraditor, ed., *Up from the Pedestal: Selected Writings in the History of American Feminism* (New York: Quadrangle Books, 1968), p. 8.

[42]See Anne Farnam, "Woman Suffrage as an Alternative to the Beecher Ministry," *Portraits of a Nineteenth-Century Family*, eds. Earl A. French and Diana Royce (Hartford: The Stowe-Day Foundation, 1976).

[43]Daniel Scott Smith, "Family Limitation, Sexual Control, and Domestic Feminism in Victorian America," *Feminist Studies*, Vol. I, Nos. 3–4 (Winter–Spring, 1973), p. 48.

[44]"A Long View," p. 384.

[45]"Family Limitation," p. 48.

[46]For a study of this pattern in one New England community from its origins to the mid-eighteenth century see Daniel Scott Smith, "Change in American Family Structure before the Demographic Transition: The Case of Hingham, Massachusetts" (Unpublished paper presented to the American Society for Ethnohistory, October, 1972), p. 3.

[47]*Treatise*, p. 48.

[48]Peter Uhlenberg, "A Study of Cohort Life Cycles: Cohorts of Native Born Massachusetts Women, 1830–1920," *Population Studies*, Vol. 23 (1969), pp. 407–420.

[49]*Treatise*, p. 69.

[50]See "Woman Suffrage as an Alternative to the Beecher Ministry."

Margaret Fuller

(1810–1850)

Bell Gale Chevigny

Margaret Fuller was born on May 23rd, 1810, in Cambridgeport, Massachusetts, to Mary Crane Fuller and Timothy Fuller. Fuller attended Miss Prescott's school in Groton and then Mr. Perkins's school in Cambridge. In 1839 she translated Johann P. Eckermann's Conversation with Goethe. *By that time Fuller had left home, supporting herself by teaching. Between 1840 and 1842 Fuller edited the radically innovative magazine the* Dial, *with Ralph Waldo Emerson. She continued to write criticism for the* New York Tribune, *moving to New York for that purpose in 1844. Fuller published* Summer on the Lakes *that year, recording a visit she had made to the West in 1843. In 1845 she published* Woman in the Nineteenth Century. *Fuller had long been immersed in reform, involved in the Brook Farm communal experiment and, while in New York, visiting and writing about Sing Sing and Blackwell's Island prisons. Fuller's last book was* Papers on Literature and Art *(1846). That year the* Tribune *sent Fuller to Europe as its foreign correspondent. In Rome, Fuller became the lover of Giovanni Angelo, Marchese d'Ossoli, and in September, 1848, had a son by him. They may have been married the following year. Fuller was, with Ossoli, an active participant in the Italian revolution. They became refugees when Rome fell in 1849. In Florence she worked on her history of the brief Roman republic. Fuller, Ossoli, and their child were drowned July 19, 1850, in a storm off Fire Island, New York, as she returned to publish her book in America.*

After Margaret Fuller's death, the poet Elizabeth Barrett Browning wrote of her friend, "If I wished anyone to do her justice, I should say 'Never read what she has written.' " And although Ralph Waldo Emerson, a great admirer, judged her conversation "the most entertaining in America," he also said, "her pen was a non-conductor." Countless others testify that Fuller's writing never matched the vividness of her presence and, above all, her life story.*

Certainly the barest recitation of the facts of her remarkable life command attention. Reared in the intellectually stimulating climate of Massachusetts at the turn of the nineteenth century, Fuller received a remarkable upbringing. From the age of six, she was tutored so rigorously by her father that, by her teen years, she could match wits with the brightest men at Harvard. She is supposed to have said, "I now know all the people worth knowing in America, and I find no intellect comparable to my own." She was no beauty, but her conversation was so clever and eloquent that her plainness was forgotten. A plan to go to Europe at age twenty-five was deferred for eleven years by family demands placed upon her by her father's death. Fuller was an intimate of the transcendentalists, the community of utopian literary figures including Ralph Waldo Emerson, Henry David Thoreau, and William Henry Channing, in New England. She edited their journal, the *Dial*, and taught at an experimental academy run by fellow transcendentalist Bronson Alcott, a member of the literary family from Concord, Massachusetts.

Each winter from 1839 to 1844 Fuller offered "conversations" for the leading women of Boston, a series of meetings in which the group explored intellectual issues within a broad range of topics. In 1845 she published *Woman in the Nineteenth Century,* one of the first American texts to examine the condition of women's lives. A book of her travels in the West, *Summer on the Lakes in 1843* (1844), won her a position as the first female journalist for a major newspaper—Horace Greeley's *New York Tribune.* She produced articles on social questions and a body of literary criticism that in her time was rivaled only by that of Edgar Allen Poe. A collection of these articles, *Papers on Literature and Art,* was issued in 1846. She went on assignment to Europe and became involved in literary and radical political circles, earning fame as a war correspondent when the revolutions of 1848 broke out. In Rome, she secretly became the lover of an Italian revolutionary, Giovanni Angelo Ossoli, with whom she bore a child. She remained in Rome for the brief days of the Roman republic and directed a hospital when the French held the city in siege. After the fall of Rome, she claimed that she was married to Ossoli, but offered no details or documentation. She removed to Florence with her family and prepared a book on the Italian revolution.

Her political radicalism made Elizabeth Barrett Browning, her confidante in Florence, call her "an out and out Red" and warn that her book was drenched in "the blood colours of Socialistic views, which would have drawn the wolves on her . . . both in England and America." In 1850, when she returned to America to promote her book, "the wolves" were cheated by the shipwreck that took her life—and that of Ossoli and their child—within sight of the American shore. Her great friend Henry David Thoreau spent days on Fire Island off the coast of New York's Long Island searching for her body and her manuscript—but neither were recovered. The cutting short of such a dramatic and enigmatic life has helped to keep her legend alive—tantalizing, infuriating, and elusive.

From our twentieth-century perspective, it is tempting to see Fuller as a woman of the nineteenth century nurturing a modern woman within. Such an approach helps us to analyze her problematic writing. This modern woman, wary of being trapped by the conventional language of her day, only intermittently sought expression in Fuller's life and writings. Fuller's writing strained toward a future, a transformed society, a culture that would mirror and validate her reality as nineteenth-century America could not do. Her failures were marked by romantic rhetoric, or an outlandish jargon of her own. Sometimes she saw lucidly that the language of modern feeling had to be invented and that the deep cultural change must accompany such speech. Increasingly, as she encountered such change in her last years, she found words—and her writing became easy, eloquent, and forceful.

More useful to us than Elizabeth Barrett Browning's warning is Poe's observation: "Her acts are bookish and her books are less thoughts than acts." It is interesting to read her life and work as if they formed a single text. Although Fuller's literary criticism was her most praised work within her lifetime, we now profit most from the critical light her life and work cast on the situation of American women and on the underlying social assumptions of her time.

Alexis de Tocqueville saw better than any American the unique position of women within this new democratic nation. Visiting the United States in the 1830s, Tocqueville noted that, as a "puritanical people and a commercial nation," Americans had a double motive for binding women in conventional marriages: ensuring the purity of their morals and securing order and prosperity in the home. But as a democratic people, placing high value on individual independence, Americans preferred not to repress woman's passions but rather to trust her to restrain herself, by placing "more reliance . . . on the free vigor of her will," by arming her with reason as well as with virtue.

So reared, nineteenth-century unmarried American women revealed a freedom of mind and action unmatched in Europe. But as wives, they were more submissive, dependent, dutiful, and conformist than their European counterparts. What wrought this change? Tocqueville believed it was the young American women themselves, who, in the culminating exercise of their virtue, reason, and free will, chose marriage. Tocqueville further noted that American women "attach a sort of pride to the voluntary surrender of their own will, and make it their boast to bend themselves to the yoke, not to shake it off."

Fuller, however, was one of many American women who sought to continue this youthful freedom of mind in their adult lives. As Tocqueville showed, the religious and economic objectives which defined the nation defined the American woman as a creature destined for marriage and fulfilled and useful only in the family circle. To conceive of women differently was tantamount to challenging the assumptions on which the nation was built. Ultimately, Fuller did this while living in Italy, implicitly challenging Puritanical assumptions by her sexual behavior, and explicitly questioning the economic assumptions and especially their social, and political corollaries through her writing.

Fuller's path to the understanding of herself and fulfillment of her vocation that she gained while living abroad was paved by her willingness to be considered a freak in America. According to Poe, humanity is divided into three classes: men, women, and Margaret Fuller. As others did, she saw herself as a hybrid, a union of two usually exclusive tendencies: more often than not, these tendencies were labeled "masculine" and "feminine."

By their natures, Fuller's parents reinforced American sexual stereotypes, and by their method of rearing her, they contributed to her sense of being hopelessly divided between these stereotypes. Her mother, Margaret Crane Fuller, seems to have followed without effort the model of the "true woman" esteemed at the time. As a teenaged schoolteacher she could keep rough boys in line, but as a mature woman she submitted serenely to her husband's domination, and patiently endured illness and the bearing of nine children, two of whom died in infancy.

The earliest American Fullers had arrived in Massachusetts in 1629. Individuality, and strong and even controversial, behavior seem to be the paternal legacy. Her father, Timothy Fuller, served two terms in Congress before becoming Speaker of the Massachusetts House. Something of a renegade, he opposed the expatriation of the Seminoles and the Missouri Compromise, remaining a staunch supporter of John Quincy Adams despite Adams's declining popularity. Fuller's political discouragement drove him back into the country to pursue farming as his father before him had done.

At the age of thirty, Margaret Fuller wrote an autobiographical romance, in which she gave an ideal account of her parents that connects her mother with physical nature, emotionalism, spirituality, and idealism, and her father with the social world, intellectual discipline, and practicality. The usual practice of the daughter following her mother's role was distorted in Fuller's case by her father's enormous influence on her and her mother's unusually retiring role in her life. Spurred on by his daughter's precocity, Timothy Fuller initiated an unusual and rigorous program of classical education when she was six. Quizzing her in Latin and English grammar until long past her bedtime, he rejected apology, hesitation, or qualification in her performance, effectively cutting her off from prevailing styles of female discourse. Eventually realizing the cost of his one-sided approach, Fuller urged his daughter to be less bold in speech, less bookish, and more concerned with manners. It was too late: by age twelve, his daughter had resolved to be "bright and ugly."

Fuller later wrote that her father's odd and exacting education whetted her appetite for heroic action and for meeting the challenges of the world with a disciplined will—values she associated with the ancient Romans. "I kept their statues as belonging to the hall of my ancestors, and loved to conquer obstacles, and fed my youth and strength for their sake," she wrote, as if a New England girl might simply grow into a Roman hero. On the negative side, she felt her father's nocturnal drills contributed to her nightmares as a child and later to her "continual headache, weakness and nervous afflictions, of all kinds." In addition, some deeper distortion stemmed from the imposition of the values of will and intellect at the expense of imagination and passion. "The child fed with meat instead of milk becomes too soon mature," Fuller confessed. "With me, much of life was devoured in the bud."

The effect of this rigid perfectionism of the Romans and Timothy Fuller was in some way counterbalanced by Fuller's appreciation of the Greeks, and of Molière, Cervantes, and especially Shakespeare. She wrote of the Greeks that she "loved to creep from amid the Roman pikes to lie beneath this great vine, and see the smiling serene shapes go by. . . . I loved to get away from the hum of the forum and the mailed clang of Roman speech, to these shifting shows of nature, these Gods and Nymphs born of the sunbeam, the wave, the shadows on the hill." Fuller's imagery bisects the classical world by gender: male Rome (vertical pikes, "mail," the forum) and female Greece (horizontal vines, nymphs, nature). Her earliest refuge from her father's books was the garden, significantly her mother's cherished workplace. Thus Fuller felt herself divided into separate selves. As the side nurtured by her father came into public view, that associated with her mother became private, and even invisible:

> His influence on me was great, and opposed to the natural unfolding of my character, which was fervent, of strong grasp and disposed to infatuation, and self-forgetfulness. He made the common prose world so present to me, that my . . . own world sank deep within. . . . But my true life was only the dearer that it was secluded and veiled over by a thick curtain of available intellect, and that coarse but wearable stuff worn by the ages—Common Sense.

Fuller's finding her vocation depended upon her breaking down the divisions that plagued her during childhood. She would have to learn to reject the notions of masculine and feminine that were locked into the culture, for as long as she described her problem in these terms, she conspired in delaying her progress to selfhood and freedom.

By 1824, Timothy Fuller was anxious enough about his daughter to send her, against her will, to Miss Prescott's School for Young Ladies in Groton, Massachusetts, where he hoped she would acquire "female propriety." Fuller's affection for the headmistress, Susan Prescott, had the desired effect of making her wish for womanly "tact and polish" to complement the genius she took for granted. Back at home in Cambridge in 1825, she found her studies had filled her with a "gladiatorial disposition" that prevented her enjoyment of casual society. Social ease came late to this lonely adolescent.

Cambridge in the late 1820s was full of brilliant talkers, intellectuals dedicated to the romantic cult of friendship. Margaret Fuller's arrival was a spectacular event, her style startling. Many were initially repelled by this long-necked, robust figure with eyes alternately squinting and dilating, by her dominating use of erudition and scathing wit. Unitarian minister and author William Henry Channing confessed that he initially avoided one "so armed from head to foot in saucy sprightliness," and Emerson underscored the martial image: "the men thought she carried too many guns." For an extraordinary number of men and women, however, closer acquaintance with Fuller broke down initial resistance. One woman confessed, "Though she spoke rudely searching words, and told you startling truths, though she broke down your little shams and defenses, you felt exhilarated by the compliment of being found out."

Now in her late teens, Fuller enjoyed a rich life of letters with a small circle of Cambridge friends, several from Harvard's class of 1829. Together they read the English romantics, Charles Lamb, William Wordsworth, Samuel Taylor Coleridge, and Thomas Carlyle. Then when her father, disillusioned with political life, retired to the country in 1833 and took the family to Groton, Fuller's pace changed dramatically. She found herself tutoring her siblings five to eight hours daily, and taking on an onerous share of domestic work because her grandmother, mother, and brothers were often ill. One infant sibling died in Fuller's arms. During what spare time she found, Fuller read up on architecture and astronomy, devoured European and American history, and kept up her translations of German and French romantics.

While in Groton she conceived the bold idea of writing a life of the great German writer Johann Goethe, one of her intellectual heroes, who was relatively unread and underappreciated in America. Fuller was sure she would have to go to Europe to collect data on him because none of the American scholars who knew Goethe were willing to share the details of his life with a woman. Moreover, there was no American woman who could provide a model for Fuller as a writer.

Her female forerunners were in Europe, where the institution of the salon had long given women of intelligence and wit an influential role with men of letters and politics, a role rare in America. At fifteen, Fuller had been attracted by the example of French writer Madame de Staël; her reputedly brilliant conversation, intense friendships, and influential writing had been said to have compensated amply for her plain appearance. Fuller's contemporaries later compared her with de Staël. In the late 1830s Fuller was drawn to another unconventional French writer, George Sand, despite what she called Sand's "womanish" failings: "She has genius and a manly heart! Will there never be a being to combine a man's mind and woman's heart, and who yet finds life too rich to weep over?" The "common sense" instilled in her by her father caused Fuller to disparage in women artists the emotionality she cherished in her companions.

Her father's sudden death from cholera in 1835 forced Fuller to abandon her writing projects and trip to Europe and take on the role of head of the household. She began by attempting to disentangle his financial affairs. Her next challenge was to seize control of the rearing and education of her siblings over the protestations of a domineering uncle. Most difficult of all for Fuller was being emotionally orphaned; for the next few years she searched for a father figure as well as a mentor.

When Fuller met Ralph Waldo Emerson in 1836, she felt she had found a spiritual guide. Seven years her senior, Emerson, who had had to define his own vocation, offered what her father had not: encouragement for Fuller to define her own path. When he read his essay "Nature" aloud to her, she might have drawn strength from its closing: "Build therefore your own world." Emerson's vision sanctioned a world built around individualism. Fuller thus could fashion her own world in which she could simultaneously cultivate a circle of high-minded intimates and expand her sense of private self. She praised Emerson: "From him I first learned what is meant by the inward life."

The interest each took in the other was powerful. While Emerson inducted Fuller into the worlds of solitude and natural harmony, she offered him the best of society. Sometimes Emerson was exuberantly grateful for Fuller's company and her young friends. But as Fuller eventually felt constrained by Emerson's "inwardness," so Emerson clung to his inveterate reserve. A tension grew between the two, which each expressed in similar terms. Emerson's adoption of Montaigne's phrase "Oh, *my friends*, there are no friends," was, to Fuller, "a paralyzing conviction." After one of Fuller's visits, Emerson confided to his journal, "Life too near paralyzes art." Given the ascetic basis of Emerson's craft and Fuller's craving for dynamic relationships, the friendship dwindled within a few years. In her last visit with Emerson in 1844, Fuller teased him about how Concord lacked "the animating influences of Discord."

Before Fuller discovered her own path, she drew heavily on the stimulating and steadying influence of Concord and the transcendentalists. Fuller's intellectual exchange with Emerson helped fill gaps in her knowledge of English literature while she broadened Emerson's appreciation of Continental literature. Emerson also encouraged Fuller's acquaintance with Bronson Alcott, who offered Fuller her first job at his Temple School. Although teaching was the most conventional of female occupations during this era, Alcott's teaching philosophy was anything but conventional. He believed that children are nearer their "celestial origins" than adults, and directed their education inward. His principles were branded as heretical, blasphemous, and even obscene. Fuller preferred Alcott's methods to her father's forced march, although she was a critic of some of Alcott's methods. When she switched to a more lucrative and less radical school in Providence, she found herself restless after her stimulating tenure at Alcott's school.

Early in 1840, Fuller embarked on the most demanding of her transcendentalist enterprises, the editing of the *Dial*. Members of this elite literary circle, the so-called Transcendental Club, decided to produce a journal of their own. Their first editorial proposed "not to multiply books, but to report life." Despite initial enthusiasm, Fuller had to beg for contributions, and for one issue of 136 pages, had hastily provided 85 pages from her own notebooks. She was sharply criticized despite her heroic efforts. Emerson complained, "I hope our *Dial* will get to be a little *bad*," while theologian and fellow transcendentalist Theodore Parker even more pointedly suggested that the publication "needed a beard." These calls for greater boldness drove Fuller into an uncharacteristically "feminine" neutrality, resulting in work of poorer quality than most of her later efforts.

Fuller's poems and art and music criticism are too subjective for evaluation now, but her literary criticism provides us with a systematic record of critical practice in America. Fuller argued that criticism should go beyond the impressionism that chiefly characterized the critic; it should combine empathetic elucidation of literary works on their own terms with objective standards outside them.

During her twenty months in New York in 1844–46 writing for Horace Greeley's *New York Tribune,* Fuller wrote two literary pieces a week, outstripping any in her New England circle in practical criticism such as book reviews. Fuller was happy to "aid in the great work of popular education." She was uniquely able to mediate between the ordinary reader and the likes of Goethe, Byron, and Sand. Explaining the themes of these difficult writers by placing them in the contexts of their ages and options, Fuller made them accessible, even enlightening. This perspective brought her to favor American literature that was individual but not provincial. She criticized James Russell Lowell and the lionized Henry Wadsworth Longfellow, but praised Frederick Douglass, Edgar Allen Poe, Nathaniel Hawthorne, and the as yet unknown Herman Melville. She tried to rescue from literary oblivion the novelist Charles Brockden Brown (a feminist, as she read him). In private and in public, she was satirized by many, including Lowell and Poe (who thought her praise did not match his talents), although in the *Brooklyn Daily Eagle* the young Walt Whitman welcomed "right heartily" her collected criticism, *Papers on Literature and Art.*

Fuller's ideological break with Emerson was initiated in what was ironically one of her most transcendentalist works. In her *Dial* essay, "The Great Lawsuit," Fuller applied transcendentalist tenets to women, particularly the universal sacred right and duty to develop fully one's nature. Her need to prove woman's humanity shows that however warmly Fuller had been received by transcendentalist men, she was still made to feel "other."

Probably the earliest source of Fuller's feminism was her feeling for her mother. She wrote that after her father's nocturnal drills she often had nightmares of following her mother's corpse to the grave, as she had followed her infant sister. In her biography of Fuller, Katharine Anthony made this dream the keystone of her Oedipal reading of

Fuller. But a fragmentary manuscript, in which Fuller fictionalizes her parents' marriage, suggests other readings. In this fragment, Fuller takes two stunning liberties in fact. She disguises herself, the narrator, as a *son*, and tells how the mother—weakened by her husband's neglect of her inner life and destroyed by grief over her second child's death—*dies*. The narrator speculates, "had she lived there was enough in me corresponding with her unconscious wants to have aroused her intellect and occupied her affections. Perhaps her son might have made up to her for want of that full development of feeling which youth demands from love." Fuller's fictional tale incorporates her real recurrent nightmare of her mother's death, her mother's real relative absence from Fuller's rearing and inability to provide her daughter with a model, and the death of the internalized female in the child when both parents fail to value and nurture feminine characteristics. The son's fantasized rescue of the mother can be read perhaps as Fuller's attempt to *create* a mothering self that could provide the acceptance she was unable to find elsewhere.

Fuller's friendships with other women were marked by these needs to be loved and accepted *and* her desire to transform the "other." The fervent language of her friendship owes something to the cult of romanticism. In addition, the culture's rigorous separation of human qualities by gender might have encouraged women to believe only they could understand one another. But the intensity of Fuller's love of women also came from a need to heal a wound sustained in childhood, and to enlarge women's mutual understanding, and hence their capacities. "It is so true that a woman may be in love with a woman and a man with a man," she wrote of a friend in youth whom she had loved "with as much passion as I was then strong enough to feel."

Understanding women was not the same as endorsing them or their "separate sphere." As Fuller wrote sharply, "Plain sewing is decidedly immoral." Her sense that she was an exception was a habitual defense as a young woman. As she grew older, though, her desire to work for other women replaced it: Her "conversations" for women, likely inspired by her sessions with the transcendentalists, nourished a sense of herself and of possible vocations.

In 1839 Fuller proposed to assemble a circle of "well-educated and thinking women" to help them "systematize thought and give a precision and clearness in which our sex are so deficient, chiefly, I think because they have so few inducements." Her first series of conversations was on Greek mythology, but over five winters she covered fine arts, ethics, education, and women's influence of the family, school, church, society, and literature. Paying a small fee, from twenty-five to forty women gathered once a week in fellow transcendentalist and educator Elizabeth Peabody's bookstore. The aims might have been modest, but the effort had profound effects.

Fuller's very premise that women should nurture their serious responses to each other as well as their obligations to family was trailblazing. Women's rights pioneer Elizabeth Cady Stanton later found the "vindication of woman's right to think" in the conversations subtly subversive. Fuller's notion that for women the precincts of love stretched beyond the hearth and that morality is based on free choice and personal responsibility was nothing short of revolutionary. Fuller's channeling of her talents toward women's issues led her to personal wholeness and the free exercise of her power.

The conversations also helped Fuller to develop her writing style. When she published her *Dial* essay on women, "The Great Lawsuit," Thoreau praised it as "rich extempore writing, talking with pen in hand." Fuller expanded this essay into *Woman in the Nineteenth Century* while living in Fishkill, New York, before she settled in Manhattan. She was about to start work for Horace Greeley, who had offered her a job after reading her *Summer on the Lakes in 1843*. The trip to the Great Lakes and Wisconsin that inspired this book, weaned her from New England thought; *Woman* reflects her quickened sense of independence and her new interest in the claims of society and politics.

Her psychological confidence reveals itself in her treatment of female nature. Although she concurs with the cultural conviction that woman's nature is distinct, she insists that this female essence never appears unmixed: "two sides of the great radical dualism," male and female "are perpetually passing into one another," and "there is no wholly masculine man, no purely feminine woman." Another measure of transformation comes with her portrait of her "friend" Miranda—really an idealized self-portrait—who seeks to dispose of these classifications: "Let it not be said, wherever there is energy or creative genius, 'She had a masculine mind.' " Moreover, in Miranda's story, Fuller reevaluates her father's training, and the contrast is sharp. In her 1840 autobiographical romance, Fuller condemned her father's methods as his "great mistake," but here she says it stemmed from "a firm belief in the equality of the sexes." Where previously she argued that she was cheated of her female nature, now she appreciates that he addressed her as "a living mind," and not a plaything. Where the effect earlier was a life "devoured in the bud," now it is "a dignified sense of self-dependence." Both versions are polemical exaggerations, but the experience of the conversations must help explain the shift from despair to pride.

The independence that Fuller stresses for women is a combination of the transcendentalist virtue of self-reliance and the activist one of "self-impulse." She believed that until a woman represented herself she was "only an overgrown child."

In analyzing society's effects on women and the role women should take in society *Woman* is curiously hybrid. In it, Fuller's calls for various social reforms and even for militant action sound through the old music of pure transcendentalist individualism. Her homely democratic faith in the Declaration of Independence is grafted onto the philosophy of romantic self-culture. The former leads her to praise the abolitionist movement she had ignored during her conversations and admire its activists, Angelina Grimké and Abby Kelley Foster. She also calls upon women to respond as a united group to the threatened annexation of Texas and heralds public speaking and petition campaigns by women, both widely censored as immodest and offensive. She writes with remarkable candor for the time about the double standard in marriage and on women's need to understand sexuality and prostitution.

Fuller shows acid scorn for those who felt women should be sheltered within a domestic circle: "Those who think the physical circumstances of Woman would make a part in the affairs of national government unsuitable, are by no means those who think it impossible for negresses to endure field-work, even during pregnancy, or for sempstresses to go through their killing labors." At such moments, and with the calls to action, Fuller moves for the first time toward radicalism, though she appears not yet aware of its cost.

Active feminism clarified for Fuller the ways in which pure transcendentalism was inadequate for her and initiated her career of activist journalism. It also led her into wider engagement with the world. Her feminist perspective triggered her involvement with political activism and carried her beyond the struggle for women alone. In New York, Fuller celebrated the refuge of immigrants of all classes: standing in the city, she felt "the life blood rushing from an entire continent to swell her heart." She preferred New York to New England, writing, "I don't dislike wickedness and wretchedness more than pettiness and coldness."

Horace Greeley, her editor, became a teacher of sorts for Fuller. In her weekly column on social issues—the Irish, antislavery, opposition to the Mexican War—she often supported his causes. Fuller produced controversial columns stemming from her own convictions as well: She attacked capital punishment, welcomed persecuted Jews from Europe, and sought better education and broader work opportunities for the poor and for women. No longer restricted to acquaintance within her class, Fuller's concern for women in trouble flourished and her feminism grew along with her social awareness. She visited women in Sing Sing prison and helped plan the first halfway house for female convicts. As revolutionary as these ventures into worlds formerly closed to women of her class were for Fuller, they were still rather genteel muckraking.

With the beginning of America's aggressive foreign policy, particularly after the annexation of Texas and the threat of expansion into Mexico, Fuller became disillusioned with the myth of America's special destiny. She took an interest in many varieties of socialism and even translated from a German immigrant newspaper one of the earliest discussions of Marx and Engels in this country. But as no ideology could replace the myth of special destiny, it is likely that if she had not left the country to write for the *Tribune* about Europe, her perspective would simply have soured.

In August 1846, Greeley sent Fuller to England as one of the first American overseas correspondents of either sex. Although at a younger age she might have soaked up the culture and "genius" of Great Britain, during this visit she explored social conditions and intensified her commitment to reform after being shocked by the omnipresence of poverty in England. Throughout Europe, Fuller was appalled by the horrors of industrial slums—the underside of Europe's "costly tapestry"—especially the female victims "too dull to carouse" and their children fed on opium. Although we know she had toured the slums of Five Points in New York, Fuller nevertheless wrote, "Poverty in England has terrors of which I never dreamed at home." What her unconscious adherence to the democratic rhetoric of America made her miss at home, the tradition in Europe of critical political rhetoric laid bare. In addition, she was visiting France on the eve of the 1848 revolution. The life of the streets and the salons was crackling with rival socialist theories, heightening her sense of the need for political action.

An illuminating series of private events kept pace with Fuller's public tour. As Europe heated up for the revolution, experiences and encounters prepared Fuller for fundamental and irrevocable change in her personal life. In New York, a troubling romance with an opportunistic businessman of German-Jewish descent, James Nathan, had made her long, for the only time in her life, for the traditional subordinate role of woman. Apparently the relationship became too demanding or convoluted and Nathan retreated to Europe. If Fuller had come to Europe still hoping for a reconciliation, that hope was effectively dashed when she received a letter in Edinburgh announcing Nathan's engagement to a German woman.

But at the same time, Fuller found her work warmly received in Europe and intellectual discourse more comfortable for her abroad than at home. She wrote to Emerson, "I find myself in my element in European society. It does not, indeed, come up to my ideal, but so many of the encumbrances are cleared away that used to weary me in America, that I can enjoy a freer play of faculty and feel, if not like a bird in the air, at least as easy as a fish in the water." Europe offered her two crucial sensations America had denied: the shock of class consciousness and the warm bath of personal acceptance. She was more than ready for the liberating political and literary influences she encountered in London and Paris that helped her discover how to move against the social and religious pressures that bound American women in "their place."

While in England, Fuller met Giuseppe Mazzini, an Italian revolutionary in exile who was hoping to overthrow Austrian imperialists and unite the eight separate Italian states into a democratic republic. Mazzini knew the struggle would take more than idealism, and would include mobilizing the masses and taking concrete, violent action. Fuller did not succumb to hero-worship, but she did support his cause and accept Mazzini's list of his secret agents on the Continent.

While in France, Fuller met George Sand, whose work Fuller had defended in America, although always with an added regret for her lapses in private virtue. However, after meeting Sand in the freer atmosphere of France, Fuller confessed, "I never liked a woman better. She needs no defence, but only to be understood, for she has bravely acted out her nature, and always with good intentions." It was a moment of prophetic self-recognition, for Fuller would later adapt this phrase to explain her liaison with Ossoli. In Rome, historical events would combine with Fuller's capacity for change to alter transcendentalism's influence on her and to offer her an opportunity for self-realization and her most satisfying work.

When Fuller arrived in Rome during the spring of 1847 a state of optimistic excitement prevailed. The liberal Pope Pius IX, elected a year earlier, had proclaimed a universal amnesty for political prisoners, admitted laypersons into the council of state, and authorized a civic guard. These measures undermined the Pope's temporal powers and stimulated pressure for reform in Italy's seven other states.

Most of Fuller's twenty-one dispatches from Italy have more concentrated force and style than almost anything else she wrote. The effect is panoramic, a combination of quick sketches of conditions in Germany, Austria, and France with colorful and shrewd predictions of sociopolitical evolutions; denser drawings of mounting struggles throughout Italy; and a close, evolving portrait of the Pope and the people of Rome. Fuller chronicled the Pope's gradual decline and the Italian people's growing consciousness and awakening to their own civic responsibilities. Fuller's values are so focused that they make her partisan accounts of hope, restlessness, political suspense, and battle riveting reading. Something of the bite and flash said to have characterized her conversation at last dominates her prose.

Fuller sought out radicals in Genoa, Milan, Florence, and Rome. One of these, met by chance, was Giovanni Angelo Ossoli, a Roman nobleman of meager means who was expected to follow his father and three older brothers into the Pope's service. Late in 1847 the twenty-seven-year-old Ossoli defied his family and rejected his livelihood by turning his back on the Pope and joining the radicals' civic guard. During this same period he became Fuller's lover.

The couple served one another's emotional needs. Ossoli, the youngest of six children, still grieving over the death of his mother when he was six, found in Fuller, ten years his senior, an authoritative woman. Fuller cherished in Ossoli his gentleness and the way he defeated "masculine" stereotyping. An American acquaintance who knew Ossoli commented, "She [Fuller] probably married him as a representative of an imagined possibility in the Italian character which I have not yet been able to believe in." Fuller had been committed to "imagined possibilities" all her life, but she took her greatest risk in her liaison with Ossoli. She wrote to her sister later, "I acted upon a strong impulse. I neither rejoice nor grieve, for bad or good, I acted out my character."

At the same time that she committed herself to Ossoli, Fuller became more deeply involved with the Italian people in the cause of a free Italy. While most American visitors in Italy at this time saw the Italian people as becoming a frightening rabble, Fuller saw in them a heroic struggle. She now saw no Americans more worthy of honor than the abolitionists (to whom she apologized in print for earlier assessments), for with the exception of antislavery, Fuller felt that the "spirit of America flares no more" but had leaped the ocean to blaze in Italy. So, until 1850, she refused the entreaties of Emerson and her family to return home, believing she had more to say to Americans from Italy.

Her refusal to repatriate demonstrates Fuller's repudiation of Emerson's perspective. Fuller denied the mythic specialness of American destiny and offered herself to the struggles of a foreign people as a guide to completing the American Revolution and entering "brotherhood of nations." So Fuller remained in Italy, anchored by political as well as personal ties.

In January 1848, when uprisings flared across Europe like a string of firecrackers, Fuller, nearly thirty-eight and chronically ill, discovered that she was pregnant. She may well have feared survival scarcely less than death in childbirth, for without much more money, Ossoli's marriage to a foreign Protestant radical would probably be impossible. Moreover, Fuller had strong reservations about marriage. Unwell and unsure of her personal circumstances, Fuller turned with relief to the public crisis—devouring news of the February revolution in Paris, the March uprising in Vienna, and especially the "Five Glorious Days" in Milan when the Autstrian garrison was expelled. "It is a time such as I always dreamed of," Fuller wrote, and she contemplated becoming its historian. Seeking seclusion ostensibly to write her history, Fuller withdrew to the Abruzzi mountains. That summer she awaited with equal anxiety the birth of her child and news of friends in reoccupied Milan. Angelo Eugenio Fillippo Ossoli was born September 4, 1848, in the village of Rieti. Fuller was overwhelmed with joy at being a mother, yet she felt obliged to leave the child in November with a wet nurse in the hills and to rejoin Ossoli in Rome. She sent enthusiastic reports to the *Tribune* of the murder of the Pope's minister, the Pope's flight to Naples, and the dignity of Romans in their first attempt at self-government.

On the eve of the declaration of the Roman republic in February 1849, Fuller begged the United States (in the pages of the *Tribune*) to send a sensitive and statesmanlike ambassador to the new nation, adding, "Another century and I might ask to be made Ambassador myself." But even with the triumphal return of Mazzini to preside in the new republic, America was only willing to send a lowly chargé d'affaires. Then France, in the full sway of reaction, sent its army to defeat isolated Rome. During the long siege of June, with news of her child cut off from her, Fuller stayed behind with Ossoli in Rome while other Americans fled the city. Fuller worked long hours as director of a hospital while Ossoli remained at his battery command, but the city's bombardment and the wounded made her "forget the great ideas" and confess she was not of the heroic "mould." After Rome fell, Fuller, Ossoli, and their child moved in the autumn of 1849 into exile in Florence, where she reexamined the events of the past few months and began a broader social critique.

There is no minimizing her sense of loss. "Private hopes of mine are fallen with the hopes of Italy. I have played for a new stake and lost it," she wrote. Had the republic triumphed, work for Fuller and Ossoli might have emerged and continued to give form to their lives. But even defeated and living in Florence, which was again under despotic rule, facing a future empty of earlier promise, Fuller and Ossoli tasted great happiness. Fuller wrote of the "power and sweetness" of Ossoli's presence and rejoiced in the love of their child. Ossoli's love for her seemed to deepen during this period as well; Fuller wrote that he "loves me from simple affinity." More illuminatingly, Fuller compares the tenderness of Ossoli's love for her with that of her mother and expresses confidence that they, in particular, will love each other when they meet.

Yet Fuller's announcement of her marriage and motherhood in the summer of 1849 was not without problems. There was gossip about a "Socialist marriage, without the external ceremony." No document or reliable account survives. Fuller was either lying and avoiding embroidery as much as possible, or telling the truth in such a way as to signal the unorthodox view she had of legal unions. She had advanced ideas about her liaison: "Our relation covers only a part of my life," but "I do not feel constrained or limited." Further, she believed that Ossoli, being younger, might one day love another, in which case she pledged, "I shall do all that this false state of society permits to give him what freedom he may need."

The family was dogged by the fear of police surveillance and poverty, and Fuller, the breadwinner, felt she could no longer rely on presents and loans to support them. Work for the *Tribune* had stopped inexplicably. Believing that her book was the most important project she had undertaken, she decided to sell it in person in America. Yet she knew that at home she would face "the social inquisition of the United States." Both she and Ossoli were superstitious about sea-travel. Moreover, on the eve of her May departure, some good friends, in consultation with Emerson, urged her to remain in Italy for the time being.

This warning was clear: the person she had become could not return to America. The long trajectory of her short life was not circular. To learn to respect herself as an intellectual woman, Fuller had first had to use what was at hand in America, the idealism of the transcendentalists. When this had made her strong enough, she left New England and began in New York to apply her energies more directly to herself, to society, and to the world, but her repressed sexuality and her simplistic faith in divinely ordained national destiny reveal she was still subject to the limits of American attitudes. Only her European experiences, especially those in Italy, could illuminate for her the meaning of her most intimate prayer, "Give me truth, cheat me by no illusion."

Despite fears and warnings, Fuller, Ossoli, and their child set sail on what became an ill-fated journey. The details of Fuller's death remain uncertain. We know that within sight of American shores, her ship struck rocks off Fire Island. During the twelve hours between the time the ship began to sink and when it finally went under, Fuller was on deck watching some swim to safety and others drown. She repeatedly refused to leave the boat. She saw the lifeboat brought to the beach by persons unwilling to risk a rescue. We know she told the ship's cook, "I see nothing but death before me." We do not know whether or not she tried to swim ashore, clinging to a board. Her body and those of Ossoli and her child were never recovered. After her drowning, Emerson confided to his journal, "I have lost in her my audience." As for Fuller's audience, it remained to be created.

Note

* The longer version of this essay may be found in Leonard Unger and A. Walton Litz, *American Writers: A Collection of Literary Biographies* (New York: Scribner's 1981).

PART IV

Divided Loyalties

The dramatic challenges faced by American women during the first half of the nineteenth century were overshadowed by events taking place at mid-century. By 1860, the ferment of reform and the explosive impact of sectional politics on national policy led America into civil war. All women felt the impact of this national calamity, except perhaps those on the far western frontier. The Civil War (1861–1865), an attempt to preserve the Union against the forces of secession, eventually would determine the fate of slavery. Because of women's disproportionate role in the antislavery movement, they can be said to have contributed decisively to the momentum toward war.

After the election of Abraham Lincoln in November 1860, the southern states—led by South Carolina—began a slow but steady departure from the federal Union to form their own Confederacy. The mobilization for war tore families apart as many women watched helplessly as their kin divided over choosing sides. Lincoln's own wife, Mary Todd, saw members of her family fight and die with the Confederacy. Further, women's feelings about the war effort changed over time. At the outset women might have gaily waved their men off to war; however, as the casualties mounted, they watched reluctantly as men donned uniforms to join in prolonged and bloody military campaigns. The issue of war pulled women's emotions and energies in different directions. Both as individuals and as a group, women faced a crisis when the nation erupted into a full-scale armed conflict.

In the wake of the Mexican War in 1846, many women abolitionists launched a pacifist crusade, forming the New England Non-Resistance Society. Yet the firing on Fort Sumter in April 1861 galvanized most antislavery women into enthusiastic support of the Union. The talents and skills which they had brought to bear in the fight to end slavery were put to invaluable use by Federal authorities. Following the Fort Sumter battle, three thousand New Yorkers attended a benefit at Cooper Union Hall. The New York Central Association of Relief tapped this patriotic outpouring for donations and volunteers. This group was one of over seven thousand local organizations that collected and distributed supplies, trained nurses, and aided widows and orphans. Out of this effort, the U.S. Sanitary Commission established itself as an ambitious and effective conduit for civilian resources. The administration of this quasi-official organization was primarily male, but women quickly established competence as fundraisers, supply collectors, and recruiters of medical staff. In their zeal to promote the cause, female agents of the Sanitary Commission, especially in the Midwest, frequently exceeded their authority, issuing orders independently without consulting supervisors in times of urgent need. However, the circumstances of war made the freely donated labor of women more valuable than the maintenance of feminine submissiveness. Hundreds of women gained valuable experience and enormous confidence through their wartime service in the Commission.

Women also joined the war effort by volunteering in hospitals, rolling bandages and performing other menial but essential labor. Another important group (including Louisa May Alcott, better known as the author of *Little Women*) joined the effort by serving as skilled nurses. Young women from a wide range of class and ethnic backgrounds supported the Union—and themselves. Social reformer Dorothea Dix became Superintendent of Nurses for the Union Army in 1861. Some nurses served not only in hospital wards, but on the battlefield as well; women such as Mary Ann ("Mother") Bickerdyke were a welcome sight for the wounded at battle sites. Self-taught in "botanic" medicine, the early widowed Bickerdyke simply went to work on her own in the filthy hospital tents near her home in Illinois. She eventually joined Grant's army along the Tennessee River and was present at some of the bloodiest contests of the war—at Fort Donelson, Lookout Mountain, Missionary Ridge, and the sieges of Vicksburg and Atlanta.

Southern "ladies" set propriety aside to participate in activities usually reserved for servants or slaves. Sally Tompkins of Richmond borrowed the home of a friend to set up a clinic for the Confederate wounded. The female members of the upper class staffed her hospital, performing menial and taxing labors. By war's end, Tompkins had been commissioned as a captain by Confederate President Jefferson Davis, and well over 1,000 men had been successfully treated at her facility.

African-American women also made significant contributions during the war as illustrated by the career of Charlotte Forten, a schoolteacher who went south to help freedpeople at Port Royal,

South Carolina. The most famous of black nurses during the war, former slave Suzy King Taylor, began work in the camps as a laundress before serving as a nurse in the Union Army. During Reconstruction she launched her career as an educator.

Women on both sides of the conflict entered government service, working alongside men for the first time as clerks. With men away at war, female labor was crucial to both the efforts in Washington and Richmond, the Confederate capital. Increasingly, widows and mothers sought employment as well as pensions and charity. Even with jobs, single mothers and widows faced mounting difficulties. Though Confederate women were especially hard hit by wartime inflation which made minimum wages nearly worthless, families North and South were confronted with the harsh realities of war. Mary Todd Lincoln and Varina Davis witnessed enormous suffering from their respective White Houses; the numbers of homeless and hungry increased rapidly during wartime.

While almost all women felt a sense of dislocation and loss, one group viewed the war as a means to gain that most precious commodity: freedom. African-American women in the North and South identified the Confederacy as their enemy and saw the war as a necessary evil. Those slave women who watched beloved men march off to battle knew that their sacrifices might bring peace and improved conditions for future generations. Blacks were enlisted on both sides, but predictably the Confederacy was more reluctant to use slave labor and was willing to contemplate using African-Americans as soldiers only in sheer desperation during the war's final weeks.

The North did drag its heels when it came to utilizing willing and able African-American soldiers—including free blacks from the North and the "contraband" slaves who deserted masters for the protection of the Union Army in droves. However, following the Emancipation Proclamation in January 1863, black soldiers took a more decisive role in the war against the Rebels. The arming of African-Americans changed the nature of the battle for white soldiers who fought alongside blacks, as well as for the white soldiers at the end of black gunsights. Certainly the presence of African-American soldiers in the occupied Confederacy broke the famed southern spirit during the prolonged period which preceded surrender. But even more importantly, African-

American soldiers were empowered by their fight on their own behalf, for a freedom so long denied.

When Lee surrendered at Appomattox in April 1865, more than half a million soldiers had perished: the North lost over 360,000 and the South 260,000. Four long years of conflict wiped part of a generation of young men off the face of the earth. The human toll was even larger, as many more were maimed and towns were filled with scores of one-legged or one-armed men. Those wounded by war also included the widowed and orphaned, the displaced and devastated women left homeless after surrender.

In the years immediately following the war, hundreds of men and women traveled south in hopes that education would provide a boost to the recently emancipated African-Americans. Yankee "schoolmarms," whom W. E. B. DuBois deemed crusaders, planted schools in a barren and hostile environment. Not only was black illiteracy a problem, but white illiteracy in the South was the highest in the nation. Some northern women ventured south during wartime, such as black educator Charlotte Forten who settled at Port Royal, South Carolina, and Laura Towne, a white reformer from Philadelphia, who set up her Penn School on St. Helena Island off the coast of South Carolina in September 1862. By the war's end, these crusaders had grown in number to over four thousand Yankee women laboring in Freedmen's Bureau schools throughout the South. With the withdrawal of federal troops from the South in 1877, which signalled an end to Reconstruction, most women abandoned their posts—although Penn School founder Laura Towne, and others similarly dedicated, remained south.

Northern women in the Reconstruction South found themselves drawn not just into educational issues, but into all aspects of reform. Women began to petition against the abuses of the apprentice system which was used virtually to re-enslave many African-American children. They petitioned, too, for land reform and other economic and civil measures to stem exploitation of freedpeople as well as white sharecroppers. But women, white and black, confronted the immovable force of southern racism and many felt defeated.

Women's rights advocates who believed that the end of war would signal rewards for their loyalty to the Union cause were equally disappointed. When Elizabeth Cady Stanton, wife of abolitionist Henry Stanton, along with Lucretia Mott, a Philadelphia Quaker abolitionist leader, and other organizers launched their campaign for women's rights at Seneca Falls in 1848, they had linked the battle for female status with an end to chattel slavery. Throughout the 1850s, at conventions in New York and Ohio, Susan B. Anthony and Sojourner Truth preached the gospel of abolitionism along with women's rights.

Reform efforts resulted in the Married Women's Property Acts. These guaranteed married women control over the property that they brought into marriage with them as well as any they might inherit. Other statutes liberalized divorce. Wealthy legislators were not opposed to amending *feme covert* principles. Under English common law and in American statutes, a woman who was adult and single had *feme sole* status, or "legal personality." However, when a woman married she relinquished this status and became *feme covert*. Her legal personality was subsumed by her husband's rights over her person and property. Some husbands were interested in protecting their property from creditors by passing on assets to their wives. They also wanted their own property controlled by deserving daughters rather than by sons-in-law exclusively. In 1839 the Mississippi legislature approved such a measure. However, in other states, such as New York, reform proceeded much more slowly. A similar law, first introduced by women's rights advocates in Albany in 1836, was not finally approved until 1848; and then only the real and personal property of women was protected. It took another twenty years before wives could retain control over their own wages, and mothers might be given equal consideration in child custody.

Many feminists hoped that the cataclysm of war would accelerate their gains—pushing up the timetable for legislative reforms—and even lead to a rapid acceptance of women's suffrage, the goal of radical activists during the antebellum era. To many female activists, northern victory symbolized a triumph of reform; advocates of woman's suffrage believed they should be rewarded with the franchise, as ex-slaves had been by Constitutional amendment. Too many male reformers failed to agree. Frederick Douglass, the most famous African-American of his day, had championed woman's suffrage from Seneca Falls onward. Women reformers stood firmly behind the 13th Amendment which abolished slavery but, when controversy flared in

1867 during debates over the 15th Amendment, even Douglass declared that it was "the negro's hour."

Outraged by the exclusion, Susan B. Anthony, Elizabeth Cady Stanton, and many feminist supporters abandoned the Republican party and aligned with the Democrats in 1867 in exchange for the party's support of woman's suffrage. When this strategy failed miserably during a referendum campaign in Kansas and local elections in New York, Stanton and Anthony abandoned party politics altogether and formed an independent political organization in 1869: the National Woman Suffrage Association (NWSA). Additionally, in 1875, feminists tackled the courts with the *Minor v. Happersett* case, proposing that suffrage was a right conferred on all national citizens. The Supreme Court, however, ruled that the vote was a privilege granted by individual states and not guaranteed through federal protection.

Victoria Woodhull had been an early proponent of the strategy to sue for the vote, based on rights protected by the Constitution. An unusually flamboyant personality, Woodhull's early life was marked by upheaval: she and her sister Tennessee Claflin travelled with their parents' medicine and fortune-telling show. Married at fifteen, she divorced her husband in 1864 after bearing two children. Four years later she captured the interest of Cornelius Vanderbilt, a widowed millionaire, who set up Woodhull and her sister in a successful stock brokerage business. In 1870, the sisters established a women's rights paper, *Woodhull and Claflin's Weekly* which advocated dress reform, free love, legalized prostitution, and other radical reforms. In 1872, she organized an "Equal Rights" party and accepted their nomination as President. Her designated running mate, Frederick Douglass, chose not to participate as a candidate; nonetheless, the protest campaign brought Woodhull and feminist issues attention in the national press.

Relatively few women were even exposed to the kinds of feminism espoused by Woodhull, Anthony, and Stanton. While radicals like Stanton and Anthony formed the NWSA, a separate organization, the American Woman Suffrage Association (AWSA), was established by Lucy Stone, Henry Blackwell and Henry Ward Beecher (Catharine and Harriet's brother). This rival group provided a more moderate framework for reform, which appealed to those unwilling to join beneath the banner of NWSA's journal, the *Revolution*. The reunification of the movement would await a later generation of women.

It was not surprising that race tore apart the suffrage movement. The whole of white American society was preoccupied with racial issues in the nineteenth century: at first over the issue of slavery, and once slavery was ended, over the issue of extending rights and recognizing African-Americans as part of free society. The 1860s witnessed the rise of several white supremacist organizations in the South, most significantly the Ku Klux Klan. Many northern whites, even some who had dedicated their lives to abolitionism, exhibited racist attitudes when it came to granting blacks full and equal membership within society.

Nativist movements (groups of white "native born" people) gained support both North and South. Groups such as the American Protective Association (APA) founded in 1887, hoped to limit immigration and to enforce stricter naturalization laws. Xenophobia and religious intolerance flourished in the postwar years.

The *real* native Americans, Indians, found their already reduced land holdings being sacrificed to the wave of white pioneer farmers and ranchers moving westward. From the Gold Rush of 1849 onward, white settlers began a steady march to fill up the Great Plains and the Pacific seaboard. Congress enacted the Homestead Act in 1862, which allowed any twenty-one-year-old or head of household to stake a claim of 160 acres for $14, a provision which benefited women as well as men. White settlers demanded Indian land, pushing the government to break treaties in order to guarantee the fulfillment of the nation's "manifest destiny." Thus in 1887 Congress passed the Dawes Act, which provided for individual land holdings, voiding the Indian custom of collective ownership. This led to the further economic and political disintegration of native peoples.

The scope of these human developments in nineteenth-century America was matched by another major transformation in the wake of the war—the expansion of heavy industry and a revolution in transportation. Mining, manufacturing, shipping and railroads all boomed in the postwar era. The gleaming gold of the closing spike that joined the two tracks of the first transcontinental railroad in 1869 symbolized not only the unification of the continent but the seemingly "golden" opportunity for expanding markets and continuing economic growth. By 1890 there were six transcontinental lines, with settlements and businesses flourishing from coast to coast. These transformations propelled women as well as men into the modern industrial era.

Elizabeth Cady Stanton
(1815–1902)

Bruce Miroff

Elizabeth Cady was born in Johnstown, New York, in 1815. Educated at Johnstown Academy and at the Troy Female Seminary (now the Emma Willard School) in Troy, New York, she married abolitionist Henry Stanton in 1840. When in that year she and Quaker lecturer Lucretia Mott were outraged by the exclusion of female delegates from the floor of the World Anti-Slavery Convention in London, they decided to call for a women's rights convention. Although the plan was not immediately carried out, a meeting of Stanton, Mott, and three other women in 1848 resulted in the first women's rights convention, which began a few days later in Seneca Falls, New York. At this convention, Stanton drafted the Declaration of Sentiments, which called for economic and social equality and suffrage for women. In 1851, she began a lifelong collaboration toward this goal with Susan B. Anthony. Busy rearing her seven children, born between 1842 and 1859, Stanton nonetheless worked continuously in the women's movement and successfully advocated married women's legal rights in New York state. During the Civil War she and Anthony organized the National Woman's Loyal League to support Abraham Lincoln's party and to petition Congress for the immediate abolition of slavery by constitutional amendment. Stanton was president of the National Woman Suffrage Association, which she founded with Anthony in 1869, for twenty-one years, and of the National American Woman Suffrage Association from 1890 to 1892. She wrote and lectured all her life, and with Anthony, edited the radical periodical, the Revolution *(1868–1870). Together they published three volumes of the documentary* History of Woman Suffrage *(1881–1886). Stanton also published* The Woman's Bible *(1895–1898) and her autobiography,* Eighty Years and More *(1898).*

221

At the first women's rights convention in America, held in her home town of Seneca Falls, New York, in 1848, Elizabeth Cady Stanton discovered the vocation that would shape the remainder of her life. She would become a public voice for women's grievances and a prophet of genuine equality between the sexes. Battling for this vocation against the ridicule of men, the fears of women, and the continuing claims of her own family upon her, she emerged after the Civil War as the most vocal agitator and the most penetrating thinker in the ranks of nineteenth-century American feminists. Stanton's subsequent public career was not without disturbing episodes. The pain of women's exclusion from the rights of citizenship led her, on occasion, to outbursts of nativist and racist sentiments. Yet her career was always animated by a profound insight into women's subjugation and a passionate commitment to the freedom of all women.

Prior to the convention at Seneca Falls, Elizabeth Cady Stanton had struggled unsuccessfully against the dominant social convention of "separate spheres," which reserved the fields of politics and business for men, while restricting women to the "sphere" of domesticity. She was born in 1815 in Johnstown, New York. Her mother was a strong woman, but it was Elizabeth's father, a wealthy landowner and judge, who exercised the decisive influence on her childhood. When her father became distraught over the death of his only son, Elizabeth, then aged ten, resolved to take her brother's place and fulfill her father's shattered ambitions. She learned to ride on horseback, studied Greek, and became a star student at the local academy.[1]

But as much as her father loved her and took pride in her accomplishments, he set strict limits as to how far Elizabeth could breach the proprieties of a "woman's sphere." When the male classmates that she had bested in school competitions went off to college, he forbade her to go. Many years later, in one of her most popular lectures, "Our Young Girls," Elizabeth Cady Stanton would tell a story of a "proud girl" who, rejecting "these invidious distinctions" between the sexes and feeling herself to be "the peer of any boy she knows," would find everything conspiring to defeat her aspirations. Perhaps remembering her own defeat, she would conclude the tale by asking: "But what can one brave girl do against the world?"[2]

Although Elizabeth's father insisted that her life follow a conventional path of marriage and domesticity, he could not prevent her from following that path into unconventional circles. Making frequent visits to the Peterboro, New York, home of her older cousin, Gerrit Smith, a prominent antislavery leader, she came into contact with numerous abolitionists and other reformers who congregated

223

under the hospitable Smith's roof. Among these was Henry Stanton, a romantic young abolitionist agitator, whom she married in 1840. Elizabeth was now drawn into the most radical network in antebellum America. Like a number of other women in this network, she responded passionately to its language of equality, finding in the arguments directed toward emancipating the slave a potent vocabulary for women's needs as well. Still, her husband was the public actor, and she was his domestic counterpart. Elizabeth's only public identity was as Henry Stanton's wife.

The Stantons settled in Boston, the capital of political and intellectual reform, in 1844. For Elizabeth, domestic life in Boston, balanced as it was by intellectual and social stimulation, was pleasurable. She threw her enormous energies and talents into housekeeping and motherhood (she had two small children at the time), and imagined the home as an arena for female power. But when the family moved a few years later to the town of Seneca Falls in the Finger Lakes region of New York, domesticity lost its savor. Cut off from the wider world in the isolated environs of Seneca Falls, Elizabeth was exhausted and sometimes depressed by the demands of a growing household. To her cousin, Elizabeth Smith Miller, she wrote: "I am desperate sick of working and attending to the fleshly needs."[3]

With her rebellious temperament and her grounding in reform movements, Elizabeth Cady Stanton was not likely to succumb to isolation and depression, or to accept domesticity as defeat. Instead, she began to view her own confinement in the home as representative, her own hunger for a larger life as a metaphor for women's hunger for political and social equality. The slogan of the modern women's movement—"the personal is political"—would have come as no surprise to Stanton. From her personal discontent with women's restricted "sphere," she derived a fundamental insight into an oppression that needed to be combatted through political action. Stanton had ample amounts of the frustration, passion, and vision necessary for the founding of a feminist politics in America. All that she lacked was a catalyst.

That catalyst was Lucretia Mott. Stanton had become friendly with Mott, a pioneer abolitionist and feminist, at an international antislavery gathering in London in 1840. The two had been outraged by the overwhelming majority vote at this convention to exclude women as delegates, and had talked of convening a meeting to discuss women's rights as soon as they returned to America. Although this plan was not carried out, Stanton remained in touch with Mott, whom she came to look upon as her mentor and role model. In the summer of 1848, Mott came on a visit to Waterloo, a town near Seneca Falls. Meeting there with her and three other women on July

13, 1848, Stanton knew that at last she had a sympathetic audience for her rebellious thoughts. As she recalled in her autobiography, *Eighty Years and More,* "I poured out, that day, the torrent of my long-accumulating discontent, with such vehemence and indignation that I stirred myself, as well as the rest of the party, to do and dare anything. . . . We decided, then and there, to call a 'Woman's Rights Convention'. . . ."[4]

Lacking a model of feminist political discourse, the five women seized upon the Declaration of Independence as a framework for their Declaration of Sentiments. It was a fortunate choice. As Stanton reworked the language of the Declaration of Independence, it became a potent vehicle for women's declaration of independence. In her adaptation, men as a class stood accused of practices as onerous as those the American colonists had ascribed to George III: "The history of mankind is a history of repeated injuries and usurpations on the part of man toward woman, having in direct object the establishment of an absolute tyranny over her."[5] The Declaration of Sentiments listed eighteen grievances, the same number as the colonists had advanced, in a revolutionary indictment of men's oppression of women.

The Declaration of Sentiments was Stanton's first venture into political theory and rhetoric, but it already contained the marks of her distinctive feminist style. Stanton took a classic American idiom and infused it with a radical message not contemplated by its authors. She took the most democratic and egalitarian American values and turned them against a dominant culture that claimed to uphold them. The Declaration of Independence was genuinely sacred to Stanton, who remained throughout her life a passionate believer in the republican ideals of liberty, equality, and virtuous citizenship. At Seneca Falls, she discovered the feminist possibilities in those ideals.

On July 19, 1848, only six days after Stanton had poured out her personal discontents, the first women's rights convention began. The hastily organized convention was well attended. Several hundred women and several dozen men came from a radius of fifty miles to the small Wesleyan chapel at Seneca Falls to hear Stanton and her colleagues proclaim a new struggle for female equality. The response of the audience was favorable; at the conclusion of the convention, sixty-eight women and thirty-two men signed the resolutions that Stanton had prepared.

Stanton's speech at the convention refuted every ground—physical, intellectual, moral—for men's self-proclaimed superiority over women. This speech was more, however, than a brief for women's equality; it was also a personal declaration of vocation.

Propelling herself from domesticity to public activity in a single leap, Stanton made herself into a political voice for her sex. In the opening lines of her speech, she announced her life's work:

> I should feel exceedingly diffident to appear before you at this time, having never before spoken in public, were I not nerved by a sense of right and duty, did I not feel the time had fully come for the question of woman's wrongs to be laid before the public, did I not believe that woman herself must do this work; for woman alone can understand the height, the depth, the length, and the breadth of her own degradation. Man cannot speak for her. . . .[6]

That women must speak for themselves, that they must find their own public voice, was, for Stanton, the key to their struggle. Men had monopolized public speech up to now, and had used their monopoly to define women into subservience. The Declaration of Sentiments spelled out the consequences of man's power over public discourse: "He has usurped the prerogative of Jehovah himself, claiming it as his right to assign for her a sphere of action, when that belongs to her conscience and to her God. He has endeavored, in every way that he could, to destroy her confidence in her own powers, to lessen her self-respect, and to make her willing to lead a dependent and abject life."[7]

Stanton insisted that the voice of a woman also be the voice of a citizen. It was through her efforts that suffrage for women became a demand of the Seneca Falls convention. Lucretia Mott did not want to include enfranchisement of women among the proposed resolutions, fearing that it would make the convention appear foolish. Henry Stanton warned his wife in much the same terms. But Elizabeth Cady Stanton swept aside these cautions. With the support of black abolitionist Frederick Douglass, she carried her suffrage resolution—the only one not to receive unanimous approval—by a small majority.

Because Stanton and other pioneer feminists entertained inflated hopes for women's suffrage as an instrument of political reform, it has been common for later observers to criticize their focus on voting rights as misguided and naive. Ellen Dubois has countered this criticism by pointing to the radical meaning of women's suffrage in the context of a culture divided into sexual spheres: "By demanding a permanent, public role for all women, suffragists began to demolish the absolute, sexually defined barrier marking the public world of men off from the private world of women."[8] Stanton did exaggerate the benefits that would flow from the enfranchisement of women. But she was correct to stress that the suffrage was an indispensable prerequisite to women's freedom and dignity.

With the Seneca Falls convention of 1848, Elizabeth Cady Stanton began a public career that would span more than half a century. But before she could fully come into her own as a feminist leader, she would have to surmount a series of formidable obstacles. The first of these obstacles was the ridicule of men. In her speech at the convention, Stanton had predicted that the women's protest would raise a storm. But she and her colleagues were unprepared for the sarcastic contempt with which their handiwork was greeted. Newspapers throughout the nation vied in lampooning the Seneca Falls declaration and resolutions. And they sharply reproached Stanton and her colleagues for forgetting their proper "sphere." In the words of a Philadelphia paper: "A woman is a nobody. A wife is everything. A pretty girl is equal to ten thousand men, and a mother is, next to God, all powerful. . . ."[9]

Stanton soon learned to counter or ignore male ridicule. A more disturbing obstacle than the sarcasm of men was the silence of women. The great majority of American women did not immediately flock to the banners that had been unfurled at Seneca Falls. Some agreed with the new feminist arguments, but held back from public support out of a fear of male disapproval. A larger number clung to the dominant conventions of "separate spheres." The imperviousness of the latter group to a discourse of equality sometimes stung Stanton into vehement exclamations of frustration. In 1857, when Susan B. Anthony reported her failure to stir a meeting of female teachers to demand equal pay with male teachers, Stanton wrote back:

> What an infernal set of fools these schoolmarms must be!! Well, if in order to please men they wish to live on air, let them. The sooner the present generation of women die out the better. We have jackasses enough in the world now without such women propagating any more.[10]

The obstacles to Stanton's feminist leadership were also closer to home. She was a founding mother of the women's rights movement in a literal as well as a figurative sense; by 1859, she had seven children to bind her to the domestic sphere. Her husband, frequently absent on legal and political business, expected her to stay at home and place maternal and household cares above feminist endeavors. Her father, the person whose approval she wanted most desperately, warned her that she would pay an emotional and financial price for her public voice, threatening to disinherit her if she became a feminist lecturer. (He carried through with the threat, but later relented.) Loving her children intensely, glorying in her experiences as a mother, Stanton still repeatedly lamented the restricted public role that seemed to be the concomitant of her motherhood. Writing to

Susan B. Anthony in 1852, she cried out: "I am at the boiling point! If I do not find some day the use of my tongue on this question, I shall die of an intellectual repression, a woman's rights convulsion!"[11]

Throughout these years of domestic confinement, however, Stanton was honing her feminist consciousness. Anthony came often to visit, bringing Stanton news of the suffrage movement, and temporarily relieving her of household duties so that she could write the speeches and tracts that made her the leading theoretician of the women's cause. The laments about how domestic cares hobbled the public career for which she yearned were balanced by a realization that those cares strengthened her identification with other women and deepened her perception of what a women's movement would have to overcome. Stanton recognized that she would have to bide her time, waiting for a period when the demands of domesticity would recede and her rebellious feminist spirit could have full play. In 1857, she laid out her future in a prescient prediction to Anthony: "You and I have a prospect of a good long life. We shall not be in our prime before fifty, and after that we shall be good for twenty years at least."[12]

Shortly before she turned fifty, Stanton shed the remaining constraints of domesticity—there were no more babies to bind her to home—and took up a full-time public career amid the heated political atmosphere of the Civil War and Reconstruction. Once the dominant political forces of the Reconstruction era began to promote the rights of black men, while ignoring the rights of the women who had labored for their emancipation, she threw herself into what was to be the most painful episode in her entire public life. In the name of a passionate and outraged defense of women's rights, Stanton broke with her former abolitionist and radical Republican allies, and opposed passage of the Fourteenth and Fifteenth Amendments because they excluded women. She went beyond principled opposition to black manhood suffrage to articulate a racist and nativist position that violated her own egalitarian convictions. Fighting for women's cause with every weapon at her command, she helped to shape a more autonomous women's movement—but at a heavy cost to her own democratic vision.

The abolitionists and radical Republicans with whom Stanton and Susan B. Anthony had long associated themselves emerged as an influential bloc in the postwar politics of Reconstruction. But as the abolitionists began to press for black legal equality and then for black manhood suffrage, they also made it plain that any similar advances for women would have to wait. In their view, to couple suffrage for women with suffrage for the freedmen would ensure the defeat of both. Feminists were thus advised that this was "the negro's hour," not theirs. For some Republican politicians, the question was one of expedience; their concern in pushing black manhood suffrage was to guarantee Republican political dominance in the South. For lifelong champions of the slave, though, the sense of urgency in obtaining black rights and black manhood suffrage was sincere. Without a federal guarantee of black rights, the former slaves would have no chance to make economic progress. Without a federal guarantee of black voting power, the former slaves would be at the mercy of white violence and terror.

If there was a strong case to be made for the priority of the rights of black men, there was also a strong one to be made by Elizabeth Cady Stanton for placing women on a par with black men. Stanton insisted that Reconstruction must be "the woman's hour also. . . ."[13] Once the most progressive political forces appeared to be in the driver's seat, they should seize the moment to fulfill the equal rights promise of the Civil War struggle. The time for reform was brief; if the cause of women's rights was deferred for a few years to give precedence to black rights, it would be lost for a generation. Stanton charged her former male allies not only with political timidity, but with political hypocrisy as well. Champions of republican equality, they were proposing a universal manhood suffrage that made all men a superior and all women an inferior caste. Former patrons of the suffering slaves, they were transferring half of the emancipated population—black women—from bondage to the slavemaster to bondage to the black male. Stanton eloquently deployed the rhetoric of universal rights that the abolitionists and radical Republicans had largely abandoned, turning that rhetoric against its former practitioners: "We demand in the reconstruction, suffrage for all the citizens of the Republic. I would not talk of negroes or women, but of citizens."[14]

The initial impulse of Stanton and Anthony in the Reconstruction era was to win back erstwhile male allies to the standpoint of universal rights. But as the majority of abolitionists and Republicans opposed or evaded their arguments, they began to search elsewhere for support for the women's cause. They turned first to the Democrats—a party that included the Copperhead (pro-slavery) elements they had excoriated during the Civil War. Elizabeth Cady Stanton's and Susan B. Anthony's abolitionist friends were appalled by their association with George Francis Train, a strong supporter of women's rights but also a self-promoting crank whose Copperhead past was reflected in flagrant racist rhetoric. Train's patronage furthered—yet did not initiate—Stanton's and Anthony's own turn to the rhetoric of racism.

Although many of Stanton's arguments against giving priority to black men over women were principled and cogent, her use of racism showed her at her worst. Stanton began to devalue blacks and immigrants as a way of boosting the claims of women. One of her frequent rhetorical devices during the Reconstruction period was to project middle-class white women as the only possible saviors of the American republic from the dangerous hordes empowered by universal manhood suffrage: "In view of the fact that the Freedmen of the South and the millions of foreigners now crowding our shores, most of whom represent neither property, education, nor civilization, are all in the progress of events to be enfranchised, the best interests of the nation demand that we outweigh this incoming pauperism, ignorance, and degradation, with the wealth, education, and refinement of the women of the republic."[15] Her language of class superiority sometimes became overtly racist: "If woman finds it hard to bear the oppressive laws of a few Saxon fathers, of the best orders of manhood, what may she not be called to endure when all the lower orders, natives and foreigners, Dutch, Irish, Chinese, and African, legislate for her and her daughters?"[16]

In the search for new friends to back the cause of women's rights, Stanton and Anthony soon discovered the limits of the Democratic party and its racist elements. Rebuffed by the Democrats in 1868, Stanton and Anthony associated the women's movement with the National Labor Union, and Anthony took the lead in organizing working-class women. During the brief period when militant unionism provided a framework for Stanton's thought, the language of racism was supplanted in her speeches and articles by a language of collaboration between women and blacks. She became inspired by a vision of fundamental political and economic change in which all of the oppressed would work together: "The producers—the workingmen, the women, the negroes—are destined to form a triple power that shall speedily wrest the sceptre of government from the non-producers—the land monopolists, the bondholders, the politicians."[17] The coalition that Stanton envisioned was, however, to be short-lived, doomed both by sexist traditions among male unionists and middle-class biases on the part of the feminists. And with its unraveling, coupled with the fresh outrage to women of their exclusion from the Fifteenth Amendment, Stanton returned to the rhetoric of racism.

Elizabeth Cady Stanton could hardly have been comfortable in employing racist and nativist rhetoric. Her republican faith, expressed with great fervor during the Civil War, made her a passionate advocate of equality and a sworn enemy of caste and class distinctions. Racial prejudice was not a part of her makeup; after the Reconstruction struggles were past, Stanton would again become a defender of the rights and the dignity of blacks. Why, then, did she choose during the Reconstruction era to adopt a rhetoric so at odds with her own values?

Stanton's turn to racism was, in part, an expression of frustrated hopes for justice. To Stanton, the proclamation of a "negro's hour" that excluded women was more than another extended postponement of equality for women, more even than a betrayal by revered male allies. It was an outrageous demonstration of the gendered nature of justice in America. Asked to keep silent and to wait, women were in reality being told, as always, to subordinate their own needs and aspirations to the requirements of a group of men. They were being told that they should sacrifice their interests to those of black men, reproducing in public life the ethic of domestic self-sacrifice dictated to women by the doctrine of "separate spheres."

But Stanton's racist rhetoric also reflected her class bias. Coming from a background of privilege, and living the life of a bourgeois matron as well as a feminist agitator, Stanton's vision was obstructed by the blinders of her class. Believing that the emancipation of the freedmen placed them on a par with middle-class white women—both groups lacking only the ballot to attain full equality— she failed to grasp the beleaguered economic position of southern blacks in the new industrial-capitalist order. Stanton's Reconstruction rhetoric was, finally, a descent into political expedience. She employed racist language deliberately in an attempt to persuade middle-class white males that they needed their female counterparts as allies if they hoped to control the rising political power of immigrants and blacks. In so doing, she pitted the political aspirations of one excluded group against those of another, rather than seeking common ground among the oppressed.

Neither Stanton's principled arguments nor her racist ones made much headway. The Reconstruction era advanced black rights but left women just as excluded from public freedoms as before. For Stanton, the pain of this failure was only exacerbated by the anguish of her break with old friends. She emerged from Reconstruction shaken but undaunted. If women's immediate political prospects were bleak, the commitment of Elizabeth Cady Stanton and Susan B. Anthony to continue the fight for equal rights was underscored by their formation of the National Woman Suffrage Association in 1869. The Reconstruction era had produced a more autonomous women's movement, interested in alliances with other progressive forces but insistent on avoiding the subordination of women's cause to any other. The fashioning of this movement has been hailed by Ellen Dubois as "the greatest achievement of feminists in the post-war period. . . ."[18]

The three decades remaining to Stanton after Reconstruction, up to her death in 1902, were filled with the vigorous public activities of a feminist agitator. In the 1870s, her principal role was as a traveling lecturer, spreading her feminist views across the nation. In the 1880s, she joined with Susan B. Anthony and Matilda Joslyn Gage to compile the multivolume *History of Woman Suffrage,* preserving the words and deeds of early feminists for later generations. During the final years of her life, she became convinced that religious teachings about the inferiority of women stood in the way of equality between the sexes, and produced *The Woman's Bible* as a critical commentary on the biblical depiction of women. This work was repudiated by an increasingly conservative and Christian women's movement, leaving the elderly Stanton isolated but proudly defiant in her prophetic feminist militancy.

If we turn to examine Stanton in her roles as an agitator and theorist, we find a figure of rich feminist complexity. As an agitator, Stanton had a striking public personality. The feminist vision she voiced was explosively radical for her time. Stanton went beyond the demand for equality for women in every sphere of life, and insisted upon profound transformations of both the public and the private spheres. She was a critic of marriage and a proponent of sexual radicalism. Yet this voice that threatened the political and social proprieties of nineteenth-century America came from a woman whose appearances in public were unthreatening, indeed reassuring. On the public platform, Stanton was matronly, charming, genial. She dressed in respectable black silk, with white lace collars and cuffs.

How can this peculiar combination of militant feminist and middle-class matron be explained? According to biographer Elisabeth Griffith, Stanton's radical message was her real public personality; the feminine garb and style were her mask. As Griffith puts it: "At the same time that she was moving out of her domestic sphere, Stanton began to use her maternal role to legitimize her public activities. She shrewdly chose to appear matronly, respectable, charming, and genial."[19]

There is some evidence that Stanton did self-consciously attempt to make her radical message more palatable. But the femininity and maternity she displayed on the public platform were not masks, but essential facets of her character. Stanton was not only the mother of seven children, but a woman who prided herself on her knowledge and skills at mothering; she was genuinely eager to present herself as a sort of supermother. She loved beautiful clothes and graceful appearances. While she knew moments of private rage against male oppression, she was generally a genial and humorous person in private as well as public. Stanton was just what she appeared to be: a militant feminist *and* a middle-class matron.

If Stanton's public personality seems contradictory, especially to a modern observer, such contradiction may have made her more effective as a feminist agitator. Her public personality embodied the experiences of the majority of women, making it easier for her audiences to identify with her. That personality spoke to the ambivalence that many women, torn between prevailing codes of femininity and feminist visions of changed womanhood, seemed to be feeling in nineteenth-century America. What appears in one light as contradiction can even be seen, in a different light, as an essential attribute of Stanton's feminism. Through her public personality, as much as through her public arguments, Stanton was asserting that women did not have to give up valued experiences *as* women—such as motherhood or the expression of a special moral sensitivity—in order to stake their claims to share all the domains that men had previously monopolized. What she wrote in 1885—"surely maternity is an added power and development of some of the most tender sentiments of the human heart and not a limitation" upon women in politics—she lived out on the public stage.[20]

Stanton drew power as an agitator from her contradictory public personality, but she did not want her particular fusion of feminism and femininity to be obligatory for other female activists. She often praised the unstinting efforts that unmarried women, such as Susan B. Anthony, were able to provide to the feminist movement. She defended these women against charges that they were "masculine," arguing that men hurled this epithet at the bravest and most independent women. If Stanton remained attached to beautiful clothing and gloried in the signs of her motherhood, she was not without knowledge of the price women paid for these feminine pleasures. She knew that woman "is a slave to her rags."[21] And she knew the ambiguous joy of feminist motherhood. Upon her return home from a brief political trip in 1855, she wrote to her cousin, Elizabeth Smith Miller: "The joy a mother feels on seeing her baby after a short absence is a bliss that no man's soul can ever know. There we have something that they have not! But we have purchased the ecstasy in deep sorrow and suffering."[22]

Possessing a compelling personality and an eloquent tongue, Stanton enjoyed her role as an agitator. First initiated into politics through the abolitionist movement, she had powerful role models in William Lloyd Garrison and Wendell Phillips. Although Stanton was more willing than Garrison or Phillips to work within the framework of political parties, she shared their disdain for the politician and their pride in the stance of the agitator.

An agitator, in Stanton's self-conception, was to be guided by the truth of a principle rather than by the numbers who adhered to it. Agitators should anticipate an initial hostility and scorn from the majority rather than understanding and applause: "The history of the world shows that the vast majority in every generation passively accept the conditions into which they are born, while those who demand larger liberties are ever a small, ostracised minority whose claims are ridiculed and ignored."[23] The task of the agitator was both to defy and to transform public opinion. Confronting a majority steeped in outmoded customs and unjust values, the agitator sought to open their eyes to political rights and moral responsibilities. Stanton held to a simple, even naive, faith that true principles, if effectively agitated, would ultimately be accepted by the majority. In 1888, writing in her diary, she observed: "If I were to draw up a set of rules for the guidance of reformers, . . . I should put at the head of the list: 'Do all you can, *no matter what*, to get people to think on your reform, and then, if the reform is good, it will come about in due season.' "[24]

Stanton's pleasure in agitation was matched by her dislike for organizational politics. She viewed organizational responsibilities as cribbing her independent and militant voice. Her avoidance of organizational duties might have weakened her influence on the women's rights movement, had she not been fortunate to enjoy a close partnership with Susan B. Anthony. Where Stanton was delighted when she could obtain her freedom from organizational constraints, Anthony was most happy and most effective in the organizational milieu that suited her special talents. While Anthony organized the growing ranks of women's suffrage supporters, Stanton developed a political vision that spoke to women's most profound aspirations for changes in their lives.

Stanton's feminist vision was as complex—and often seemed as contradictory—as her public personality. Conflicting strains and impulses pulled her thought in different directions. She emphasized that women were no different than men in their mental qualities and capacities—but also argued that they were fundamentally different through their special proclivity for morality and mercy. She demanded equal access for women to all the spheres of life that men currently monopolized—but also demanded a revolution in male-female relations. She reshaped the liberal ideal of self-reliance into a doctrine of female individualism—but also bound women together through a vision of sisterhood.

On one level, these strains and conflicts in Stanton's thoughts reflect inconsistency. On another level, they are signs of a legitimate tension at the heart of her feminist vision. Recognizing the sharp dichotomies in prevailing codes of male domination and female subordination, Stanton constantly struggled to transcend them. She wanted to deny that women had to choose between their identity as women and their complete freedom and equality. She wanted to affirm that women could value their distinctive experiences, ethics, and solidarity, while still overcoming any limits placed upon them by men.

In Stanton's comparisons of women with men, arguments from women's sameness and arguments from women's difference from men were sometimes mixed together in the same speech or letter. Writing to an Ohio women's rights convention in 1850, she complained that "it is impossible for us to convince man that we think and feel exactly as he does; that we have the same sense of right and justice, the same love of freedom and independence." In the very next paragraph, however, she made it plain that women did not "think and feel exactly" like men: "Had the women of this country had a voice in the Government, think you our national escutcheon would have been stained with the guilt of aggressive warfare upon such weak, defenseless nations as the Seminoles and Mexicans?"[25]

Whether Stanton emphasized sameness or difference was, as she once candidly admitted, in large part a matter of tactics, of what made the most compelling case for women's rights. Philosophically, she wanted to push beyond the existing dichotomy between male and female. At her most visionary, she proclaimed that "in the education and elevation of woman we are yet to learn the true manhood and womanhood, the true masculine and feminine elements."[26] Stanton recognized that male oppression and female subordination had distorted the qualities of both genders. What women and men would truly be like was a question that only the future could answer. Yet that future was not predestined; it was the task of the feminist movement to create it.

Stanton always demanded equality for women—but the equality she sought had multiple meanings. One of these meanings was equal rights for women, principally in the area of the suffrage, but also in such fields as ownership of property and access to trades and professions. The disfranchisement of women was, in her view, a basic disability that lay at the core of women's grievances. Deprived of political power, women could not gain equal opportunity in any sphere of life. Deprived of citizen responsibilities, they could not gain equal respect either. Throughout her long public career, Stanton condemned what she called "the degradation of disfranchisement."[27]

If much of Stanton's case for women's equality stressed equal opportunity within existing structures, her conception of equality could not be satisfied merely by inclusion of women into the political and economic status quo. Increasingly, she came to regard the home, even more than the state, as the locus of women's oppression. In the home, she wrote, "the woman is uniformly sacrificed to the wife and mother."[28] Law reinforced custom in making the marital bond into "the man marriage," in which "the woman is regarded and spoken of simply as the toy of man . . . ."[29] Feminists must not, Stanton argued, ignore inequality in the home in their campaign for equality in the state.

Tracking down inequality in the home, Stanton courageously ventured into the domain of sexuality. She came to argue that men's power over women was anchored in an autocratic assertion of sexual prerogative. To be genuinely equal with men, women would have to fight for their sexual self-determination: "Man in his lust has regulated long enough this whole question of sexual intercourse."[30] Stanton wanted women not only to be able to say no to their husbands, but to have the personal and economic freedom to dispense with marriage if they found it oppressive. She thus championed liberalized divorce laws, and advocated greater freedom of sexual choice. Bringing the political back to the personal, Stanton fought for a radical transformation of relations between the sexes.

Just as Stanton was pulled toward the opposing poles of sameness and difference, of equal opportunity and radical transformation of gender relationships, so was she tugged toward the opposing poles of individualism and sisterhood. The language of individual freedom and self-development was one of the enduring themes in her rhetoric after 1848. Stanton's individualism only reached its apogee, however, with her 1892 speech, "The Solitude of Self." In this speech (which she considered her best), she declared that women's campaign for equality had its ultimate justification in the solitariness of each human life.

> The strongest reason why we ask for woman a voice in the government under which she lives; in the religion she is asked to believe; equality in social life, where she is the chief factor; a place in the trades and professions, where she may earn her bread, is because of her birthright to self-sovereignty; because as an individual, she must rely on herself. No matter how much women prefer to lean, to be protected and supported, no matter how much men desire to have them do so, they must make the voyage of life alone. . . .

At times in the speech, Stanton spoke a language of individual development reminiscent of Ralph Waldo Emerson, whom she admired. At the end of the speech, however, she underscored with bleak images the distances separating each individual from all others: "There is a solitude which each and every one of us has always carried with him, more inaccessible than the ice-cold mountains, more profound than the midnight sea: the solitude of self."[31]

As a sermon on the need for women to take responsibility for their own lives, "The Solitude of Self" was powerful and moving. But when Stanton posited freedom as the condition of a solitary self—even making reference to "an imaginary Robinson Crusoe, with her woman, Friday, on a solitary island"—she neglected the bonds of sisterhood that sustained women in their struggles to overcome oppression.[32] It was precisely those bonds that pulled Stanton away from her own "solitude of self."

Stanton's broad sympathies for women of all kinds were especially evident during the same period in which she produced "The Solitude of Self." In the final decades of the nineteenth century, the women's movement grew increasingly narrow. Shedding more radical demands and concentrating only on suffrage, the movement was now dominated by white, middle-class, Christian women who sought respectability in the eyes of the powerful. Elizabeth Cady Stanton found herself at odds with such a movement—and with her closest friend, Susan B. Anthony, who accommodated herself to the new conservatism—because it no longer spoke for all of women's needs or for all classes of women. Against the new tendency to work only for suffrage, Stanton insisted on a struggle in every arena in which women were oppressed. Against the new tendency to push only the claims of the most respectable women, she called upon feminists to regain an enlarged vision of sisterhood. Speaking before the founding convention of the National American Woman Suffrage Association (formed by the merger of the National Woman Suffrage Association and the American Woman Suffrage Association) in 1890, Stanton swam against the conservative tide:

> Wherever and whatever any class of women suffer whether in the home, the church, the courts, in the world of work, in the statute books, a voice in their behalf should be heard in our conventions. We must manifest a broad catholic spirit for all shades of opinion in which we may differ and recognize the equal right of all parties, sects and races, tribes and colors. Colored women, Indian women, Mormon women and women from every quarter of the globe have been heard in these Washington conventions and I trust they always will be.[33]

Elizabeth Cady Stanton could be self-righteous in her feminist individualism. Her proud self-assertion sometimes conveyed an air of superiority. But the principal force in her public life was always a sense of outrage at the degradation of women and an empathy for all women confronting that degradation. The individualist who plumbed her own "solitude of self" never forgot her bond to the multitudes of women whose redemption she once described as her "whole-souled, all-absorbing, agonizing interest."[34]

Notes

[1]For biographical details on Stanton, see Elisabeth Griffith, *In Her Own Right: The Life of Elizabeth Cady Stanton* (New York: Oxford University Press, 1984) and Alma Lutz, *Created Equal: A Biography of Elizabeth Cady Stanton* (New York: The John Day Company, 1940).

[2]Elizabeth Cady Stanton Papers, Vassar College Library.

[3]Ibid.

[4]Elizabeth Cady Stanton, *Eighty Years and More: Reminiscences, 1815–1897* (New York: Schocken Books, 1971), p. 148.

[5]Elizabeth Cady Stanton et al., *History of Woman Suffrage*, vol. 1 (Rochester: Susan B. Anthony, 1881), p. 70.

[6]Ellen Carol Dubois, ed., *Elizabeth Cady Stanton/Susan B. Anthony: Correspondence, Writings, Speeches* (New York: Schocken Books, 1981), p. 28.

[7]Stanton et al., *History of Woman Suffrage*, vol. 1, p. 71.

[8]Ellen Carol Dubois, "The Radicalism of the Woman Suffrage Movement: Notes toward the Reconstruction of Nineteenth-Century Feminism," in Anne Phillips, ed., *Feminism and Equality* (New York: New York University Press, 1987), p. 130.

[9]Stanton et al., *History of Woman Suffrage*, vol. 1, p. 804.

[10]Stanton Papers, Vassar College Library.

[11]Theodore Stanton and Harriott Stanton Blatch, eds., *Elizabeth Cady Stanton as Revealed in Her Letters, Diary and Reminiscences*, vol. 2 (New York: Harper & Brothers Publishers, 1922), p. 41.

[12]Ibid., p. 71.

[13]Elizabeth Cady Stanton et al., *History of Woman Suffrage*, vol. 2 (Rochester: Susan B. Anthony, 1881), p. 319.

[14]Stanton and Blatch, eds., *Elizabeth Cady Stanton as Revealed*, p. 120.

[15]Stanton et al., *History of Woman Suffrage*, vol. 2, p. 181.

[16]*The Revolution*, 24 Dec. 1868.

[17]Ibid., 1 Oct. 1868.

[18]Ellen Carol Dubois, *Feminism and Suffrage: The Emergence of an Independent Women's Movement in America: 1848–1869* (Ithaca: Cornell University Press, 1978), p. 164.

[19]Griffith, *In Her Own Right*, p. 143.

[20]Susan B. Anthony and Ida Husted Harper, *History of Woman Suffrage*, vol. 4 (Rochester: Susan B. Anthony, 1902), p. 58.

[21]Stanton and Blatch, eds., *Elizabeth Cady Stanton as Revealed*, p. 45.

[22]Ibid., p. 61.

[23]Elizabeth Cady Stanton et al., *History of Woman Suffrage*, vol. 3 (Rochester: Susan B. Anthony, 1886), p. 56.

[24]Stanton and Blatch, eds., *Elizabeth Cady Stanton as Revealed*, p. 252.

[25]Stanton et al., *History of Woman Suffrage*, vol. 1, p. 811.

[26]Stanton et al., *History of Woman Suffrage*, vol. 2, pp. 189–90.

[27]Anthony and Harper, *History of Woman Suffrage*, vol. 4, p. 176.

[28]Stanton et al., *History of Woman Suffrage*, vol. 1, p. 22.

[29]Ibid., p. 722.

[30]Stanton and Blatch, eds., *Elizabeth Cady Stanton as Revealed*, p. 49.

[31]Dubois, ed., *Elizabeth Cady Stanton/Susan B. Anthony*, pp. 247–54.

[32]Ibid., p. 247.

[33]Ibid., p. 226.

[34]Stanton and Blatch, eds., *Elizabeth Cady Stanton as Revealed*, p. 81.

Mary Todd Lincoln

(1818–1882)

Jean Baker

Born into the household of a wealthy Kentucky slaveholder in 1818, Mary Todd received an unusually good education for a woman of her day. In 1839 she went to live with her sister in Springfield, Illinois. There, Mary Todd entered the social circle that included the brightest young men in Illinois politics, and attracted the attention of one of them, Abraham Lincoln, a local lawyer. Despite her family's objections and a troubled courtship, in November 1842 the couple were married. Abraham Lincoln's legal career flourished, and he was elected to the state legislature and then to Congress. The Lincolns had four sons and a marriage that appears to have been a happy one. When her husband was elected president in 1860, and with the outbreak of the Civil War, Mary Todd Lincoln came under attack as a Southern woman married to the Union president, and because of her expensive tastes in creating a lavish White House. Tormented by the criticism and by the death of one of her sons (another child had died earlier), Mary Todd Lincoln became increasingly prone to melancholy and distress. With her husband's assassination in 1865, she was left homeless and with little money. During her later years she was confined to a sanitarium by her only living son on claims of her "insanity," but she was eventually able to secure her freedom. She died in Springfield, Illinois, in 1882.

Mary Todd Lincoln's prominence depended upon her connection to her husband. Her life suggests much about the relation of women to successful husbands and to the public world of nineteenth-century politics. Although the privilege she gained through marriage allowed her a voice in the public arena, it made her a target for the hostile prejudices to which outspoken women were subject.

$\mathbf{A}$t the end of her life, Mary Todd Lincoln referred to herself as "poor me" and exhorted "the ruler of us all to soften the pathway I have been called upon to tread." Her advice to anyone who would listen—and few did—was to have a good time, "for trouble comes soon enough." Surely this was the lesson she had learned from a life of exaggerated misery; others—from male contemporaries to later biographers of Lincoln—would try to make Mary Lincoln's story a cautionary tale of what respectable women should *not* be. Yet, earlier, it had seemed that hers would be the easy, pampered existence of the Lexington gentry—a life framed by the affections and the money of the Kentucky Parkers and Todds and the conventions of female behavior in the early nineteenth century. In these circumstances, like too many women, she would have disappeared from history's view, but Mary Todd Lincoln ensured her historical remembrance by her marriage to an American hero, her interpretation of the role of First Lady, and the tragedies that she sustained during her life.[1]

Like most American women of her time, it was marriage that defined Mary Todd Lincoln's adult status. Yet, before his election to the presidency in 1860, Abraham Lincoln was neither a hero nor even a suitable choice for a young woman of Mary Todd's social and economic background. Born a poor farmer's son in a Kentucky setting that shared little besides geographic proximity to Mary Todd's Lexington, Abraham Lincoln, like so many young men of his generation, had moved to town, first to New Salem and then to nearby Springfield, Illinois. A self-taught lawyer who had less than a year of formal schooling, he nonetheless impressed some of the Springfield community with his intelligence and common sense. Still, even after four terms in the state legislature in the 1830s and 1840s, Lincoln was twice defeated for the United States Senate, and his selection as the Republican nominee and his subsequent victory in the 1860 presidential election were explained by his surprised contemporaries as the result of a split in the Democratic party, which ran two candidates in the election. Nor was Lincoln a heroic figure during the war. His election in 1864 over the Democrat and former commanding general of the Union forces George B. McClellan was only assured by the votes of soldiers in the field.

Only after his assassination did Lincoln emerge as the symbol of the American Union. For blacks and antislavery whites, the sixteenth president became the "Great Emancipator" who had freed from bondage nearly four million slaves. After his death, Lincoln was seen to have dedicated his life to the restoration of the American Republic, and the leader who was assassinated the very week that Robert E. Lee's Confederate army surrendered seemed to symbolize the 600,000 young Americans who had died in military service. The wartime gibes about "Old Abe—The Black Gorilla" were forgotten, as even the South after Lincoln's death came to locate in him more benign approaches to the problem of reconstructing the Union. And as the myths around Lincoln grew and moved farther and farther away from the historical reality of his life, his wife's reputation deteriorated. Like a see-saw, the greatness of the husband provided a contrast to the myths that clustered, unfairly, around the wife. But in the beginning of their relationship, it was Mary, not Abraham, who was the more socially respectable.

Mary Todd was born in Lexington, Kentucky, in 1818, the daughter of Eliza Parker Todd and Eliza's distant cousin Robert Smith Todd; she died in 1882 at her sister's home in Springfield, Illinois. Christened Mary Ann after her father's sister, she began life as a member of an expanding household of siblings and slaves in a town that had been organized by her grandfathers and great-uncles. The Todd brothers—Levi, John, and Robert—had named Lexington after the famous battle fought in 1775 in faraway Massachusetts. With an energy and spirit that the Todds would pass along to many of their descendants, including Mary, the founders expected to transform a grassy meadow surrounded by woods into a center of culture and commerce. In these frontier times, their wives, daughters, and sisters wove textiles; bore, raised, and fed their families; took care of the livestock; and worked in the hemp and corn fields as well as the small gardens that provided this generation with its herbs and vegetables.

By Mary Ann Todd's day Lexington had become a sophisticated city of over six thousand residents with good schools, a college (Kentuckians boasted that Transylvania was the best institution in the country), stores that catered to the rich planter families of Fayette county, and an economy that depended on the transportation of agricultural products and slaves to the markets in New Orleans. But when steamboats began making the journey upstream from New Orleans to rival Louisville on the Ohio River in only three weeks, the Todds' great expectations for Lexington to become "the Athens of the West" floundered.

So too did young Mary Todd's attachment to the place. In 1826 her mother died of puerperal fever, an infection that often followed childbirth and that made childbearing a life-threatening event in every woman's life. Like most Kentucky women, Eliza Todd had a child every two or three years, a spacing dictated not by any conscious control over the process of reproduction, but rather by the natural form of contraception afforded by lactation. At a critical age to lose a mother, Mary promptly lost some of her father's affection to her mother's replacement, just as earlier she had lost part of her name to a younger sister Ann. For all her virtues, Robert Smith Todd's new wife proved to be an uncongenial stepmother.

Surrounded by a growing household that would eventually number fourteen children and ten slaves along with her parents, Mary stood out because, unlike her three sisters and five half-sisters, her behavior crossed some of the barriers of gender that separated young boys and girls in Lexington, and indeed throughout the United States. First she went to school too long; by the time Mary finished both John Ward's day school and Madame Mentelle's French School for Young Ladies she had completed twelve years of schooling, and though Lexington was well known for its educated women, only a handful of women in the United States had that much education. By the 1840s, Catharine Beecher, Mary Lyons, and Almira Phelps would make the case for girls' schooling not so much for their husbands' and children's benefit, but so that women could become schoolteachers. Still, girls were not supposed to compete as intellectual equals with boys, and Mary violated this taboo when she argued with the tutor brought from New England to advance the learning of the Todd sons. And no doubt she also set herself apart from the other girls at the Lexington parties through her book-learning. "[L]iterary topics," advised one southern woman, "make [the boys] run from you as if you had the plague."[2]

So, too, did political topics. Women who talked about public affairs, except perhaps those who consoled male relatives who had lost an election, risked gossip. Evidently Mary did not care. She may have hoped to catch a busy father's attention, for Robert Smith Todd was an important member of the Whig party, a major political party of the time, by the 1830s. She may have been influenced by a home where politicians came to grumble about President Andrew Jackson's veto of a Bank Bill and, worse, his veto of the Maysville bill that would have allocated federal funds to a road connecting northern Kentucky counties to the Ohio River. She may have been influenced by the great Whig senator, Henry Clay, who lived across the pike from her boarding school. In any case, Mary proclaimed herself a Whig, and in an early display of what became an enduring characteristic, she took an active interest in politics. This was in a time when well-born women, especially those in the South, shunned any interest in the public world, instead making their contributions to the private realm of home, family, and church. Those few who did not, like Angelina and Sarah Grimké, the daughters of a South Carolina slaveholder, found it necessary to leave the South.[3]

Mary Todd took her interest in public affairs to Springfield, Illinois, where, by 1839, she lived with her older married sister as an exile from her stepmother's house. For a time, like many young women of her class and time, she went to parties, read, sewed, and formed a close, affectionate relationship with another woman. The modern historian Caroll Smith-Rosenberg calls this "the female world of love and ritual" and means by it a female culture shared by those excluded from the male life of politics, work outside the home, and special meeting places such as taverns, coffee shops, and clubs. Women prohibited from public places made the home and the church their special preserve, while at the same time creating strong bonds with other women. Certainly, Mary participated in this female world in her friendship with Mercy Levering, and their intimacy is apparent in the letters that they wrote when separated by what Mary once called "so many long and weary miles." Wrote Mary in 1840 to Mercy: "You know the deep interest I feel for you. . . . [T]he brightest associations of the past years are connected to thee." Both of these women expected to marry; it was their obligatory status and one that would determine their future in a consuming way that would not be the same for their spouses. During this time of idleness both Mary and Mercy courted; Mary's dance cards were always full and she had an eye for men of politics. But after the parties she and Mercy shared an affection which was not necessarily sexual or erotic but which was a common response to the separated spheres of men and women.[4]

In time, Mary made her choice, and it was Abraham Lincoln, the Whig legislator and lawyer whom she married at a small ceremony held at her sister's house in November 1842. Some thought him the ugliest man in Springfield, and Mary's sister and brother-in-law had opposed the marriage on the grounds that Abraham would not go far. But behind his country manners and clothing, Mary appreciated his potential, and she also sensed his tolerance for women and his desire for the partnership that she believed marriage must be. Traditionally, the husband had been the head of the family, and the comparison of the family to a little kingdom with the wife and children as subjects was a familiar one during the colonial period. But in the nineteenth century a newer style of domestic feminism enabled wives to make crucial decisions about childrearing, the allocation of family resources, and childbearing, even if they did not control the household pursestrings. And as all Springfield soon knew, Abraham Lincoln, according to his friend, and biographer, William Herndon, "exercised no government at home."[5]

It is through an appreciation of Mary's domesticity, and her conventional years as a mother, wife, and homemaker in the western town of Springfield, that we gain an understanding of the experiences shared by many if not most American women of her era. For eighteen years, from 1842 until 1861, when the Lincolns left for the

White House, Mary Lincoln ran the household at Eighth and Jackson. She organized the menus, relying on *Miss Leslie's Cookery and Miss Leslie's House Book* for the recipes that she had never learned in Lexington, where household slaves had done the cooking. She took care of her husband in the nurturing manner that was expected of self-sacrificing middle-class women of this generation who were to smother their own individuality and autonomy with the needs of others. For according to one of the popular prescription manuals of the day:

> Best pleased to be admired at home
> And hear reflected from her husband's praise
> That her house was ordered well,
> Her children taught the way of life.[6]

Certainly it was Mary Lincoln who molded the character and values of her four sons. While Abraham Lincoln was an example of the more companionate father of the future, he was usually absent from Springfield for over a third of the year. Both business and politics took him to the dusty courtrooms of the Eighth Judicial Circuit, leaving Mary Lincoln at home with the boys for long stretches of time. In the permissive mothering style of the future, she organized games and gave large birthday parties. At a time in which most mothers were not so child-directed, she nursed her babies longer than most women, and she erupted in anger if anyone criticized her boys. She also provided most of the medical care for her children, for this was a time and Springfield was a place where the only treatments for the bacterial infections that threatened the young were ineffective drugs such as calomel, a purgative, along with the bloodletting that remained a respectable method of dealing with many diseases. Like most women, Mary Lincoln lost a child to disease; young Eddie Lincoln—"My Angel Boy," as she called him—died at age four of tuberculosis, the most common of the infectious diseases in children under five.[7]

Besides cooking and childraising, Mary was also responsible for keeping the house and the clothes clean. Washing in an age without any electrical devices was a dreaded three-day chore, and Mary paid servants to heat the water, lather the clothes, rinse them in cast-iron tubs, beat them dry, and finally iron them with the awkward stove-heated contrivances of the mid-nineteenth century. She was also responsible for clothing the family, though increasingly—and especially for the boys and her husband—she could buy ready-made clothes in the shops along the courthouse square where Abraham Lincoln kept a second-story office. Unlike her grandmothers, she did not work outside the home, for town living in the mid-nineteenth century provided no possibilities for gardening. Still, the expanding definitions of middle-class domesticity provided a ceaseless round of activities. No doubt it was Mary who organized and paid for the renovation and continuing improvements of the Lincoln cottage, which by the mid-1850s had become what Americans who wanted to summon up an image of the ideal setting for their families called "The House Beautiful."[8] Increasingly, the Lincoln house required more time and energy to maintain the bric-a-brac and the Belgian carpets purchased (for Springfield had no such luxurious goods) in St. Louis. Despite the hard, repetitive labor devoted to uninteresting tasks, Mary would look back on her years as a homemaker as among her happiest. After all, she wrote her daughter-in-law later, all women should hold as their ideal what she once had enjoyed—"a nice home, a loving husband and precious child."[9]

She was busy in Springfield but never too busy to talk politics or to encourage her husband's participation in a career that had stalled after four terms in the state legislature followed by one term in Congress. He wanted to be a United States Senator, but lost twice, once in 1854 and then again after the debates with Democrat Stephen Douglas in 1858. Throughout, Mary Lincoln played more than a supporting role: she wrote patronage letters, she calculated the partisan choices of the legislature that would vote for the senator, she tried to encourage in her husband the conviction that he could become president, and she entertained those who might help what she considered their mutual campaign. To a prominent state politician in 1858, she extended an invitation when Abraham Lincoln was out of town: "I would be pleased to have you wander up our way. . . . I should like to see you." The hospitality she offered was strawberries and cream and conversation, but the subject of her meeting with the Illinois secretary of state was the future of what she came to think of as "our Lincoln party." One lawyer in Springfield admitted that she "did a great deal to educate Lincoln up to action," but in so doing she trespassed onto territory reserved for men in the nineteenth century. When the Republican National Committee traveled to Springfield to notify her husband of his nomination for president, they met an accomplished hostess—the most genteel of ladies—who had set a fashionable table of cakes, sandwiches, and under the table so as not to upset the temperance vote, a bottle of champagne.[10]

Other women, especially in the Northeast, had begun to campaign for public roles for women—the right to address public meetings without being harassed, the right to sign contracts and control property as married women, and even, at the Seneca Falls convention in July 1848, the right to vote. Mary Lincoln thought such activities unladylike, yet she revealed her opposition to a system that denied women their natural rights through her bold involvement in her husband's political life. Like most Americans in this time when "all the world was politics" and three of four voters turned out to vote in elections, she was fascinated with the great game of partisanship. But she chose to challenge the system in a different way from most other politically aware women of her time.

March 1861 marked the beginning of Mary Todd Lincoln's notorious years in the White House, and like so much of her life, the experience was simultaneously grandiose and tragic, unusual and conventional. From the moment of her arrival in Washington, Mary Lincoln continued to trespass into the public world reserved for men. First she intended to improve what she considered the shabby interior of the thirty-one-room White House. While each president was granted $20,000 for repairs and maintenance, the allocation had never supported redecorating. For Mary Lincoln the appearance of the president's house represented more than just a frivolous effort to show off her good taste. Rather, in her redecoration of the Green and Red Rooms, she sought to provide a symbolic statement of the power of the Union during a Civil War when the impressions of foreign diplomats posted in Washington might determine the recognition of the Confederacy by their governments. Soon after the Confederate guns of Charleston fired on the Union batteries at Fort Sumter in April 1861 and her husband began his long toil of winning a war, Mary embarked on her campaign to redo the White House.

To New York and Philadelphia the "President's Lady" went to buy the best wallpaper and furnishings along with expensive dresses; she was soon christened the "First Lady" by a perceptive English correspondent.[11] In the past, presidents' wives had retired to the second-floor family quarters, their names forgotten, as the Commissioner of Public Buildings supervised the maintenance of a house that Europeans dismissed as no grander than "the country house of a merchant."[12] Mrs. President Lincoln (as she became officially known), however, took charge as the lady of the house and served as the interior decorator as well as the director of the social occasions that served as informal opportunities not only to meet the president, but also to discuss military affairs and politics.

Although in so doing she had only transplanted her domestic feminism from one setting to another, she was soon the butt of Washington gossip. In fact, the criticism had begun before she had even gotten to Washington and as such it represented—for Washington was a Southern city—an attack on her Republican husband who was bringing a "vulgar Western wife from the prairies" to the capital's high-toned society. After Mary Lincoln overspent the congressional appropriation and was rumored to have spent $6,800 for French wall-

paper and $3,195 for a magnificent set of state china with an en-
twined gold border signifying the union of North and South, the
newspapers forgot their earlier commentary on her supposed un-
couthness and instead printed stories of her extravagance. In addition, some Republicans suspected Mary Lincoln of disloyalty, in part
because of her ineradicable Southern drawl, and in part because her
three stepbrothers were fighting in the Confederate army. Meanwhile, Abraham Lincoln, who was accustomed to turning over the
management of the home to his wife, bristled at the expenses, which
Mary with some success tried to persuade others to pay. The public-
ity that enveloped what some were calling the "Presidentess" infuri-
ated many members of the government; at the same time, Mary
Lincoln became a symbol of elegance and success for others.

But for the subject of this gossip, her status as a celebrity provided
alternating cycles of elation and humiliation. She could never forego
reading about herself as a fashion-queen, dressed, according to one
description in the *Washington Chronicle,* in a "rich-watered silk
deeply bordered, with camellias in her hair and pearl ornaments," but
such praise was offset by harsh accounts of the Illinois "queen" who
was aping Louis Napoleon's empress, the red-haired beauty Eugenie.
To harassed officials trying to find funds to buy blankets and muskets
for the hard-pressed Union army, there was an inappropriateness and
bad timing to Mary Lincoln's efforts. In time Mary complained that
she had become the "scapegoat for both North and South," although
she was also the victim of the prevailing attitude toward women that
bound them to the private sphere of family, home, and selflessness.[13]
Despising what she called the unfeminine women who took up
causes, Mary Lincoln suffered because nowhere could she find a precedent for her role as President Lincoln's active partner.

Some of the complaints against Mary Lincoln focused on her incur-
sions into politics. In Springfield she had known Abraham Lincoln's
colleagues personally and believed that her special intuitiveness as a
woman provided a scanning device to be used for her husband's
benefit. But in Washington her husband presided over a vast war-
inflated patronage. Mary Lincoln was not deterred by this, for she
continued to claim appointments for her friends and relatives, and at
the same time to offer advice to her husband and to his cabinet
officers. But the cabinet members were often offended by what they
considered her impertinent demands, for their own wives did not
interfere in public affairs.

Early in her years as First Lady, Mary Lincoln organized a party that
revealed the style of her life in the White House. She intended, during
the dull winter of 1862, to give a lavish affair that would display the
economic power of a government that had been hammered on the

battlefield by the Confederate troops at Bull Run and by Nathan Forrest's Confederate cavalry raids in the West. The First Lady invited the most important members of official Washington—Union officers, the diplomatic corps, and leading Republicans. Certainly, as Mary Lincoln reasoned, their acquaintance might be useful in the future, and in the refurbished public rooms of the White House she would advance her husband's career, and through him, her own ambitions as hostess, First Lady, and promoter of what she described as "our Lincoln party." The painters had only just repainted the Gold Room walls scarred by the damage of federal troops billeted there to protect the Lincoln family from a rumored Confederate raid; all was in readiness. But like so much in her ill-starred life, as the guests streamed into the state dining room for the magnificent buffet produced by a New York caterer, young Willie Lincoln lay dying of typhoid fever. This favorite son died two weeks after the party.

Then three years later, in another of those family abandonments that had begun with her mother's death, Mary Lincoln lost her husband as they sat holding hands, enjoying the popular farce *An American Cousin* at Ford's Theater. For most of the Union it was a time of celebration. Robert E. Lee had surrendered his Confederate army only five days before, and on April 6 Mary had toured Richmond, the defeated capital of the Confederacy. But Mary Lincoln's life was always counterpoint. At a time when she looked forward to peacetime Washington and an end to the violence of the Civil War (of which her eldest son Robert was now a part as a member of Grant's army), her husband was murdered. "Alas," she wrote a friend, "all is over with me," and in the poignant expression of her grief she echoed the agonies of thousands of American widows.

The Civil War with its 620,000 dead, along with another 50,000 civilian casualties, had widowed many women, North and South. Widowhood was an especially cruel fate for those who had been trained to see themselves as dependent adjuncts to their husbands. With a characteristic sense of her specialness, Mary claimed that "No *such sorrow* was ever visited upon a people or family, as when we were bereaved of my darling husband, everyday, causes me to feel more crushed and brokenhearted. . . . Time, does not soften [my grief] nor can I ever be reconciled to my loss until the grave closes over the remembrance and I am reunited with him."[14]

For the next sixteen years, from April 1865 until her death in July 1882, Mary Lincoln dressed in the traditional mourning clothes required by her time. Most women gave up the widow's weeds (garments) after the prescribed two years, but Mary Lincoln continued to mourn, and was never able to absorb the memories of her husband into a new life. No matter where she was—for now she had no home as well as no husband—she remembered her losses, of brothers and sisters, of two elder sons and in 1871 of her youngest son Tad, and always of her husband—whom she called "my All."

She also suffered another problem common to widows—a lack of money and of experience in financial affairs. For three years she had no idea what the size of her husband's estate would be. Innocent of interest rates and money matters, she was neglected by both her son Robert and the administrator of her husband's estate, the Supreme Court Justice David Davis, who believed her a spendthrift. As was the case with most women, the bars of the male experience had separated her from the business world, and so she struggled to provide for herself. She had no profession, and other than hiring herself out as a schoolteacher or governess, there was—given the restrictions of her class—little she could do. The possibility of boarders disappeared when she could not afford the taxes and maintenance on the house she purchased in Chicago in 1866 with the $22,000 congressional donation of her husband's residual salary for 1865.

But in 1868 Mary Lincoln decided on a bold plan. She would sell her clothes, the only asset she like most other widows possessed, and though she at first tried to do so anonymously, soon everyone in America knew of Mary Lincoln's Second-Hand Clothing Sale. "Was there ever such cruel newspaper abuse lavished upon an unoffending woman as has been showered on my head?," she wondered, and there were those, including her son Robert, who believed that the most charitable construction that could be put on the behavior of what one newspaper called "this mercenary prostitute" was that she was insane.[15]

Deeply humiliated, Mary Lincoln took her son Tad and left for Germany. Before she went, with suspicious suddenness (for the probate process had languished under Judge Davis's authority until the Second-Hand Clothing Sale), her husband's estate was distributed, and along with Tad and Robert she received $36,000. She was by any standard a rich woman, though her own sense of herself as "poor me" made it impossible for her to be comfortable. Certainly the size of Lincoln's estate testified to her frugality, for the success of her efforts to get others to pay her bills had permitted the president to invest his money in Civil War bonds.

Now began Mary Lincoln's restless years. She had no home and so traveled with her son Tad until his death in 1871, and then by herself. Increasingly, Mary Lincoln turned to spiritualism for the solace that her Presbyterian faith did not provide. While the conviction that the dead could return to visit the living was not restricted to women, it was nonetheless a preeminently female approach to dealing with death. It was also a dangerous one. In Illinois a Presbyterian minister, Reverend Packard, had recently declared his wife Elizabeth a lunatic on the grounds of her spiritualism; in effect, Elizabeth Packard had been institutionalized for two years in a state asylum solely because her belief in the spirits of the other world challenged her husband's ideas. But because of the laws of the time, Reverend Packard needed no other testimony than his own to convince the superintendent of the asylum that his wife was mentally ill.

After the Civil War a growing number of institutions clamored to cure the neurasthenic, the maniacal, and the hysterical, and for the first time in American history women outnumbered men in institutions, although both, according to the U.S. Census, were at equal risk for lunacy. Among the more common diagnoses was that of *mania*, a catchall term used by doctors to include spiritualism.

But for a lonely woman, female mediums provided companionship and the opportunity to talk to a dead husband—through what the believers in the spirit world knew as "hovering," the presence of the dead in the nearby atmosphere. Since Willie Lincoln's death, spiritualism had become an essential part of her life. As Mary Lincoln had told her half-sister Emilie, sometimes Willie returned by himself or with his dead brother Eddie, and once he came with her Todd half-brothers who had fought and died in the Confederate army. With no one left of her family but her eldest son Robert, Mary listened carefully to the medium's appraisals of her eldest son's health.

In 1875 he was, according to her voices from the spirit world, about to die. Terrified, she hastened back to Chicago, where a healthy Robert, a rising star in Chicago's legal circles, met her at the station. Soon Mary Lincoln was living in a Chicago hotel and filling her days with what Robert considered unnecessary shopping. It was easy enough for Robert to persuade his medical friends that his mother was mentally ill. And in this shabby episode of family business, in May 1875 Mary Lincoln was brought before an Illinois jury, charged with being *non compos mentis* (not mentally competent). Convicted in a humiliating public trial, she was sentenced to an asylum for an indefinite period.

In this episode Mary Lincoln suffered the results of a gender system that removed women from the economic and legal sources of power and gave them the insufficient substitute of a male protector. During her trial her lawyer had been chosen by her son, not herself, and the doctors who testified against her had been paid by a son anxious in his paternalistic understanding to do "the best thing" for his mother. During the trial, Mary Lincoln was not called to testify, though had she been, she would have explained the reasons for her undeniably "different" behavior that was the legacy not of lunacy, but rather of the emptiness created by her family losses.[16]

Once in the private asylum outside Chicago, Mary Lincoln began a campaign for freedom that demonstrated her rationality and feminism. She needed an ally to effect her emancipation. For different reasons, both her son and the superintendent of the institution would extend her confinement indefinitely. But given the censorship of all outgoing mail it was difficult to find a supporter to challenge the lawfulness of her continuing confinement. In the end it was a sympathetic woman—one engaged in public activities that Mary Lincoln used to disparage as unfeminine—who accomplished her release. Without Myra Bradwell's intervention it is doubtful that Mary Lincoln would ever have left the mental institution that she likened to prison.

Myra Bradwell was a lawyer who, having successfully completed law school, had subsequently sought to be the first woman practicing attorney in the United States. Debarred from her profession by the state courts of Illinois, she appealed to the Supreme Court, which based its ruling on the ancient doctrine that a married woman was not an independent autonomous being, but instead was "one with the husband and he the one." The court's ruling followed the prejudice with which Mary Lincoln had earlier agreed—that "the paramount destiny and mission of women are to fulfill the noble and benign offices of wife and mother." Given this social understanding, a married woman could not sign contracts or represent clients, for she was not, as common law had long held, an autonomous individual.[17]

But Bradwell was more successful in Mary Lincoln's case than her own. First she found a home for Mary at Mary's sister's and then, familiar with the legal world of writs, grand juries, and appeals, she negotiated Mary's release with the grudging approval of Robert and the superintendent of the asylum.[18] No doubt Mary's notoriety helped, for hers was a case for the reporters who since her husband's assassination had chased her everywhere. Other women were not so lucky, and there is no way of knowing how many women of this generation became the permanent victims of a system that was organized to their disadvantage.

After her release Mary again fled to Europe, this time to France, an exile from the United States and the son whom she never forgave. But even before she left, the reality of her life had disappeared into two myths that determined her historical reputation. Both mirrored the attitudes of American society towards women and their proper status.

Even before her death, Mary Todd Lincoln was viewed as a shrew, a termagant, a virago, and these gendered terms—for there are no equivalents for men—were used about her on the floor of the United States Senate during the debate over her pension. She was, according to one aggrieved senator, "[a]n unrepublican, unAmerican, unfeminine" creature.[19] In such thinking the humanity of a great assassinated leader was expanded through the supposition that his selfish, ill-tempered wife had created for her husband "a domestic hell. . . . For the last twenty-three years of his life, Mr. Lincoln had no joy," wrote William Herndon, the biographer who helped to shape American opinion on Lincoln. Thus Lincoln was thought to have learned the tolerance he displayed with generals, freed slaves, and Republican politicians from navigating his allegedly tortured relations with his wife.[20]

The second myth of Mary Lincoln's historical reputation made her responsible for the trials she endured. Such feelings were a residual effect of the American reliance on Providence, for the idea that nothing happened save through God's will suggested a Job-like punishment for those who sinned. In the way that victims are often blamed for the evil that befalls them, Mary was judged guilty of neglecting her children for the glory that she sought not for her husband but for herself. This prevailing view emerged mainly from the necessity of a male-ordered society to maintain its system of male supremacy during a time of changing roles for women. It was easy enough to convict this prominent, disorderly woman of being an unruly female who violated the separated spheres of the sexes. From such a perspective, it was not surprising that history remembers her as ending her days (for her quick release was often forgotten) in a mental institution.

Today we do better to remember Mary Todd Lincoln as a conventional Victorian woman whose endurance amid the disasters of her life displays the strength that was characteristic of thousands of other American woman.

Notes

[1]Justin and Linda Turner, *Mary Lincoln—Her Life and Letters* (Knopf, 1972), p. 633; Insanity File, Letter Fragment, Lincoln National Life Library, Fort Wayne, Indiana.

[2]Katherine Helm, *The True Story of Mary, Wife of Lincoln* (Harpers', 1928), p. 52; Bertram Wyatt-Brown, *Southern Honor: Ethics and Behavior in the Old South* (Oxford, 1982), p. 201

[3]For development of this point, see Jean Friedman, *The Enclosed Garden: Women and the Community in the Evangelical South, 1830–1900,* (University of North Carolina Press, 1985). Also Gerda Lerner, *The Grimké Sisters,* (Schocken Books, 1971).

[4]Caroll Smith-Rosenberg, "The Female World of Love and Ritual: Relationships between Women in Nineteenth Century America," *Signs*, 1 (Autumn 1975), pp. 1–29.

[5]William Herndon and Jesse Weik, *Herndon's Life of Lincoln* (Cleveland Publishing Company, 1930), pp. 344–45.

[6]*The Mother's Assistant*, vol. 6(January, 1845), pref.

[7]United States Census, Seventh Census, Mortality Schedule, Springfield, Illinois, "Causes of Death," 1850.

[8]David Handlin, *The American Home: Architecture and Society, 1815–1915*, (Little,Brown, 1979), p. 232.

[9]Jean H. Baker, *Mary Todd Lincoln: A Biography*, (W. W. Norton, 1987), p. xiv.

[10]Turner, *Mary Lincoln*, p. 60; Herndon and Weik, *Herndon's Lincoln*, p. 201; Gustave Koerner, *Memoirs of Gustave Koerner*, vol. 2 (Torch Press, 1909), pp. 93–95.

[11]William Howard Russell, *My Diary North and South* (Breadbury, 1863), pp., 132,269; Edna Colman, *Seventy-Five Years of White House Gossip* (Doubleday, 1926).

[12]W. O. Stoddard, *Inside the White House in War Times*, (Webster, 1890).

[13]*Washington Daily Chronicle*, 4 Mar. 1863, 10, 23 May 1863, 17 Nov. 1863, 15 Dec. 1863; *Independent*, 10 August 1882; Helm, *The True Story*, p. 225.

[14]Turner, *Mary Lincoln*, pp. 260, 268.

[15]*Columbus (Ga.) Advertiser*, 4 October 1867.

[16]Baker, *Mary Todd Lincoln*, pp. 318–330

[17]*Bradwell vs. Illinois*, U.S., 30 (1873).

[18]Robert Spector, "Woman against the Law: Myra Bradwell's Struggle for Admission to the Illinois Bar," *Journal of the Illinois State Historical Society* 68 (June 1975), pp. 228–42.

[19]*Congressional Globe*, 41st. Cong., 2nd sess., pp. 5559–60.

[20]Herndon and Weik, *Herndon's Lincoln*, pp. 180–181, 348–350, 105–113.

Varina Howell Davis

(1826–1906)

Joan Cashin

*Born into the wealthy planter class in Mississippi, Varina How-
ell enjoyed the trappings of privilege that were conspicuous in
the antebellum South. Her upbringing had many Northern influences, however, for her father, William Burr Howell, was from
New Jersey. He sent his young daughter to an academy in Philadelphia, and on her return home engaged for her a tutor from
Massachusetts. Varina Howell met the widower Jefferson Davis,
a member of a Mississippi planter family, when she was sixteen.
Two years later, in 1845, they married. Varina Howell Davis's
strong personality sometimes countered the behavior expected
of her as a Southern "lady," and caused conflicts between
Varina and her husband's family, and often between her and
Jefferson. After early years marred by these conflicts and by
separation, Varina Davis joined her husband in Washington and
settled into the busy social life of a senator's wife. In Washington, Varina Davis bore four children, to whom she was devoted,
and gathered a circle of prominent figures as friends. With the
secession of the Southern states and Jefferson Davis's selection
as the president of the Confederacy in 1861, Varina Davis took
on the role of First Lady of the Confederacy. She maintained the
Confederate White House in Richmond and bore two more children, at the same time becoming a visible First Lady, a role that
brought her much criticism. As the fortunes of the South fell, so
too did those of the Davises, as one of their children died in an
accident, and Jefferson Davis was imprisoned for treason at the
end of the war. After Jefferson Davis's release the family faced
illness, financial worries, homelessness, and the loss of two
other children. Varina Davis also faced another estrangement,
as her husband took up residence on the plantation of a wealthy
widow. Reconciled later, the Davises lived together until Jeffer-*

son Davis died in 1889. Despite the trouble that had sometimes characterized their marriage, Varina Davis was devastated by her husband's death, and set out to write a memoir of him in which she defends him. In 1892 she moved to New York, where she lived until her death in 1906.

Like Mary Todd Lincoln, Varina Howell Davis did not choose the public spotlight, but became prominent because of her marriage to a leading political figure of the time. The similarity of their lives, despite being identified with opposite sides of the Civil War, suggests the centrality of marriage in shaping women's lives in the nineteenth century—how much women were invested in marriage for their self-esteem, social status, and even perhaps, their reason for living.

V arina Howell Davis was probably the most famous Southern woman of the nineteenth century. The wife of Jefferson Davis, president of the Confederacy, she was a fascinating person in her own right, an intelligent, dynamic, and sensitive woman. One of the most important themes of her life concerns her deep ambivalence about her identity as a Southern woman. Varina Howell Davis was born into the slave-owning elite and accepted many of the conservative values of her region, race, and class, but she could never abide completely by the rules of behavior appropriate to a Southern "lady." Her ambivalence had its origins in the particular circumstances of her personal background, but it was compounded by the oppressive conditions that she and every planter woman faced as a member of the slave-owning class.[1]

Her story begins in Mississippi, where her father, William Burr Howell of New Jersey, settled after his service in the War of 1812. Howell was the scion of a distinguished family; his father Richard was a major in the Revolutionary War and in the 1790s was governor of New Jersey. A talented but irresponsible man, William Howell dabbled in several occupations until he married Margaret Kempe, the daughter of a wealthy slave-owner, in 1823. Margaret Kempe's father gave the young couple a plantation in Warren County, Mississippi, near the banks of the Mississippi River, as a wedding gift, so Howell began a career as a Southern planter. Over the next several decades, the Howells reared their six surviving children. Varina, the second child and oldest daughter, was born on May 7, 1826.

In the 1830s, when Varina Howell was a girl, the role of the Southern "lady" coalesced, part of the South's response to the abolitionist attack on slavery. When Northerners criticized bondage as cruel, immoral, and unchristian, Southerners responded with a battery of arguments defending slavery, among them the notion that the wife of a slave-owner, the plantation mistress, humanized and softened the institution by her kind treatment of slaves. The ideal had larger implications for a woman's role in all of her relationships. She was supposed to defer in all things to her husband, who gave her security, protection, and guidance in return. She should be literate and know something about the arts, but she should not become so well educated that she forgot that her most important duty was to care for her family. Languid, gentle, and retiring, she lived entirely in the private world of the family. The image took deep root in Southern culture and remained the standard by which the behavior of women of the planter class was measured throughout the generation before the Civil War.

In reality, planter-class women had great responsibilities and few freedoms in this conservative, patriarchal society. They typically received poor educations, married at young ages, bore many children, and lived on isolated plantations where they performed a great deal of work—well documented by historians—in rearing children and managing slaves. But these responsibilities did not translate into decision-making power within the family. Men made the key decisions, such as where the family would live, as well as the smaller decisions, such as when women would be allowed to visit their relatives on distant plantations. If a man violated his marriage vows, mistreated his wife or children, or abrogated his responsibilities to provide for his family, his wife had few alternatives. Divorce was illegal in many Southern states, and it was extremely difficult to obtain even in states that did permit it; the stigma was so terrible that most women would rather endure an unhappy marriage than get a divorce.

It is true that elite Southern women had privileges that poor white women did not enjoy; they were literate, lived in physical comfort, and had the assistance of slave house servants in running their households. But they were also denied the freedoms enjoyed by Northern white women of the upper classes or even the middle classes, such as sound educations, the opportunity to work outside the home, and the stimulation of town and city life, and through it all they had to live up to the demanding ideal of the lady. Varina Howell Davis escaped some of these strictures, partly because of her family's Northern roots and partly because she married a man who became a national figure, but she too had to struggle all of her life to behave as a lady, and she was often confronted with her powerlessness in the family.

Her difficulties began, ironically, with her education, which was almost completely Northern in orientation. She attended an elite girls' academy in Philadelphia and then studied at home with a private tutor, George Winchester of Massachusetts, a stern Yankee who recognized that his pupil had a keen, lively mind. He gave her a rigorous education in the classics, history, literature, and languages, and he nurtured her love of reading, something that stayed with her for the rest of her life. Winchester also imparted his political views to her—he was a confirmed Whig but no abolitionist—and encouraged her to take an interest in current events. Perhaps most important of all, he taught her to think for herself and value her own intelligence. Varina Howell did not attend college, but she was better educated than most Southern women (and most men) of her generation. Throughout her life, she showed a hearty interest in cultural and political matters, an interest that was considered bold and unfeminine.

As Varina Howell grew up, it became clear that her personality would not conform to the ideal of the lady. She was an energetic, affectionate, and brave girl, who felt things vividly and tended to say exactly what she thought. She took on family responsibilities at an early age, helping to run the household at the family's plantation, the Briers. As the oldest daughter, she helped her mother care for the other children, and she once saved her siblings from a housefire. Margaret Howell, reared in Louisiana, was much like a typical lady, completely submerged in family life, not very well educated, and deferential toward her husband. She was also a loving woman and understood her daughter's temperament. Varina in turn was devoted to her mother, but she could not play the ideal female role as her mother did.

Varina Howell's relationship with her father was more complex and much more strained. Although William Howell gave her a far better education than most young women received, he expected her to behave like a typical lady, and he never encouraged her to aspire to any occupation other than wife and mother. Furthermore, there was an emotional barrier between them. When she was in her thirties, she remarked that her father did not like children, and some of his missives to her have a callous, indifferent tone. One letter he wrote after the birth of one of her children, when Varina nearly died from puerperal fever, a common post-childbirth infection, was so cold that she burst into tears. Nor was he a good provider for his family: he squandered his wife's dowry and lost the plantation in 1850, when he moved to New Orleans to work as a customs official. Margaret Howell suffered quietly as her husband went deeper into debt, but Varina resented his irresponsibility. She stepped into the vacuum and guided the education and upbringing of her younger siblings; after she married, several of them lived with her, rather than with their parents, for long periods of time. At an early age, Varina began learning a hard lesson: men did not always behave consistently or provide the security that was their duty to provide as fathers and husbands.

Yet the young Varina Howell was not completely at odds with the Southern world in which she grew up. She enjoyed the status, privileges, and physical comforts that went with being a lady. All of her life she loved beautiful clothes, good food, and elegant homes, and she wanted to be around powerful, accomplished people. In fact, she was always an elitist, feeling distaste and pity for whites who were not members of the slave-owning class. Her racial views were also representative of the planter class: she saw blacks as inferior, childlike, and untrustworthy, and she accepted slavery as a God-given institution. By the time Howell was in her teens, she had been socialized as a member of the planter class, but she was not completely at one with its values. Her education and her family background prevented her from becoming a lady in the traditional mold.

When sixteen-year-old Varina Howell met Jefferson Davis at a Christmas party in 1843, she was a tall young woman with pale skin, dark hair, and great dark eyes, and she already had a reputation as a wit. In an observant letter to her mother, she described their meeting: "He impresses me as a remarkable kind of man but of uncertain temper, and has a way of taking for granted that everybody agrees with him when he expresses an opinion, which offends me." She added, "He is the kind of person I should expect to rescue one from a mad dog at any risk, but to insist upon a stoical indifference to the fright afterward." Yet he could also be "most agreeable" with "a winning manner of asserting himself," and he was a gentleman, handsome, "refined," and "cultivated," even though he was a Democrat. Jefferson Davis left no account of their meeting, but he told his brother soon afterwards that she was beautiful and had a fine mind. The couple fell in love, but they had a rocky courtship, and Margaret Howell initially opposed Jefferson's suit because he was a widower and considerably older than Varina. She finally gave them her blessing, and the couple was married at the Briers on February 26, 1845.[2]

Seventeen years older than Varina, Jefferson Davis was the son of Mississippi planter Samuel Davis, who died in 1824 when Jefferson was sixteen years old. The oldest son, strong-willed Joseph, completed Jefferson's upbringing, sending him to Transylvania College and then to West Point Military Academy, from which he graduated in 1828. He served in the army in the Midwest, where he fell in love with Sarah Knox Taylor (called "Knox"), the daughter of Colonel Zachary Taylor. His brother Joseph gave him slaves and a plantation called Brierfield near his own plantation in the Mississippi River Delta so that Jefferson might begin a new career as a planter. Jefferson married Knox Taylor in 1835, and the couple proceeded on a honeymoon trip to the South where the bride was to meet the Davis family.

Little is known about Knox Taylor Davis, but she seems to have been much like the ideal lady—sweet, pliable, and even-tempered. Her new in-laws adored her. But the marriage ended tragically when the newlyweds both contracted malaria while visiting relatives in Louisiana. Knox Davis died only three months after the wedding. Jefferson Davis plunged into a profound grief, retreating to Brierfield, where he saw few people other than his own relatives. For eight years, he lived virtually alone, spending his time reading and talking to his brother Joseph when he was not working on his plantation. The brevity of the marriage allowed Jefferson and everyone else to idealize Knox, and he mourned for her for years.

The death of Knox Davis probably accentuated the austere, rigid aspects of Jefferson Davis's personality. Even as a boy, he was dignified and self-controlled, and as an adult many people found him aloof, as Varina Howell did when they first met. He suffered from bad health for most of his life, enduring a variety of neurological disorders, eye problems, and recurring bouts of malaria, so that his nerves were easily frayed. Yet Jefferson Davis worked hard at whatever task he chose, driving himself whether he was a soldier, planter, or politician. There was a warmer, more humane side to his makeup. With intimates he could be funny and engaging, and some of his letters to his family members were surprisingly sweet. He was idealistic and devoted to principles as he understood them, but he could easily become self-righteous. It would soon become clear that he had very conventional attitudes about women's roles. These unappealing qualities appeared early on in his marriage to Varina Howell.

The match was shadowed from the beginning, and not only by the ghost of Knox Taylor Davis. For several years, both Davises believed (falsely, as it turned out) that they could not have children, and for reasons that are not clear, they both thought the problem lay with Varina. When the couple settled in 1845 on Jefferson's plantation, domestic peace was disrupted by heated conflicts between Joseph Davis and his new sister-in-law. The elder Davis first suggested that the couple share living quarters with one of Jefferson's widowed relatives, but Varina objected. Then she found that Joseph Davis had drawn up a will that prevented her from inheriting Jefferson's plantation; since Joseph had never given his brother title to the property, he still had control over its disposition. Joseph had initially approved of his brother's second marriage, but he had then taken a deep dislike to Varina, probably because of her strong personality and the fact that she was much better educated than the other women in the Davis family. Joseph, Jefferson, and Varina exchanged harsh words over all of these issues.

Jefferson Davis was offended by the conduct of both his brother and his wife, but he seems to have blamed Varina for much of the conflict and, more generally, for the incompatibilities that surfaced in the marriage. Jefferson and Varina Davis had very different personalities, and Jefferson was in the habit of commanding others, whether in the military or on the plantation. Varina tried hard to please him and behave as a submissive wife, but she resented the punishing behavior of her brother-in-law and her husband. During the first year of their marriage, the couple became estranged. In the midst of this turmoil, Jefferson Davis was elected to the House of Representatives, serving briefly in Washington, D.C., before he left to join the American army in the Mexican War. Varina Davis remained in Mississippi with in-laws who were increasingly uncharitable to the teenaged bride and subtly reminded her that she was not Jefferson's first love. The Davises ostracized her much of the time, so that she even ate her meals alone, telling her mother that "my one plate looks very lonely, and I tear my food in silence." She moved from one household to another, living alternately with her brothers- and sisters-in-law until her husband returned from Mexico in 1847.[3]

Their reunion was not a happy one, aggravated by Jefferson Davis's ill health and continuing rancor over Joseph Davis's will. Jefferson Davis had become a war hero after the battle of Buena Vista, and he was appointed to serve in the United States Senate. He left his wife in Mississippi and went alone to Washington, where he wrote her a series of blistering letters. In one letter, he lambasted Varina for "suspicions and threats . . . equally unjust and unnecessary" and told her to act in a way "demanded by your duties as a wife," when in fact Joseph Davis was clearly trying to stop Varina from obtaining property that should have been hers as the wife of Jefferson Davis. Varina's response to this letter is not recorded, but no doubt she was angry that her interests were being shunted aside; when her in-laws discussed these property disputes, she raged that "it has not been thought proper to inform me" about the outcome. Few letters survive from this fateful year in their marriage, possibly because Varina or Jefferson later destroyed them, but by mid-1848, the couple reconciled on his terms. Joseph Davis's will remained unchanged, but Varina joined her husband in Washington, where she lived for most of the next twelve years. She somehow forgave her spouse, whom she still loved, but she never forgave Joseph Davis, and her relationships with most of the Davis family were cool and formal.[4]

Thus in the early years of her marriage Varina Davis was confronted with the power, and the inconsistency, of two of the most important men in her life. Her brother-in-law, a prototypical Southern patriarch, deprived her of property that should have been hers, and her husband did not take her side or protect her interests. Her spouse also had the power to decide when, or if, she could live with him in Washington. Her response was one of initial rebellion followed by eventual acquiescence, which became a recurring pattern in the Davis marriage. Jefferson Davis loved his wife and respected her intelligence, but he expected her to submit to his will; he simply accepted the sex roles of his era and never understood or sympathized with her frustrations, which he tended to dismiss as the outbursts of an emotional woman. He had the decision-making power in the relationship in matters large and small. Varina once told her mother that she had been "begging" her husband to allow her to visit her family, but added, "He does not say yea or nay."[5]

The marriage nonetheless had its compensations and satisfactions. The couple seemed to be sexually compatible, according to the few oblique comments they made in their letters. Jefferson once told his wife that he longed to "clasp my own Winnie [his nickname for her] in my arms." And when the couple finally had children, both parents delighted in them. Varina bore four children in the 1850s, Samuel, Margaret, Jefferson Jr., and Joseph. Varina Davis worked as her husband's secretary, helping him read and write letters when his vision troubled him, and they often discussed books and politics together. Davis's political career flourished, as he served as secretary of war under President Franklin Pierce and for a second time in the United States Senate in 1857. Varina gave up her Whig sympathies for his Democratic views, and she was proud of her husband's success. But even his triumphs had a bitter edge: she regretted his long absences from home, and as an old woman she wrote that long before the Civil War she realized that the lot of a politician's wife was a lonely one.[6]

Varina Davis was a hard-working mother as well as a wife. She occasionally had the help of female slaves who worked as house servants, but she longed for the assistance of her mother at home, whom she missed very much. She raised her children, a "precocious" bunch with "unbroken wills," with little help from her busy husband. Varina nursed her offspring herself, and her letters are filled with anxious accounts of their many illnesses. Medical knowledge was primitive in the mid-nineteenth century, and every childhood ailment was a potentially serious one. Her firstborn, Samuel, died in 1854, probably from the measles, and his death traumatized

Varina. Yet the Davises were able to comfort each other and devote themselves to their other children.[7]

In the 1850s, Varina Davis developed her distinctive views on the subject of women's roles, reflecting her experiences and those of her friends. She had a number of close female friends in Washington, and she remarked after the birth of her son Joseph in 1859 that they "did everything in the world for me." A friend later commented that "clever women" tended to gravitate toward Varina Davis, and in this decade she forged friendships with such vital women as Mary Boykin Chesnut, the wife of Senator James Chesnut of South Carolina. Davis believed that there were deep differences between the sexes and that intimacy between men and women was difficult, if not impossible; she could share her most private thoughts, her inner self, only with other women. She also believed that the many demands made on women in their capacities as wives and mothers were unfair, an opinion she expressed throughout her life. In 1858, at age thirty-two, she told her mother that young wives had to take on the responsibilities of adulthood at too early an age. She lamented that "Cares do wear out one's youth," but added, "I think they refine, and purify at the same time." Here Davis's innate conservatism was evident: she objected to the heavy burdens of being a woman in a man's world, and she probably regretted her early marriage, but she strove to find something redeeming in her sacrifices. These views she expressed privately in her correspondence, never in public, and she showed no interest in the burgeoning woman's rights movement of the mid-nineteenth century.[8]

Varina Davis did find time to take part in the social life of the capital. As the wife of a cabinet member and senator, she attended dinners, teas, and other social events with the most powerful people in the nation. She became known for her wit, which was sometimes cutting, but her warmth and spirit won her a wide circle of friends, including President Franklin Pierce, his wife Jane Pierce, President James Buchanan, and Judah P. Benjamin, the senator from Louisiana. Davis was a shrewd observer of human nature, and her writings contained some wise judgments and funny comments about political figures of the day. She once went to a masquerade ball dressed as Madame de Staël, delivering "caustic repartee" in French and English. She relished the social and intellectual stimulation of the capital that life on a Southern plantation could not provide.[9]

Varina Davis was very much alarmed by the secession crisis of 1860–61. Although she believed that slavery had to be protected and that the Southern states had the right to secede from the Union, she prayed for peace and wished that she had lived in an another age. She

was anything but optimistic when her husband was chosen president of the new Confederacy in February 1861. Davis allegedly told a
friend in 1860 that if the South seceded "the whole thing is bound to
be a failure," and she confided to her mother in 1861 that the North
had a great advantage in manufacturing power. She described her
husband as "depressed" about the Confederacy's prospects, but he
accepted the office as his duty. Varina Davis did her duty and followed him to Montgomery, Alabama, and then to Richmond, Virginia, when it was selected as the Confederate capital.[10]

As First Lady of the Confederacy, Varina Davis was once again part
of a brilliant social circle. She resumed her friendship with Judah
Benjamin, the canny Louisianian who held several posts in the Davis government, and she became the confidante of the equally gifted
Mary Chesnut, whose husband was an aide to President Davis. She
was a highly visible First Lady, sparkling at parties and dinners, so
much so that her sister-in-law, Eliza Davis, the wife of Joseph Davis,
left a disapproving account of Varina's behavior in the summer of
1861. She received callers every evening, so that the parlors of the
Confederate White House were "filled with strange gentlemen" and
"[A] few ladies." (Eliza Davis, by contrast, kept to her room.) What
made Varina Davis's behavior even more unsuitable was the fact
that she was pregnant with her fifth child. In and of itself, this was a
serious transgression of proper behavior for a Southern lady, and it
helps explain why Varina became such a controversial individual.[11]

Varina Davis repeatedly violated other standards of genteel feminine behavior, and now that her husband was president she came in
for criticism from many sides, not just from her sister-in-law. Jefferson Davis's political enemies criticized his wife as imperious, and
some said that she dominated her husband. The blue-blooded ladies
of Virginia shunned her, and one of them derided her as a "coarse
western woman." Men and women said that her forthright, spirited
manner was unrefined. Davis did have an exuberant sense of humor
with an especially acute sense of the ridiculous, which got her into
trouble. She once attended a dinner during which a general's wife
said that the underdrawers for an entire regiment had mistakenly
been made with two right legs. Davis burst out laughing, much to
the horror of the other guests. The First Lady was just as controversial in the eyes of the Confederate public, and for much the same
reasons. A plantation mistress in North Carolina remarked that
Varina Davis was not "Ladylike" in her dress or her conduct and that
she was not a "truehearted Southern woman."[12]

Jefferson Davis did not publicly rebuke his wife for her behavior,
although we will never know what he said to her in private. He was
too traditional a man to be dominated by Varina, but it is clear from

letters written when they were occasionally separated during the war that their relationship was much like it had been in Washington. He discussed military developments with his wife and gave her his frank views about the capabilities of Confederate generals and politicians. She played a supportive role in their correspondence, agreeing with his opinions and passing on rumors and information she heard from various sources. These letters also demonstrated the love that Varina still felt for her husband. In 1862, when she and the children had to evacuate Richmond because a Union invasion seemed imminent, she felt "every months [*sic*] absence an irreparable loss."[13]

The Davis family continued to grow in the 1860s, as two more children were born, William in 1861 and Varina Anne in 1864, but for Varina motherhood continued to bring worry and sorrow. Much of her time was taken up with rearing and caring for her children, just as it had been before the war. Doctors, nurses, and female slaves attended them, but Davis herself tended to her children through their many illnesses. She lost another child in a freak accident in 1864, when five-year-old Joseph died after falling from the second story of the Confederate White House. Davis was distraught, and her husband walked the floor at night, consumed with grief.

As the war went on, both Davises continued to take a pessimistic but stoical view of the conflict. In the spring of 1865, Varina and the children fled Richmond once again, heading south. Her husband followed after the city fell to the Union army, and the family reunited, planning to go to Texas, where Jefferson Davis hoped to continue the fight. After a nightmarish flight, they were captured in southern Georgia near the town of Irwinville by a contingent of Northern troops. When the soldiers closed in on Jefferson Davis, Varina apparently threw a shawl over his head to disguise him, giving rise to the rumor that he had tried to escape in the dress of a woman. Both the Davises denied the rumor for years afterwards because it called Jefferson's courage into question, but the incident is just as interesting for what it reveals about Varina, who once again refused to play the helpless lady.

Soon after his capture, Jefferson Davis went to prison for treason in Fort Monroe, Virginia, and the children left for Canada in the company of their grandmother Margaret Howell. Varina lived near the prison with her infant daughter, feeling "very desolate" about the fate of her husband and scattered family. The couple wrote regularly to each other and were allowed to visit occasionally; in 1866 she confided to a friend that her husband had changed a great deal since he had gone to prison, growing weaker as the months and years went by, and she later wrote that during all of the postwar years she never once heard her husband laugh, suggesting that something vital had gone out of him forever. Meanwhile, Varina handled their financial problems, borrowing money from friends to support her mother, her children, and herself. It was a harbinger of days to come, because Jefferson Davis was never able to provide for his family after he was released from prison in the spring of 1867.[14]

Now began a period of homelessness, poverty, and illness for Varina Davis and her family. The Davises traveled to Canada and rejoiced to see their children, but Varina lost her beloved mother a few months later when Margaret Howell died of typhoid fever. The family set sail for England in 1868 in hopes that a change of scene would improve Jefferson's health. The family spent two years abroad, living in a succession of hotels, while Varina cared for her sick and restless husband. "I watch over him unceasingly," she told a friend, and lived "in terror" that he would collapse and die. She also struggled to care for her brood of children and was determined that they should get the best education the family's limited means could permit. She sent her sons and daughters to several noted schools, such as an academy in Karlsruhe, Germany, where she placed young Varina Anne.[15]

The Davises were still public figures, and they were sometimes cheered on the streets of England and France by sympathetic strangers. They received social invitations from the European elite, including members of the British aristocracy and the emperor of France, who were curious about the ex-president. Varina was grateful for the kindnesses she received, especially when her children fell ill, but she longed for quiet and privacy. They occasionally met other Confederate exiles, such as Judah Benjamin, who had begun practicing law in England and eventually built up a lucrative practice. Jefferson Davis lacked Benjamin's resilience, however, and found it very difficult to adapt to the postwar world.

In 1870, the family returned to the United States, where Varina faced a new round of struggles. Her husband accepted a job as head of the Carolina Life Insurance Company in Memphis, Tennessee, but he had no experience in business, and the company foundered. The Davises lost yet another of their children, William, who died of diphtheria in 1872 at age eleven. Another family dispute marred these difficult years, when Jefferson Davis sued to break the will of his brother Joseph, who died in 1870 without leaving Jefferson the title of the plantation, Brierfield, which he had given him in the 1830s. Jefferson Davis won the case in 1878, but the plantation brought in little revenue, so he moved to Beauvoir, a plantation owned by Sarah Dorsey on the Gulf coast of Mississippi, and decided to begin writing a history of the Confederacy. Varina Davis, who had developed heart trouble, was in England being cared for by a physician. She was furious when she discovered where her husband had relocated.

Jefferson Davis's decision to live on the estate of Sarah Dorsey, a widow whom the Davises had known for many years, seems surprising even today. Sarah Dorsey idolized Davis and may have been in love with him; in any event, she quickly usurped his wife's role, acting as his secretary and helping him with his book. He rented a separate cottage on the estate, but he had nonetheless abandoned his wife while she was ill and gone to live with a woman who was not his wife. Davis's behavior may have been part of a more general deterioration in his judgment and personality that seems to have begun while he was in prison. Varina Davis was wounded and mortified by his settlement at Beauvoir, which soon became a subject of gossip. When she returned from England, she lived in Memphis with her daughter Margaret for almost a year.

This episode illustrates not only the issues in the Davis marriage, but also suggests the outlines of sex roles for women in the postwar South. Historians still know little about how the upheavals of the Civil War and Reconstruction era changed the lives of women from the old slaveholding class, but these events resulted in more burdens on Varina Davis and only exacerbated the inequities in her marriage. Despite Varina's growing responsibilities and her husband's inability to provide for his family, he nonetheless retained the power to do as he wished, to forsake the role that he as a Southern man, husband, and father should have played. This was Joseph Davis and William Howell all over again, and Varina acquiesced once again, as a proper lady and loyal wife had to do. If she ever considered divorcing her husband, she never mentioned it in writing. She finally went to Beauvoir in 1878 on the most humiliating terms, living with her husband in the main house with Sarah Dorsey.

The wretchedness of this era in Varina's life had not yet come to an end. Her last surviving son, Jefferson Davis, Jr., died of yellow fever at age twenty-one in Memphis, and his death sent both of his parents into a still, silent grief. Once again Varina was robbed of a home when Sarah Dorsey, who died in 1879, willed Beauvoir to Jefferson Davis and his daughter Varina Anne, also called "Winnie," excluding Varina from ownership altogether. The Davises continued to live in the house because they could not afford to go elsewhere. When in 1881 Jefferson Davis published his history of the Confederacy—a dry account that justified the right of secession—it sold poorly and brought in little revenue.

The last years of Varina Davis's married life were somewhat more contented. The household brightened when her daughter Winnie returned from abroad to live with her parents. A delicate, thoughtful woman, Winnie wrote poetry and fiction, and like her parents, she was an avid reader. She soon became her father's constant companion. The family received many visits from old friends and inquisitive strangers, such as Oscar Wilde, who came to Beauvoir in 1882 to meet the ex-president and his wife. Jefferson himself became ever more frail and suffered from insomnia. Winnie and Varina both cared for him, writing letters, helping him with articles and speeches, and reading to him into the night when he could not sleep. Davis tended to relive the war years, fighting battles again and discussing them endlessly with his wife, daughter, and friends. Varina became the mainstay of the household, its greatest source of vitality and strength.

She showed little interest when Southerners began celebrating the war and the "Lost Cause" in the late nineteenth century, even though she was a natural candidate, as the wife of the ex-president, for some role in these activities. Varina seems to have valued her privacy too much to give it up, and she may have thought that she had already sacrificed enough for the Confederacy. Her daughter Winnie did play a ceremonial role and became something of a public figure in the 1880s. Born in 1864, she had been nicknamed "The Daughter of the Confederacy." She had spent most of her youth abroad and knew little of the South when she came home, but when she appeared at a meeting of Confederate soldiers in Atlanta in 1885, the crowd gave her a thunderous ovation. Soon Winnie was appearing at other reunions and public gatherings. She apparently played this role out of love for her parents, especially her father, rather than her personal commitment to the "Lost Cause." In the 1880s, she fell in love with a Northerner, Alfred Wilkinson, Jr., who was the grandson of a noted abolitionist. Jefferson Davis opposed the match on these grounds, but later reluctantly consented when he realized how deeply she loved Wilkinson; Varina did not relent, however, and objected even more strongly when she discovered that Wilkinson was not as affluent as he pretended to be. Winnie finally broke the engagement, and she never married.

Varina Davis had long suspected that she would outlive her husband, and his death finally came in December 1889. Jefferson contracted acute bronchitis on a trip through New Orleans, brought on because he characteristically insisted on traveling on a cold rainy day. She rushed to New Orleans to care for him, and she was holding his hand at his bedside, sobbing and calling his name, when he died. The funeral was an enormous public event, but the widow behaved with dignity and maintained her composure. She collapsed afterward, however, and went into a period of deep mourning, at one point telling a friend that she felt that her life was over. Varina had indeed devoted most of her life to her husband's needs, like so many nineteenth-century Southern women, and she never publicly criticized her husband or voiced what must have been her considerable anger at his behavior with Sarah Dorsey. The death of her spouse, despite the many problems in the marriage, was a great loss to Varina.

She then threw herself into the task of writing a book about her husband. Published in 1890, the memoir is a monumental work, a total of 1,638 pages in two volumes. Like many nineteenth-century biographies, it includes excerpts from Jefferson Davis's speeches and correspondence interspersed with Varina's own account of events. Written in clear, strong prose, the book has some poetic touches, such as her description of the wildflowers at Brierfield which shone like "banks of gold." The memoir is a valuable source of information about Varina Davis herself, especially her early life, and it wonderfully evokes the lush tropical beauty of the Southern countryside and the rhythm of plantation life.[16]

It is somewhat disappointing, however, as a commentary on her forty-four-year relationship with Jefferson Davis, since her chief purpose seems to have been to vindicate her husband, and in doing so, to justify the many sacrifices she made throughout their life together. She depicted her late husband in reverential terms as a noble, principled man, and she did not mention most of the conflicts and tensions that plagued the marriage, such as her long-standing feud with Joseph Davis. She did discuss her husband's sojourn with Sarah Dorsey, which may indicate how much she was hurt by it. Obviously attempting to dispel the rumors surrounding the incident, she emphasized that Sarah Dorsey acted as her husband's secretary "at stated hours during the day." The only critical remark she made about her husband was that he should have been a general during the Civil War because he "did not know the arts of the politician, and would not practise them" if he did know them. Varina may have thought that his entire career as a politician was a mistake; she knew that he lacked the flexibility necessary for successful political leadership, a judgment later reached by many historians of the Confederacy.[17]

Her ambivalence about the South was also evident in certain passages of the memoir. She continued to believe that the states had the right to secede, and she praised the courage of Confederate soldiers, but she still bristled at the restrictions of the role of the Southern lady. Varina Davis commented on the role indirectly in her description of the Virginians who had snubbed her during the war. They were cold, merely "practical," and not very cosmopolitan—a sharp retort from a woman who had received an invitation from the emperor of France. She ridiculed attempts to prevent women from reading widely and freely in the 1840s and 1850s, when authors such as

Charles Dickens were considered too dangerous for the female mind—something that still galled Davis over forty years later. Yet nowhere in the book did she directly challenge traditional sex roles, despite her manifest unhappiness with the role proscribed for her.[18]

In 1892 Davis decided to leave Beauvoir and live elsewhere. For the first time in her life, she was able to decide for herself where she wanted to live, and she moved to New York City. Her choice stunned many Southerners, who felt betrayed when the former Confederate First Lady settled in the North. Davis had several practical reasons for the move: New York was full of ex-Confederates, some of them prosperous, who were willing to befriend the family. She hoped that Winnie's literary abilities might be recognized in the metropolis, and she wanted to escape the hot climate of the Deep South, which had begun to bother her as she aged. These reasons were all plausible enough, but at the heart of her decision there was nonetheless an unmistakable rejection of the South itself. After all, cities in the Upper South such as Richmond or Baltimore offered similar attractions. Davis wanted the cosmopolitan atmosphere that only a great Northern city like New York could provide.

So mother and daughter settled in the Marlborough Hotel, the first of many hotels Varina was to inhabit for the rest of her life. They worried constantly over money, writing articles for pay and receiving financial help from friends and family members. It was a precarious existence, but an interesting one. Members of the city's social and cultural elite flocked to her door, drawn by her fame, charm, and conversational powers. Her life was filled with improbable encounters: she became a good friend of John W. Burgess, a prominent intellectual and political scientist, and in 1893 she met Julia Dent Grant, the widow of Ulysses S. Grant, with whom she had an extended, friendly conversation.

Varina Davis lost yet another child, however, when Winnie died of some gastro-intestinal disorder in 1898 at age thirty-three. Varina felt very much alone, deprived of her daughter's "precious companionship and sympathy." She was also wracked with guilt, not only because she had insisted that Winnie take the trip Varina thought had precipitated the illness, but because she had been primarily responsible for Winnie's broken engagement. She had put tremendous energy into her role as a mother, raising six children, but only one of her offspring lived long enough to marry and have children, and this daughter had settled far from her mother. Margaret Davis had wed Addison Hayes, a bank officer, in Memphis in 1876, and the couple moved to Colorado Springs in the 1880s for Addison's health.[19]

The remaining years of Varina Davis's life she lived on her own terms. She supported herself by writing articles on the Civil War and other subjects for such publications as the *New York World*. She continued to draw friends, relatives, and acquaintances to her sitting room, and she took part in the city's cultural life, attending the opera, the theater, and concerts. Freed of her demanding duties as a wife and mother, she was able to control the use of her time and indulge her taste for accomplished people, good books, and good conversation. She remained a fundamentally conservative woman, however, and to the end of her life she was a tireless defender of her husband. Yet there was a breach in her conservatism, as always; she maintained her views that women were treated unfairly. In her old age, she opposed woman's suffrage, but on the grounds that women already had enough responsibilities. Varina Davis felt that "my duties have always been more numerous and arduous than I could satisfactorily perform." It was a sad comment, a confession of failure after a lifetime of trying to conform to the ideal of the Southern lady.[20]

Varina Howell Davis died of pneumonia in New York on October 16, 1906, and was buried beside her husband in Richmond. Raised in the South, she absorbed many, but not all, of its values, and she could never be wholeheartedly loyal to it. The First Lady of the Confederacy was always ambivalent about her identity as a Southern lady, and her feelings were evident throughout her long, turbulent life.

Notes

[1]I am writing a full-scale biography of Varina Howell Davis, the first professional historian to do so. Students seeking information on her life have to go to a variety of sources: Davis's memoir of her husband, Varina Davis, *Jefferson Davis, Ex-President of the Confederate States of America: A Memoir*, 2 vols. (New York: Belford Company, 1890); Haskell M. Monroe, Jr., James T. McIntosh, Lynda L. Crist, and Mary S. Dix, eds., *The Papers of Jefferson Davis*, 5 vols. (Baton Rouge: Louisiana State University Press, 1971–1985); Eli N. Evans, *Judah P. Benjamin, The Jewish Confederate* (New York: The Free Press, 1988); C. Vann Woodward, ed., *Mary Chesnut's Civil War* (New Haven: Yale University Press, 1981); Bell Irvin Wiley, *Confederate Women*, Contributions in American History, no. 38 (Westport, CT: Greenwood Press, 1975). Ishbel Ross, a journalist, wrote the most recent biography, *First Lady of the South: The Life of Mrs. Jefferson Davis* (New York: Harper & Brothers Publishers, 1958). I thank the National Endowment for the Humanities for a Travel to Collections Grant that enabled me to conduct some of the research for this article.

[2]Varina Banks Howell to Margaret K. Howell, 19 December 1843, *The Papers of Jefferson Davis*, vol. 2, *June 1841–July 1846*, ed. James T. McIntosh (Baton Rouge: Louisiana State University Press, 1974), pp. 52–57.

[3]Varina Davis to Margaret Kempe Howell, 4 January 1847, Jefferson Davis Papers, University of Alabama.

[4]Jefferson Davis to Varina Davis, 3 January 1848, *The American Scene: A Panorama of Autographs 1504–1980*, Paul C. Richards (n. p., n. d.), p. 66; *The Papers of Jefferson Davis*, vol. 3, *July 1846–December 1848*, eds. James T. McIntosh, Lynda L. Crist, and Mary S. Dix (Baton Rouge: Louisiana State University Press, 1981), pp. 301–304; Varina Davis to Margaret Kempe Howell, n. d. [January 1848], Jefferson Davis Papers, University of Alabama.

[5]Varina Davis to Margaret Howell, 15 September 1858, Jefferson Davis Papers, University of Alabama.

[6]Jefferson Davis to Varina Davis, 5 November 1850, original owned by Joel Webb.

[7]Woodward, ed., *Mary Chesnut's Civil War*, p. 595.

[8]Varina Davis to William B. Howell, 1 September 1859, Jefferson Davis Papers, University of Alabama; Woodward, ed., *Mary Chesnut's Civil War*, p. 80; Varina Davis to Margaret Howell, 21 November 1858, Jefferson Davis Papers, University of Alabama.

[9]Virginia Clay-Clopton, *A Belle of the Fifties: Memoirs of Mrs. Clay, of Alabama, covering Social and Political Life in Washington and the South, 1853–66*, Put into narrative form by Ada Sterling (New York: Doubleday, Page & Company, 1905), p. 134.

[10]Woodward, ed., *Mary Chesnut's Civil War*, p. 800; [Varina Davis] to [Margaret Howell], n. d. [June] 1861, Mrs. Jefferson Davis Letters, Iowa Department of History and Archives, Copy at Jefferson Davis Papers, Rice University.

[11]"Aunty" [Eliza Davis] to "Dear Mattie" [Martha Harrison?], 10 August 1861, Lise Mitchell Papers, Tulane University.

[12]Woodward, ed., *Mary Chesnut's Civil War*, p. 136; Catherine Anne Devereux Edmonston, 20 May 1862, *"The Journal of a Secesh Lady"*: *The Diary of Catherine Ann Devereux Edmonston, 1860–1866*, eds. Beth G. Crabtree and James W. Patton (Raleigh: Division of Archives and History, Department of Cultural Resources, 1979), p. 180.

[13]Varina Davis to Jefferson Davis, 28 June 1862, original owned by Jefferson Hayes-Davis.

[14]Varina Davis to William Preston Johnston, 2 November 1865, Johnston Family Papers, The Filson Club. William Howell died in 1863.

[15]Varina Davis to Mrs. Howell Cobb, 22 October 1868, *The Correspondence of Robert Toombs, Alexander H. Stephens, and Howell Cobb*, ed. Ulrich Bonnell Phillips, 2 vols. (Washington, D. C.: Ninth Report of the Historical Manuscripts Commission, 1913), 2: 704.

[16]Varina Davis, *Jefferson Davis*, 1: 475.

[17]Davis, *Jefferson Davis*, 2: 828, 12.

[18]Davis, *Jefferson Davis*, 2: 202.

[19]Varina Davis to Charles Dudley Warner, 2 October 1898, Charles Dudley Warner Papers, Watkinson Library, Trinity College.

[20]"Should Women Vote," in unknown newspaper, n. d., Kate Cumming Collection, Alabama Department of Archives and History.

Charlotte Forten

(1837–1914)

Brenda Stevenson

Born in 1837 into a prominent free black family in Philadelphia, Charlotte Forten lost her mother when she was three. After her father's remarriage, Forten spent much of her childhood under the guidance of relatives living in the Forten household, who encouraged the young girl in her studies, and influenced her with the abolitionist and other reform ideals. In 1853 she was sent to Salem, Massachusetts, where she received an excellent education and was again exposed to prominent African-American activists. Despite her shyness, Forten carved out a career for herself as a teacher, became self-supporting, and continued to live in Salem. In 1858 she was forced by illness to resign her position and returned to Philadelphia to the home and care of maternal aunts. While recuperating, she published essays and poems in antislavery journals and taught her young cousins. The great challenge of her career came during the Civil War, when Forten moved in 1862 to the Sea Islands of South Carolina to work as a teacher among "contraband" slaves (those who had escaped and were under the protection of the Union army). Forten was one of the first black teachers to join this educational effort and was the first and only one at her outpost on St. Helena Island. Her journals of this period provide scholars with an invaluable record of this dramatic historical experiment and epoch. A two-part article chronicling her experience, "Life on the Sea Islands," appeared in The Atlantic Monthly *in May 1864. At this same time, faced with another bout of illness and the impact of her father's death, she returned to the North, traveling and living for short periods in both Pennsylvania and Massachusetts. She returned to the South in 1871, to teach a year in Charleston, South Carolina, after which she moved to Washington, D.C., to teach at a black preparatory school. During these years in Washington,*

279

Forten met her future husband, Francis Grimké. Married in 1878,
the couple had one child, who died in infancy. The couple spent
most of their lives in Washington, with Francis Grimké pursuing
his career as a minister and Charlotte Forten retiring from teach-
ing to continue her interest in writing and reform. Forten died in
Washington in 1914.

Charlotte Forten was born on August 17, 1837 in Philadelphia,
Pennsylvania. She was the only child of Robert Bridges Forten
(1813–1864) and his first wife, Mary Virginia Woods Forten (1816–
1840), who died when Charlotte was only three. The Forten family
was among the most prestigious and wealthy of the Philadelphia free
black community. Moreover, they used their financial and social
standing to support local and regional reform movements, most particularly the efforts to abolish slavery and to establish legal equality
for free blacks. Charlotte's earliest paternal ancestor in this country
had been an African slave, but that was five generations before her
birth. She represented the fourth generation of Fortens who were
born free, a generation that would live long enough to realize some
of the political goals that her family of activists advocated.

James Forten, Sr., Charlotte's paternal grandfather, initially articulated these ideals that so profoundly influenced the lives of his children and his granddaughter in particular.[1] In 1800, Forten was
among other prominent Philadelphia free blacks who, led by the
Reverend Absalom Jones, petitioned the U.S. Congress to end the
African slave trade, establish guidelines for the gradual abolition of
slavery, and provide legislation to weaken the Fugitive Slave Act of
1793.[2] Congress voted 85 to 1 not to consider the petition.[3]

Forten and his peers, however, were not discouraged in their determination to gain legal and economic equality for blacks. In 1813,
Charlotte's grandfather published a pamphlet of five letters rebut-
ting statements supportive of legislation that would ban the en-
trance of free blacks into the state of Pennsylvania. Moreover, he
was an adamant critic of the American Colonization Society. The
members of the society, which was formed in December 1816, proposed the voluntary removal of free blacks from the United States to
some location in Africa or elsewhere. Most members did not support
abolition, but offered a ready remedy for the social and economic
problems that they believed free blacks imposed on American society. Colonizationists, as they were called, couched their appeal to
blacks in "benevolent" terms, asserting that prejudiced whites in
the United States would never accept blacks as full citizens. Outside

the country, however, blacks could live more peaceably and "freely." Forten and other free black activists, on the other hand, believed that blacks and whites had equal intellectual and physical capabilities, and that blacks had contributed much to the creation and development of the United States as a nation, and thus should have equal access to the country's resources and equal protection under its laws. Free blacks should not be forced to move elsewhere, Forten maintained, but should receive the appropriate training to enable them to live productive lives in American society. He supported protest meetings against the colonizationist movement in both 1817 and 1819.

In 1830, Forten was one of the driving forces behind a National Negro Convention held in Philadelphia. Participants of this convention not only condemned colonizationist efforts, but also discussed strategies to expand the rights of free blacks and abolish slavery. Black reformers held several similar meetings during the 1830s, and Forten figured prominently in all of them.[4] This was an important decade for all blacks within the nation, for it was during these years that disparate antislavery efforts became united in powerful organizations, locally and regionally. James Forten and most of the adult members of his household were at the forefront of these efforts. Thus, the Forten home of the 1830s was a hub of radical thought and activity, and certainly none of its members could have escaped the influence of such dedication and activity.[5] Into this household Charlotte Forten was born in 1837.

James Forten and his wife, Charlotte, Sr. (1784–1884), taught their children to take responsibility both for their lives and for the fate of their race. Scholarship, morality, achievement, selfless dedication to the improvement of the political and economic conditions of blacks—these were the important elements of the socialization process that took place at 92 Lombard Street during Charlotte's childhood as well as during her father's. James and his wife had eight children, four sons and four daughters. Among them, Margaretta, Sarah, Harriet, and Robert Forten were the most politically active.[6]

Forten's daughters, his wife, and his future daughter-in-law (Mary Virginia Woods)[7] were all founding members of the Philadelphia Female Anti-Slavery Society in 1833, an organization that figured prominently in their activities. Margaretta (1808–1875), teacher and administrator of a school for black children in Philadelphia, had a special interest in education and served on the society's educational committee for several years. Moreover, she was one of the few remaining founding members who still supported the organization when it dispersed in 1870. Sarah, her younger sister, also served on the Female Anti-Slavery Society's Board of Managers, representing the organization at the Anti-Slavery Convention of American Women in 1837. Harriet Forten herself was a delegate to this conference in 1837 and 1838.[8]

Sarah Forten and her sister Harriet also were active supporters of women's rights and representative of a growing number of antebellum women who believed in the equality of the sexes. They especially understood the great social and political changes women could help to effect and believed women had a contribution to make to society. Their husbands, the brothers Robert and Joseph Purvis, held similar views. Harriet's spouse, Robert, was a particularly influential abolitionist as well as an advocate of temperance and women's rights. Young Charlotte Forten was very impressed with her Uncle Robert's activism and enlightened perspective, and she drew personal comfort and intellectual delight when in the company of her Aunt Harriet's family. In their home and in her grandparents' Charlotte met and heard some of the most important members of the abolitionist movement, locally and nationally.

Her father, Robert Bridges Forten dedicated himself to efforts to improve the status of blacks in America. It was a commitment that his father demanded of him and that he expected of his daughter. Born in 1813 and educated privately, Charlotte's father was considered by family, friends, and acquaintances as the most talented of his clan. As a young man, he was known locally as a mathematician, poet, and orator. It was during his youth that he constructed a nine-foot telescope that was exhibited at Philadelphia's Franklin Institute. And it was at an early age that he began to participate in various antislavery organizations and activities. Forten was a member of the Young Men's Anti-Slavery Society of Philadelphia and served on its Board of Managers from 1835 to 1836. He also was a member of the Philadelphia Vigilance Committee and the New England Anti-Slavery Society.[9]

Robert Forten's activities document his dedication to antislavery and civil rights, and yet the years of frustration and anger he sustained while growing up as a talented black man in a racist society took its toll. He found it impossible to live a productive and happy life in the United States and moved abroad, first to Canada in 1855 and then to England in 1858.

In 1862 Robert Forten returned to the United States to enlist in the Union forces then at war with the Confederacy. Although his family counseled him not to expose himself to the harshness of military life, he was determined to join the U.S. Army and did so at Camp William Penn on March 2, 1864. His initial rank was that of a private in Company A of the 43rd U.S. Colored Infantry. A month later, he was promoted to sergeant-major and transferred to Maryland, where he was to help recruit black soldiers. Forten became ill almost immediately after reaching Maryland and, on April 18, 1864, requested sick leave to return to his family home in Philadelphia. Robert Forten died of typhoid fever on April 25, 1864. He was the first black to receive a military funeral in Philadelphia.[10]

Charlotte's father and other politically active family members must have had a tremendous impact on her. She grew up in a home where abolition and equal rights for blacks were key issues to discuss and act upon. Daily she was in the presence of important designers and participants in the abolitionist and civil rights movements. William Lloyd Garrison, John Greenleaf Whittier, Harriet Martineau, William Nell, and Charles Remond were but a few of the prominent abolitionists who visited the Forten and Purvis homes. Moreover, there were present in her family and their groups of friends several impressive female activists who served as important role models for Charlotte. Her mother, grandmother, and aunts were all well-educated, hardworking, morally upright, socially astute women who quite willingly gave much of their energy, financial resources, and time to abolition, civil rights, and the general improvement of conditions within the free black community. Charlotte's mother, Mary Virginia Woods Forten, who was described by her contemporaries as a "beautiful mulatto," was herself a member of a prominent abolitionist family of Philadelphia. Undoubtedly, the young mother believed that her little girl too would grow up to participate in such worthy activities. Unfortunately, Mary Virginia Forten died when Charlotte was quite young and thus was unable to influence her child directly.[11] Yet Charlotte's relatives provided recollections of her mother that served as an inspiration to her as she grew older.

After Mary Virginia Forten's death, Charlotte's paternal grandmother, Charlotte Forten, Sr., and her aunts—particularly Margaretta, who was unmarried—took over the maternal role in her life. Because her aunts and their families lived so near each other, Charlotte benefited from an extended family network that was particularly close-knit. She spent many of her childhood days at the Forten family home at 92 Lombard Street, but also would often visit her aunts Sarah and Harriet Purvis who had moved to nearby Bucks County. She adored her cousins and the beauty of the land surrounding their homes, spending many summer days riding, reading, playing games, acting out plays, discussing important issues, picking flowers and berries, and generally enjoying herself. And it seems she never was as relaxed or happy as when surrounded by family. After she moved to Salem in late 1853, Charlotte often thought of the happy times she had spent with her large family and wished once again to be in their presence. Yet she was not one for leisurely vacations at home. She left Philadelphia to complete her education. Her personal needs, even family affection, she maintained, were unimportant in comparison.[12]

On May 24, 1854, Charlotte Forten began to keep a daily journal. At the time, she was sixteen years old and had moved to Salem, Massachusetts, from her native Pennsylvania just six months before. At home, Charlotte had received years of private instruction from tutors since Robert Forten refused to send her to the poorly equipped and racially segregated schools designated for black children in Philadelphia. When an opportunity came for her to receive an excellent public school education outside of Philadelphia, Charlotte was sent. Forten discovered from friends that Salem had integrated schools of sound reputation. It was also the location of a fine normal school which her father wanted her eventually to attend so that she could prepare for a teaching career. This profession, he believed, would give Charlotte some practical skill with which to aid her race, for there were few well-trained teachers available to the black community. Moreover, he surmised, such a profession would allow Charlotte some secure means of financial support.

It is not clear whether Charlotte ever really wanted to become a teacher. It seems as though she preferred the life of a scholar or writer. The young Charlotte Forten was, however, eager to please her father and to contribute to the uplift of her race and, therefore, she was determined to complete her studies successfully. "I will spare no effort to become what he desires that I should be; . . . to prepare myself well for the responsible duties of a teacher, and to live for the good that I can do my oppressed and suffering fellow-creatures."[13]

Robert Forten arranged that his precocious, but shy, daughter reside in the Salem home of old friends, the prominent abolitionist Charles Lenox Remond and his wife, Amy Matilda. Charles Remond was active as an orator and supporter of the abolitionist cause and was still in the forefront of the movement during Charlotte's stay in his home. In fact, it was while she resided with the Remonds that she met William Lloyd Garrison, Wendell Phillips, John Whittier, Abigail and Stephen Foster, Lydia Maria Child, Maria Chapman, William C. Nell, William Wells Brown, and other noted abolitionists. Many of these persons were close friends of Charlotte's family and the Remonds, and wholeheartedly welcomed her into their fold. Her host's sister, Sarah Parker Remond, did not live with her brother, but was a frequent visitor. A lecturer for the American Anti-Slavery Society, Sarah Remond inspired Charlotte with stories of her lecturing tours at home and abroad.

As time passed, Charlotte came to know and love Salem. Its climate, political activism, and particularly its intellectual offerings suited her tastes. She was well aware of the racism of some of its residents and various instances of institutionalized discrimination, but in comparison with Philadelphia, she found Salem much less oppressive. On those occasions when she had to leave New England for Pennsylvania, Charlotte was routinely apprehensive of the treatment she would receive in her racially hostile home state.

During the first year and a half of her stay in Salem, Charlotte was a student at the Higginson Grammar School. Intellectually, Charlotte thrived at the school from which she graduated with "decided éclat" in March 1855. Charlotte's poem "A Parting Hymn" was chosen as the best submitted by her class, and she gained a modest local reputation as a young poet of some merit. In fact, she had begun to submit her poetry for publication a year before. In March 1855, a poem that she wrote in praise of William Lloyd Garrison was published in the *Liberator* magazine.[14] Charlotte entered the Salem Normal School after her final examinations at Higginson and graduated in July 1856.

Charlotte lamented the end of her school days, but she pursued knowledge even more avidly in the following years. She most often spent her free time studying French, German, Latin, European and classical history, and reading the works of both her contemporaries and of the great authors of the past. Charlotte was particularly fond of good literature and searched for companions with similar tastes. Fortunately, she found such persons in her "society" of housemates and their local relations. Still, she deemed her studies her "closest friends" and approached them with a vitality and passion rarely expressed in other facets of her life. A typical week of self-imposed study was rigorous. On January 5, 1857 she noted: "Still alone, and should be lonesome were not my time so constantly occupied,—teaching all day and reading and studying all the evening. Translated several passages from the 'Commentaries,' and finished the 'Conquest of Mexico.' "[15] The following evening she read and criticized Tennyson.[16] The afternoon of the seventh she spent studying Latin.[17] The next evening she dedicated herself to translating Caesar, a task of which she wrote: "Find it rather difficult, but am determined to persevere. Excelsior! shall be my motto, now and forever."[18] On the ninth, she relaxed and attended a concert by the pianist Thalberg, but followed this with a thorough reading of the *Liberator* when she returned home.[19]

Such was the scholar's life that young Charlotte Forten chose for herself. To pursue her studies in this uninhibited manner she considered a wonderful blessing. Deeply religious, Charlotte believed that

God had indeed chosen her for a particular mission—to use her natural talents to inspire and improve her race. Denial of this calling, Charlotte believed, could jeopardize her own Christian salvation.

Charlotte's insistence on selfless dedication to her race—which in her mind denied her the right of such basic human needs as love, pride, and concern for "self-culture"—was at best a burdensome ideal that caused her immeasurable frustration during her youth. It was a goal that, in time, Charlotte came to know as unattainable. As a young adult, however, she could not accept this rationally and failed to appreciate the valuable contributions she could and did make. Thus a pervasive sense of unworthiness and insecurity characterized Charlotte's adolescence and young adulthood. Yet her unhappiness and frustration during this period not only was derived from a growing sense of failure with regard to her mission but also from the deteriorating relationship with her father.

Charlotte came to Salem in 1853 hoping her father and stepfamily would soon relocate to Massachusetts, where together they could establish a home.[20] She was crushed when Robert Forten decided in 1855 to move his family to Canada. Once he left the country, Charlotte received little communication from him, which prompted her to believe that his interest in and affection for his only daughter had somehow diminished. She felt a profound sense of parental abandonment during this important period of her development.

Charlotte's estrangement from her father posed practical problems, too, for she was left with no financial support except that which she earned herself. When her father's aid ceased, she was a full-time student at the Salem Normal School and suddenly was unable to pay some of her school expenses as well as her room and board to the Remonds. Her growing indebtedness was another source of frustration and depression. As Charlotte's relationship with her father disintegrated, she seemed to think more of her deceased mother and of the loving relationship they would have had if she had lived. Charlotte's fantasies of her mother depicted a beautiful, warm, loving woman to whom an unhappy and often ill daughter could always turn for comfort.[21] Although for days and weeks at a time Charlotte thought much about her mother, her fantasies did not bring her long-lasting comfort.

Charlotte's unhappiness and negative self-perception undoubtedly also stemmed from the racism and rejection of whites with whom she came in contact. During her adolescence and early adulthood, she keenly felt the racism of classmates and, later, of teachers in Salem. A shy, sensitive, sometimes angry and defensive adolescent, Charlotte absolutely refused to compromise her standards with regard to friends. Thus, from her experience, Charlotte grew suspi-

cious of the racial attitudes of whites and usually withheld her judgment of a person until she found out if that person held the "correct"
views on racial issues. She was, however, able to establish a few
meaningful relationships with some of her schoolroom associates,
most particularly a deep friendship with Mary Shepard, Charlotte's
principal at the Higginson Grammar School.

Despite her criticism of many of her associates, Charlotte judged
her own character and actions more harshly than she did those of her
friends and family. She was particularly generous in her assessment
of those whites whom she believed had overcome their racism and
were involved actively in the abolitionist movement. She also
praised those who, like Shepard, offered her genuine acceptance and
friendship. And while Charlotte was familiar with the overt racial
hostility of most whites in mid-nineteenth-century America, she
continued to be angered and hurt when faced with discrimination or
outright rejection.

Yet as a young adult, Charlotte Forten never realized the enormous impact that she had on those whites with whom she came in
contact. Her insecurity and extreme modesty blinded her to their
appreciation of her demeanor, intelligence, and accomplishments.
These persons—primarily abolitionists, intellectuals, and literary
artists—viewed her as exceptional in character and talent. Her close
friend, John Greenleaf Whittier, for example, described Charlotte to
Theodore Dwight Weld as "a young lady of exquisite refinement,
quiet culture and ladylike and engaging manners, and personal appearance." "I look upon her as one of the most gifted representatives
of her class," he concluded.[22] A writer for the *Salem Register* wrote
of Charlotte in 1856: "She presented in her own mental endow-
ments and propriety of demeanor an honorable vindication of the
claims of her race to the rights of mental culture and privileges of
humanity."[23] Forten never allowed herself to take such compliments seriously.

Perhaps Charlotte's negative self-esteem resulted from her subcon-
scious inculcation of popular views of black inferiority. Publicly she
never wavered in her belief in the natural equality of the races and,
indeed, dedicated her life to asserting through personal example the
legitimacy of that doctrine. Yet privately she struggled not so much
with the basic premise of natural equality, but with the question of
whether members of her race were willing to work diligently to
achieve the reality of equality, given their limited access to it. Her
criticism of blacks, as of herself, was often severe, and it was difficult for her to accept their moral nobility, much more so than it was
for her to recognize the nobility of whites. She described a good
friend from Salem, Henry Cassey, for example, as a young black man

with a "noble nature, and high aspirations, both moral and mental." She went on, however, to sharply contrast his nobility with those of other black males, noting that these characteristics of Henry made "him a different being from the generality of colored young men that one sees;—though I know that the unhappy circumstances in which these are placed, are often more to blame than they themselves."[24]

Charlotte certainly adopted white standards for beauty that caused her to think of herself as unattractive when by all accounts she was a pretty woman. While she was visiting John Whittier's home in 1862, for example, the poet's sister, Elizabeth, presented her with a portrait of an Italian woman that everyone present thought resembled Charlotte. She noted of the incident, however: "I utterly failed to see it: *I* thought the Italian girl very pretty, and I know myself to be the very opposite."[25] On another occasion Charlotte described a Caucasian acquaintance as quite attractive, with "just such long, light hair, and beautiful blue eyes. . . . She is a little poetess—a sweet, gentle creature. I have fallen quite in love with her."[26] When describing the face of a wounded black soldier in the 54th Massachusetts, she again indicated her standards for beauty. "He has such a good honest face. It is pleasant to look at it—although it is black."[27] Thus Charlotte herself internalized racist attitudes that undoubtedly would have a negative effect on her self-image.

While issues of race continued to figure largely in Charlotte's life, her health problems became a major source of frustration as early as 1856. Like so many of her friends and family, she suffered from respiratory ailments that frequently imposed an immense physical and emotional burden on her. Charlotte first began to suffer from severe headaches and respiratory illnesses in November 1856, not long after she accepted a teaching position at the Epes Grammar School. She was intermittently ill for the next six months and, in May 1857, she was forced to return to Philadelphia to rest and regain her health. Charlotte returned to Salem in July 1857 to resume her teaching position at Epes, but was forced to resign in early March 1858 due to illness.

Following her resignation, Charlotte returned to Pennsylvania where she rested, taught the younger children of Harriet Purvis, and wrote poems and essays for publication. Although her health had interrupted her teaching career, the less hectic pace of the Purvis household allowed her to focus on professional writing. She received her first payment for writing, a modest sum of one dollar, from Bishop Daniel Payne of the *Christian Recorder* magazine, on May 20, 1858, for a poem entitled "Flowers."[28] The next month, her essay "Glimpses of New England" appeared in the *National Anti-Slavery Standard.*[29] In 1859, two poems—"The Two Voices" and "The Wind

Among the Poplars"—appeared in print.[30] And in January 1860, Charlotte's poem "The Slave Girl's Prayer" was published in the *National Anti-Slavery Standard*.[31]

Charlotte remained with her family until September 1859, when she again returned to Salem to teach in the Higginson Grammar School. By the spring, however, she became ill with "lung fever" and resigned her post. Charlotte then traveled to Bridgewater and later to Worcester to seek physical therapy at the water cure establishment of Dr. Seth Rogers.[32] By the fall of 1860, she had recuperated enough to resume work, but again became seriously ill in late October 1860 and had to return to Philadelphia. There she rested but remained active in the abolitionist cause while she taught in a school for black children. Charlotte returned to Salem during the summer of 1862 to teach summer classes, and on August 9, 1862, she visited John Whittier at his home in Amesbury. It was during this visit that Whittier suggested to Charlotte that she could render a great service to her people if she went to teach among the contraband slaves who had run away to Union camps in the Confederate South.[33]

On October 22, 1862, Charlotte Forten sailed from New York for Port Royal, South Carolina, where she remained for about eighteen months. Under the auspices of the Port Royal Relief Association, Charlotte secured the position of teacher among the contraband slaves of the South Carolina Sea Islands. She was among hundreds of teachers from the Northeast who had come South for various reasons, but primarily to prepare the recently released slaves for their new role as free citizens of the United States.

Charlotte Forten was among the first black teachers in the South and, at the time she arrived, the first and only one stationed on St. Helena Island. Proportionately, there continued to be a very small number of blacks who were trained as teachers. Moreover, some agencies were less than cooperative in their efforts to place qualified black teachers in these positions. Charlotte Forten, for example, initially tried to reach South Carolina under the auspices of the Boston Educational Commission, later renamed the New England Freedman's Aid Society. After several unsuccessful attempts to gain their sponsorship in August 1862, she returned to Philadelphia where she retained the support of the Port Royal Relief Association of that city.[34]

Charlotte Forten believed that working among the contraband slaves of South Carolina would afford her an excellent opportunity to help her race. Frustrated by the restrictions of poor health, she welcomed the opportunity to travel South where she hoped the mild climate would allow her to remain tolerably healthy while she performed the "noble" task of preparing illiterate blacks for their roles as free Americans.

From the very beginning of her stay on St. Helena Island, Charlotte thought fondly of the contraband slaves with whom she came in contact. Sensitive to their plight of trying to adjust to the status of free persons, she was quick to explain that their cultural expression and lifestyles, which seemed peculiar and sometimes crude to Northerners, were largely a result of their past as slaves.[35] Yet like the other teachers and missionaries who came to instruct the contraband, Charlotte sometimes was both amused and repulsed by the social, linguistic and religious practices of the Sea Island blacks. Overall, however, she appreciated their friendly and deferential manner, their determination to gain freedom and educate their children, and particularly their affectionate treatment of loved ones and friends. Her general fondness for the adults as well as her students caused her to be solicitous of their individual and group needs, especially their health and material welfare.[36]

Forten's primary task was to teach the contraband children the rudiments of a formal education. Placed in a one-room schoolhouse with children of all ages, Charlotte taught reading, writing, spelling, history, and math. She also instructed older blacks on proper moral and social behavior. Freedman aid societies, such as the one that sponsored Charlotte's work, strongly advocated this kind of informal but instructive contact between contraband slaves and their Northern workers. Charlotte, who was an avid assimilationist, was no different in this respect from her white peers and adamantly believed that blacks would never be accepted as equals if they remained culturally distinct. Certainly she enjoyed the culture of the Sea Island blacks, especially their unique singing style, but she was greatly relieved that the contraband were conforming to Northern mores, such as solemnizing their relationships through legal marriage.[37]

Most of her time on St. Helena was happy. It was undoubtedly the most challenging period of her life, a time of immense personal growth. As the first black teacher among the contraband who resided there, Charlotte faced the mixed feelings of both teachers and military personnel. Although she reported that most of the Union whites she interacted with were pleasant, she did note that initially she felt no "congeniality" among those with whom she lived.[38] This feeling, however, changed when old abolitionist friends and acquaintances began to arrive.

Colonel Thomas Wentworth Higginson was one of the several close friends that Charlotte acquired while residing on St. Helena Island. A native of Massachusetts, Higginson had been a dedicated abolitionist who gained widespread notoriety in 1854 when he tried unsuccessfully to aid in the escape of the fugitive slave Anthony Burns, who was then on trial in Boston. Higginson was by profession a Unitarian minister and lived in Worcester, Massachusetts. When Charlotte saw him in South Carolina in the fall of 1862, she recalled that she had seen him the summer before drilling soldiers of the all-white 51st Massachusetts before they left for duty in the South, and she remembered his enthusiasm in commanding the troops. Such a man, "so full of life and energy" and so obviously dedicated to the black race, was "the one best fitted to command a regiment of colored soldiers," she thought.[39] So did General Rufus Saxton, commander of the Union forces in the Port Royal region, who decided to place Higginson in command of the First South Carolina Volunteers, a regiment of Sea Island blacks.[40] Charlotte followed closely the recruitment and training of this historic regiment. Both blacks and white abolitionists hoped that they would soon impress America with their bravery and determination.

Charlotte also befriended other military personnel, as well as teachers and plantation superintendents. She met, for example, and was very impressed with Colonel Robert Gould Shaw, son of the noted abolitionist Francis Shaw of New York and commander of the all-black 54th Massachusetts regiment. She was moved by Colonel Shaw's gentlemanly qualities, intellect, and his great appreciation for his position as commander of the first regiment of free blacks from the North to be engaged in the Civil War.[41] She was stunned by the death of Colonel Shaw at the bloody battle of Fort Wagner on Morris Island, South Carolina, on July 18, 1863.

But, by far the most important relationship that Charlotte established on St. Helena Island was her deep romantic attachment to a white surgeon in Higginson's First South Carolina Volunteers, Dr. Seth Rogers. Forten first met Dr. Rogers during the spring of 1860, when she frequented his water cure establishment in Worcester. He arrived at Camp Saxton, South Carolina, during the latter part of December 1862. When Charlotte traveled to the camp on New Year's Day 1863 to celebrate the Emancipation Proclamation, she was elated to see her friend and physician again, and their friendship flourished. Entry after entry in Charlotte's diary describe the times they spent together—taking walks and riding horseback, having dinner, traveling together to nearby plantations, playing chess, reading to one another, and just talking about themselves, their work, and literature.[42] It is not certain how profoundly Dr. Rogers felt about Charlotte, for the journal only depicts her feelings. It does tell us, however, that Rogers certainly devoted a great deal of time and energy to her while they were in South Carolina. Moreover, it was his suggestion that they write to one another when they could not visit often. He also sent her gifts, read to her when she was ill, and was generally very attentive.[43] Although his gestures appear to have been romantic in intent, Charlotte explained in a diary entry on February 2, 1863 that Dr. Rogers wanted her to think of him "as a brother." "And I will gladly do so," she responded.[44]

Charlotte did not forget that Rogers was married and white. He in turn, seeming to anticipate the possibility of a more intimate relationship with her, tried to quell it by insisting that Charlotte regard him as a brother and by reminding her of his wife. Charlotte viewed these as "noble" gestures and was apt to respond to them by feeling closer to him. Charlotte's journal indicates that she and Seth Rogers continued to have a close relationship throughout most of 1863, until he resigned from his post in the Union Army in December 1863, and went back to Worcester.

Overall, Charlotte's experiences on St. Helena Island were fruitful. She wrote of her time among the contraband in two letters addressed to William Lloyd Garrison, which subsequently were published in the *Liberator* in 1862. A two-part article, which Charlotte called "Life on the Sea Islands," appeared in *The Atlantic Monthly* in 1864.[45] It was a rewarding and exciting period of her life not only because opportunities existed for it to be so, but also because she had acquired the emotional maturity necessary to realistically perceive and act on these opportunities. After a troubled and prolonged adolescence, she was long overdue for the happiness and sense of fulfillment that she obtained while working among the ex-slaves. Unfortunately, her health began to fail again. That circumstance, and undoubtedly her father's untimely death on April 25, 1864, precipitated her decision to return to the North for good where she hoped to recover her health and draw comfort from her family.[46]

Charlotte did not remain very long in Philadelphia once she left the South. Her health was poor, and she wrote to her friend John Whittier from Detroit during the summer of 1865 to solicit his aid in securing her a place in the sanatorium of Dioclesian Lewis at Lexington, Massachusetts. For reasons that are unclear, Charlotte never went to Lexington. Instead, in October 1865, she accepted a position as Secretary of the Teachers Committee of the New England Branch of the Freedman's Union Commission for a salary of ten dollars a week.[47] Located in Boston, Charlotte socialized with her many New England friends and continued with her personal studies. Her determination to master the French language culminated in her translation of Emile Erckmann and Alexandre Chatrain's novel *Madame Thérèse; or, The Volunteers of '92*, which Scribner's published in 1869.[48] As Secretary of the Teachers Committee, Charlotte acted as liaison between the teachers in the South who tutored the ex-slaves and those in the North who supplied them with financial and material support through the auspices of the Commission. She held this position until October 1871[49], then resigned to teach for a year at the (Robert Gould) Shaw Memorial School in Charleston, South Carolina.[50] She then moved to Washington, D.C., where from 1872 until 1873 she was a teacher in a black preparatory high school (later named Dunbar High) under the direction of Alexander Crummell. Charlotte left this position to accept a job as first-class clerk in the Fourth Auditor's Office of the U.S. Treasury Department.[51]

Charlotte stayed in Washington for almost the remainder of her life. Her first few years in the capital were no doubt spent working, meeting new friends, renewing old acquaintances, writing, and studying. She also enjoyed the stimulating company of her cousin, Charles Burleigh Purvis, who was at that time a surgeon in the Freedmen's Hospital at Howard University.[52] Charlotte continued to suffer from poor health, and kind but chauvinistic friends, such as John Whittier, wished that "the poor girl could be better situated—the wife of some good, true man who could appreciate her as she deserves."[53] Several years later, Whittier's wish for "the poor girl" came true. During her late thirties, Charlotte met and fell in love with a young, black graduate student of divinity who was twelve years her junior—Francis Grimké, the mulatto nephew of Angelina Grimké Weld. Charlotte and Francis married in December 19, 1878.[54]

Intelligent, sensitive, morally upright, and fiercely dedicated to his profession and race, the Princeton-trained minister was certainly the husband Charlotte and her friends hoped that she would have some day. The two set up house in Washington, and Charlotte retired from public work. They had one child, Theodora Cornelia, who died as an infant in 1880. Given Charlotte's age and persistent bad health, it was inconceivable that she could bear another child, though she dearly loved children.

Charlotte now viewed her mission as intimately intertwined with that of her husband's. Francis Grimké used his pulpit as a religious forum to attack discrimination. He and Charlotte wrote and published many essays that were critical of racial oppression. They obviously worked well together, combining fierce intellectual acumen with a passionate commitment to alleviating the racial hostility prevalent in late nineteenth- and early twentieth-century America.[55]

In 1885, Charlotte and her husband left Washington to reside in Jacksonville, Florida, where Francis Grimké had accepted the pastorate at the Laura Street Presbyterian Church. They remained there for four years but then returned to Washington and the Fifteenth Street Presbyterian Church. Although they were both busy with missionary work and the many commitments that Francis Grimké's growing political influence mandated, Charlotte and her husband continued to pursue an active intellectual life. They both regularly attended two weekly reading groups, one on Friday and the other on Sunday, where they discussed art, literature, history, politics, religion, and any other topic of interest to the members of the societies.[56]

After her marriage, Charlotte continued her interest in writing poetry and essays. Her poems from that period include "A June Song" (1885), "Charlotte Corday" (1885), "At Newport" (1888), "The Gathering of the Grand Army" (1890), and "In Florida" (1893). Only a handful of essays that she wrote during the 1880s and 1890s survive: "On Mr. Savage's Sermon: 'The Problem of the Hour' " (1885), a lengthy letter addressed to the editor of the *Boston Commonwealth;* "One Phase of the Race Question" (1885), another letter written to the *Commonwealth* editor; "Colored People in New England" (1889), which was sent to the editor of *The Evangelist;* and "Personal Recollections of Whittier" (1893), which appeared in the *New England Magazine.* Four other essays, probably written during the 1890s, were not assigned a specific date of completion: "The Umbrian and Roman School of Art"; "The Flower Fairies' Reception"; "At the Home of Frederick Douglass"; and "Midsummer Days in the Capitol: 'The Corcoran Art Gallery.' "[57]

The last decade of the nineteenth century was a busy one for Charlotte, not only because of her intellectual pursuits, writing, and missionary work, but also because of her special relationship with her niece, Angelina Weld Grimké. Angelina Grimké was the only child of Francis Grimké's brother, Archibald. While he served as consul to Santo Domingo from 1894 to 1898 Charlotte and her husband acted as Angelina's legal guardians. Charlotte always had a deep affection for her niece, who was born just two years after her own infant daughter died. When Archibald and his wife, Sarah Stanley, separated, Charlotte became an important maternal figure in Angelina's life. Moreover, after 1905, Archibald and Angelina Grimké moved into Charlotte's home, where they remained until well after her death in 1914. Their permanent inclusion in Charlotte's house enlivened it socially and intellectually—further cementing the bond between aunt and niece. As always, Charlotte was surrounded by well-educated political activists. And she must have drawn immense pleasure from the fact that this time it was her own home that was the hub of activity. Although continually ill, she undoubtedly was happy to be among her loved ones, to be cared for by a "noble" and loving husband whose mission was so compatible with her own, and to be able to pursue her intellectual growth and development.[58] Charlotte Forten Grimké died quietly in her Washington home, on July 22, 1914, at the age of seventy-six.

Notes

Charlotte Forten Grimké (1837–1914) completed five journals. The dates and locations of each journal are as follows: Journal One, 1854–1856, Salem, Massachusetts; Journal Two, 1857–1858, Salem and Philadelphia, Pennsylvania; Journal Three, 1858–1863, Salem, Philadelphia, Boston, Massachusetts, and St. Helena Island, South Carolina; Journal Four, 1863–1864, St. Helena Island, Philadelphia, and Salem; Journal Five, 1885–1892, Jacksonville, Florida, Washington, D.C., Philadelphia, and Ler, Massachusetts. The manuscript copies of Grimké's journals are located in the Moorland-Springarn Research Center, Howard University, Washington, D.C.

[1]Gloria C. Oden, *"The Journal of Charlotte L. Forten:* The Salem-Philadelphia Years (1851–1862) Reexamined," *Essex Institute Historical Collections* 119 (1983): 121; Rayford W. Logan and Michael R. Winston, eds., *Dictionary of American Negro Biography* (New York, 1982), 233–234 (cited hereafter as *DANB*).

[2]The Fugitive Slave Law of 1793 allowed slave owners to seize their runaway slaves in any location in the United States, slave or free, and upon documentation of ownership to a federal or state magistrate, could return the fugitive to his former residence and status. Moreover, this law stipulated that it was a criminal act for anyone to knowingly harbor fugitive slaves or to aid their evasion of arrest. John Hope Franklin, *From Slavery to Freedom: A History of Negro Americans*, 3rd ed. (New York, 1967), 151–152; Peter M. Bergman and Mort N. Bergman, *The Chronological History of the Negro in America* (New York, 1969), 73.

[3]Bergman and Bergman, *Chronological History of the Negro*, 83.

[4]Howard Holman Bell, *A Survey of the Negro Convention Movement, 1830–1861* (New York, 1969), 10–37; Nell, *Colored Patriots*, 177–178; *DANB*, 235; Franklin, *From Slavery to Freedom*, 237–241.

[5]Bell, *Negro Convention Movement*, 43–53; Nell, *Colored Patriots*, 178–179; *DANB*, 235.

[6]Oden, *"Journal of Charlotte L. Forten* . . . Reexamined," 122.

[7]Mary Virginia Woods, Charlotte's mother, was not married to Robert Bridges Forten in 1833, the year of the formation of the Philadelphia Female Anti-Slavery Society. They were married in 1836. For an informative account of the lives of Charlotte Forten's parents, see Janice Sumler Lewis, "The Fortens of Philadelphia: An Afro-American Family and Nineteenth Century Reform," Ph.D. Dissertation, Georgetown University (1979), 14–128, passim; Sterling, *We Are Your Sisters*, 119–120.

[8]Lewis, "Fortens of Philadelphia," 43–44, 61; Sterling, *We Are Your Sisters*, 114, 120–121.

[9]Lewis, "Fortens of Philadelphia," 24–128, passim.

[10]Lewis, "Fortens of Philadelphia," 14–128, passim.

[11]Oden, *"Journal of Charlotte L. Forten* . . . Reexamined," 121.

[12]Journal One, September 3, 1854; Journal Two, February 14, 1857, April 12, 1857.

[13]Journal One, October 23, 1854.

[14]*Liberator*, March 16, 1855.

[15]Journal Two, January 5, 1857.

[16]Journal Two, January 6, 1857.

[17]Journal Two, January 7, 1857.

[18]Journal Two, January 8, 1857.

[19]Journal Two, January 9, 1857.

[20]Journal One, September 3, 1854.

[21]Journal Two, April 12, 1857, July 16, 1857; Journal Three, June 18, 1858.

[22]John B. Pickard, ed., *The Letters of John Greenleaf Whittier, Vol. 3, 1861–1892* (Cambridge, 1975), 97.

[23]*Salem Register*, July 24, 1856.

[24]Journal Three, June 22, 1862.

[25]Journal Three, August 9, 1862.

[26]Journal Three, April 11, 1858.

[27]Journal Four, July 23, 1863.

[28]Journal Three, May 20, 1858.

[29]*National Anti-Slavery Standard*, June 18, 1858.

[30]*Liberator*, May 27, 1859; *National Anti-Slavery Standard*, January 15, 1859.

[31]*National Anti-Slavery Standard*, January 14, 1860.

[32]Journal Three, June 22, 1862.

[33]Journal Three, August 9, 1862.

[34]Journal Three, August 13, 1862 to October 22, 1862.

[35]Journal Three, November 30, 1862; and "Life on the Sea Islands," draft in the Francis Grimké Papers, Moorland-Springarn Research Center, Howard University.

[36]Journal Three, November 7, 1862, November 18, 1862.

[37]Journal Three, October 29, 1862, November 7, 1862, November 23, 1862.

[38]Journal Three, November 23, 1862.

[39]Journal Three, November 27, 1862.

[40]Thomas Wentworth Higginson, *Army Life in a Black Regiment* (Boston, 1870), 1–3.

[41]Willie Lee Rose, *Rehearsal for Reconstruction: The Port Royal Experiment* (1964; New York, 1967), 248–250.

[42]Journal Three, January 1, 1863, January 7, 1863, January 26, 1863, February 8, 1863, February 9, 1863, Journal Four, February 19, 1863, February 22, 1863, March 2, 1863, April 11, 1863, July 25, 1863.

[43]Journal Three, January 7, 1863, January 26, 1863; Journal Four, February 19, 1863, March 2, 1863, April 3, 1863.

[44]Journal Three, February 8, 1863.

[45]*Liberator*, December 12, 1862; *Liberator*, December 19, 1862; *The Atlantic Monthly*, May 1864; *Atlantic Monthly*, June 1864.

[46]Lewis, "Fortens of Philadelphia," 126–128.

[47]Pickard, *Letters of John Greenleaf Whittier, Vol. 3*, 97, 98, nn. 1, 4. Whittier wrote to Theodore Dwight Weld concerning Charlotte Forten's desire to seek a place at Lewis's establishment, asking Weld if he could arrange a "reduced" price for her. Pickard quotes a letter of Whittier's dated September 13, 1865, in which Whittier mentions Forten's request and notes that she did not go to the sanatorium because all concerned thought it unwise. He did not give a reason for this decision, but only wrote, "To take her at all would I fear be hazardous to his enterprise, and I am sure Charlotte would not wish to run the risk of that"; Sterling, *We Are Your Sisters*, 284.

[48]Emile Erckmann and Alexandre Chatrain, *Madame Thérèse; or, The Volunteers of '92*, Charlotte Forten, trans. (Boston, 1869).

[49]Sterling, *We Are Your Sisters*, 284–285.

[50]Sterling, *We Are Your Sisters*, 283.

[51]*New National Ear*, July 3, 1873.

[52]*DANB*, 507.

[53]Pickard, *Letters of John Greenleaf Whittier, Vol. 3*, 278.

[54]Sterling, *We Are Your Sisters*, 285–286.

[55]*DANB*, 274–275.

[56]Anna Julia Cooper, "Reminiscences," Francis Grimké Papers, Moorland-Spingarn Research Center, Howard University.

[57]Copies of Charlotte Forten Grimké's writings from this period are all part of the Francis Grimké Papers , Moorland-Springarn Research Center, Howard University.

[58]*DANB*, 272–273; correspondence of Charlotte Forten Grimké, to Angelina Weld Grimké dated September 23, 1899, January 23, 1903, May 7, 1911, June 4, 1911, July 18, 1911, August 4, 1911, August 25, 1911, Francis Grimké Papers, Moorland-Spingarn Research Center, Howard University.

Acknowledgments *(continued from page iv)*

"Charlotte Forten" by Brenda Stevenson. From *The Journals of Charlotte Forten Grimké*, edited by Brenda Stevenson, 1988 by Oxford University Press, Inc. Reprinted by permission of the author.

Photo Credits

Cover and page 12, "Pocahontas." Pocahontas, c. 1595–1617. Daughter of Powhatan chief. Unidentified artist, English school, after the 1616 engraving by Simon van de Passe. Oil on canvas, 76.8 × 64.1 cm. (30¼ × 25¼ in.) after 1616. NPG.65.61. National Portrait Gallery, Smithsonian Institution; transfer from the National Gallery of Art; gift of Andrew W. Mellon, 1942.

Page 34, "Statue of Anne Hutchinson at Boston State House." Photo by Daniel L. Colbert.

Page 64, "Mansion House of Charles and Eliza Lucas Pinckney." From an engraving by Samuel Smith from Thomas Leitch's 1774 Painting of Charles Towne, Courtesy of the Museum of Early Southern Decorative Arts, Winston-Salem.

Page 82, "Stone Mortuary Figure at Etowah Indian Mounds, Georgia." Courtesy of Georgia Department of Natural Resources.

Cover and page 102, "Phillis Wheatley." From copy in Rare Book Collection, University of North Carolina Library, Chapel Hill.

Page 120, "Mercy Otis Warren." Bequest of Winslow Warren. Courtesy, Museum of Fine Arts, Boston.

Cover and page 146, "Maria Weston Chapman," Portrait from *Life of William Lloyd Garrison*, Vol. II. (1894).

Cover and page 168, "Catharine Beecher." The Schlesinger Library, Radcliffe College. Stowe-Day Foundation.

Cover and page 188, "Margaret Fuller." Picture Collection, The Branch Libraries, The New York Public Library.

Cover and page 220, "Elizabeth Cady Stanton." Courtesy of Rhoda Barney Jenkins.

Cover and page 240, "Mary Todd Lincoln." Courtesy of Lloyd Ostendorf Collection, Dayton, Ohio.

Cover and page 258, "Varina Davis." Davis, Varina Howell, 1826–1906. Wife of Jefferson Davis. John Wood Dodge, 1807–1893. Watercolor on ivory, 6.5 × 5.3 cm. (2½ × 2 in.), © 1849. NPG.80.113. National Portrait Gallery, Smithsonian Institution. Gift of Varina Webb Stewart.

Page 278, "Charlotte Forten." Moorland-Spingarn Research Center. Howard University.

About the Authors

Jean Baker is Professor of History at Goucher College. Among her most recent books are *Affairs of Party* and *Mary Todd Lincoln: A Biography.* She is currently working on a family biography of Adlai Stevenson and his family.

G. J. Barker-Benfield teaches history at the State University of New York, Albany. He has written *The Horrors of the Half-Known Life* (1976), and articles on medical and social history. He is completing a book on the culture of sensibility in eighteenth-century Britain.

Joan Cashin is Assistant Professor of History at Rutgers University at Camden. She is author of a forthcoming book on planter families, and she is currently working on a biography of Varina Howell Davis.

Bell Gale Chevigny teaches literature at SUNY-Purchase. She is author of *The Woman and the Myth: Margaret Fuller's Life and Writings* (1976), co-editor of *Reinventing the Americas: Comparative Studies of Literature of the United States and Spanish America* (1986). Her most recent work, the novel, *Chloe and Olivia* was published in 1990.

Catherine Clinton has taught at Brandeis University, Harvard University, and Union College. She is the author of *The Plantation Mistress* (1982) and The Other Civil War (1984). Currently she is completing a study of Fanny Kemble.

Marianne B. Geiger teaches in the Social Science Division of Fordham University's College at Lincoln Center. Her study of the historical writing of Mercy Otis Warren and Catharine Macaulay is forthcoming from M. E. Sharpe.

M. J. Lewis, a member of the department of Language and Literature at Clinch Valley College of the University of Virginia, is constructing the first intelligible chronology of the controversy associated with Anne Hutchinson, the foundation of a major revisionist study.

Bruce Miroff teaches political science at the State University of New York, Albany. He is the author of *Pragmatic Illusions: The Presidential Politics of John F. Kennedy* (1976) and of numerous articles on the presidency and political leadership. He is currently writing *The*

300

Tribe of the Eagle: American Images of Political Leadership, one of whose chapters concerns Elizabeth Cady Stanton.

Theda Perdue is Professor of History at the University of Kentucky. She is the author of *Slavery and the Evolution of Cherokee Society, 1540–1866* (1979), *Native Carolinians* (1985), and *The Cherokee* (1988), and is the editor of *Nations Remembered: An Oral History of the Five Civilized Tribes, 1865–1907* (1980) and *Cherokee Editor* (1983). Currently she is completing a book, *Cherokee Women: A Study in Changing Gender Roles.*

Constance B. Schulz is Assistant Director of the Applied History Program at the University of South Carolina, and co-Director of an MA/MLS program at the university in Archival Administration. She is creator of *The History of South Carolina* slide collection (1989), and *The History of Maryland* slide collection (1980), and has written articles on the history of childhood for the colonial and early national period. She is currently completing the editing for *Maryland: A History in Documents.*

Charles Scruggs is a professor of English Literature at the University of Arizona. He is the author of *The Sage in Harlem: H. L. Mencken and the Black Writers of the 1920s* and of articles on Jonathan Swift, Richard Wright, Ralph Ellison, and Jean Toomer. He is presently at work on a book-length manuscript tentatively titled *The Image of the City in the Literature of the Harlem Renaissance.*

Kathryn Kish Sklar is Distinguished Professor of History at the State University of New York, Binghamton. She is the author of *Catharine Beecher: A Study in American Domesticity,* several articles on American women's history, and editor of *Notes of Sixty Years: The Autobiography of Florence Kelley.* She is currently completing a biography of Florence Kelley.

Brenda Stevenson is a member of the history department at the University of California, Los Angeles. She is the editor of *The Journals of Charlotte Forten Grimké* (1988) and is the author of articles on the black family and women. She has just completed a study of white and black families in antebellum Virginia.

Philip Young is Evan Pugh Professor Emeritus of English at Penn State. Author of books on Hemingway, he has also published a collection of essays, *Three Bags Full: Revolutionary Ladies,* and *Hawthorne's Secret.* Presently he is writing a book on Melville.